The Collective Farm
in Soviet Agriculture

The Collective Farm in Soviet Agriculture

Robert C. Stuart
Rutgers University

Lexington Books
D.C. Heath and Company
Lexington, Massachusetts
Toronto   London

Published simultaneously in Canada.

Printed in the United States of America.

International Standard Book Number: 0-669-81265-X

Library of Congress Catalog Card Number: 77-175164

To my father,
Alexander G.R. Stuart
and to the memory of my mother,
Olive C. Stuart

Table of Contents

List of Tables

List of Figures

Preface

Soviet agricultural performance has received considerable attention from western scholars and yet the collective farm as a unique organizational form crucial to the Soviet development experience has not been adequately studied. The present work attempts to fill this gap though only on a partial basis.

When I began this study of collective farm management, it was not clear to me why such an obviously interesting and important topic had received only limited attention. Later, however, the reasons became clear—lack of appropriate data, inadequacy of the traditional tools of economic analysis to handle the peculiar features of the collective, and, possibly most important, the very broad scope and complexity of the subject matter. It will be apparent to the reader that many of the topics discussed in this study could be (and indeed some are) the subject of a separate study. Also, in working with this sort of topic, the debt to other disciplines is necessarily great. Nevertheless, I have attempted not to duplicate, but rather, where necessary, to draw upon the work of others. My debts to other researchers in the Soviet field are heavy, a situation not uncommon for those of the author's generation. While these are general debts, there are those of a more immediate nature for which acknowledgment is a minimal recompense.

While they bear no responsibility whatever for the final result—its presentation, interpretations or conclusions—the author wishes to thank the University of Wisconsin Ford Area Program, the Foreign Area Fellowship Program of the Social Science Research Council, the American Council of Learned Societies, the Ford Foundation Program in Business and Economics, and the Rutgers University Research Council for financial assistance at various stages in the preparation of this study. In addition, the author is grateful to those individuals and institutions in the Soviet Union who rendered assistance during an extended period in residence at the Timiriazev Agricultural Academy and visits to various collective farms of the Krasnodar Region during 1966, and to Professor H. Gordon Skilling and the University of Toronto-Soviet Union Cultural Exchange Program for making travel possible.

The writer is happy to extend thanks to the Russian Research Center of Harvard University and its former director Abram Bergson, who, along with staff members, assisted greatly in the provision of a most hospitable climate for scholarly pursuits.

While there are many individuals who might be mentioned, the author owes special thanks to Professors Earl R. Brubaker, Norton T. Dodge, John M. Farrell, Paul R. Gregory, Carl H. McMillan and James R. Millar, all of whom commented on some aspect of the study. In addition, Mrs. Doris K. Cunningham and Miss Beth Ann Cunningham exhibited great patience in typing the final manuscript. The author's greatest debt is to Professor David Granick of The University of

Wisconsin who has provided wise counsel, guidance, time and patience well beyond the call of duty.

Permission to include portions of my research already published has been kindly granted by *Soviet Studies* and The University of Illinois Press.

Finally, my thanks and appreciation go to my wife Beverly, and my son Craig, both of whom willingly endured the unusual demands made upon my time.

1

Agriculture and Economic Development

Since the process of economic development requires an adjustment from primarily agricultural to primarily industrial economic activity, the transitional process has been of great interest to development economists. Viewed in historical perspective, economic development has normally resulted in a rural sector which declines in importance both relatively and absolutely, and primary growth in the non-rural sectors of the economy. The Soviet economy has experienced these sorts of structural shifts during the planning era and thus differs little from what we might expect based upon historical experience.[1] The Soviet experience is most noteworthy, however, for the relative speed of transition, the socialist planning techniques utilized and the relatively minimal use of external assistance.

Economists have long stressed the importance of the agricultural sector as a contributor to the development process. A large body of non-Marxian economic theory suggests that the growth of agricultural output can serve as a stimulus to development not only for the provision of adequate food supplies for both rural and urban dwellers, but also as an important input to industrial processing, and, through the foreign trade sector, as a means of financing needed imports of machinery, equipment and technology. In addition, the agricultural sector contributes to the growth of the industrial labor force as urban-rural wage differentials stimulate a pattern of net migration towards the urban sector of the economy.

The dynamics of the urban-rural interaction during the course of economic development are complex and need not detain us here.[2] It is necessary to emphasize, however, that if the agricultural sector is to "contribute" product to the development effort, there must exist both a surplus product in the agricultural sector, and most important, a mechanism by which the surplus can be channeled from the agricultural to the industrial sector.[3] The collective farm *(kolkhoz)* played such a role in the Soviet approach to economic development.

In addition to the generation and transfer of surplus product from the agricultural to the industrial sector, the prevailing conception of the development process implies the presence of continuing structural change within the agricultural

---

[1] For a detailed discussion of comparative industrialization patterns, see Paul Gregory, *Socialist and Nonsocialist Industrialization Patterns* (New York: Praeger Publishers, 1970).

[2] For a general discussion, see, for example, J.W. Mellor, *Economics of Agricultural Production* (Ithaca: Cornell University Press, 1966).

[3] An agricultural surplus implies the existence of sectoral product above that required to maintain consumption of the rural population at existing caloric levels.

1

sector. During the early stages of the development process, production in the agricultural sector is typically labor intensive. However, to the extent that agricultural labor is attracted by and flows to the industrial sector, factor proportions in the agricultural sector must change.[4] One would anticipate a movement away from labor intensive towards capital intensive methods of production.

To the extent that capital is to replace labor in agricultural production, the level of investment in agriculture must increase. If increasing levels of investment are financed by the savings of the rural sector, enhancement of output and/or the share of output devoted to capital accumulation is implied. Hence consumption levels (in both the urban and rural sectors) and their change over time become crucial factors in the development process. If the standard of living is to increase and yet at the same time a rising portion of output is to be devoted to capital accumulation, increases in output are implied. In short, agricultural productivity must increase, and those concerned with economic development must also be concerned with the organizational arrangements suitable for such a result.

Again, the kolkhoz was, in the Soviet case, both the primary mechanism for the organization of agricultural production and at the same time the device through which the state could effectively control levels of consumption in the countryside. The kolkhoz, therefore, occupies a very important place in the Soviet approach to industrial development and modernization.

The Soviet Development Experience

During the Soviet Industrialization Debate of the 1920s and prior to the introduction of full scale economic planning in 1928, possible alternative industrialization strategies and accordingly varying roles for the agricultural sector in the development process were discussed in considerable detail.[5] Indeed, following the Revolution of 1917 and prior to the introduction of planning in 1928, the question of an appropriate relationship between the peasants and the regime was one of continuing importance. The regime viewed the peasants as both a potential political force and a crucial factor in any development effort.

Although the collective farm had not been the focus of discussion by the left wing of the Bolshevik Party during the industrialization debate, Stalin in 1928 both adopted the left wing strategy of development and saw the development of

[4]We are assuming that as the development process is initiated, the marginal product of labor in the agricultural sector is positive. For a discussion of this question, see, for example, Theodore W. Schultz, *Transforming Traditional Agriculture* (New Haven and London: Yale University Press, 1964).

[5]The standard work on this debate is Alexander Erlich, *The Soviet Industrialization Debate, 1924-1928* (Cambridge: Harvard University Press, 1960). For a concise treatment of the Soviet development model, see Nicolas Spulber, *Soviet Strategy for Economic Growth* (Bloomington: Indiana University Press, 1960).

the collective farm system as a crucial component of the model. Hence with a strong commitment to rapid industrialization, Stalin chose the kolkhoz as an appropriate mechanism to harness the peasants to the goals of economic development.

Since the inception of economic planning in the Soviet Union in 1928, agricultural production has been organized along three main lines: the collective farm *(kolkhoz)*; the state farm *(sovkhoz)*; and the private subsidiary sector. The private sector after collectivization consisted of small plots of land cultivated by peasant families (in both state and collective farms) and by some workers (located around industrial establishments and other state institutions). The state farm is essentially a factory in the countryside in the sense that the same organizational structure and ideological basis is common to both.

The primary form of organization in agriculture, unique to the Soviet experience, has been the collective farm (Table 1-1). The introduction of the collectives into the Soviet countryside in the early 1930s was both rapid and costly.[6] While 1.7 percent of peasant households were in collective farms as of 1928, this figure rose to 93 percent by 1937, a social upheaval of major historical importance.[7] In addition to a loss of human lives from famine and the collectivization

Table 1-1

The Organization of Agricultural Production in the Soviet Union: Selected Indicators

	1928	1932	1940	1953	1955	1960	1965	1968
Number of collective farms ('000)	33.3	211.7	236.9	97.0	87.4	44.9	36.9	36.2
Sown area of kolkhozy as a portion of total sown area (%)	1.2	–	78.3	83.9	80.2	60.6	50.2	49.4
Cattle held in kolkhozy (not including private) as a portion of all cattle (%)	–	–	36.8[a]	49.7[b]	45.7[c]	49.7	41.0[d]	41.3

Source: *Narkhoz-1960*, pp. 389, 450, 492, *Narkhoz-1968*, pp. 338, 394, 423.
[a]1941.
[b]1954.
[c]1956.
[d]1966.

---

[6]The most detailed treatment of the early years of the collectivization experience is M. Lewin, *Russian Peasants and Soviet Power* (London: George Allen and Unwin, 1968).

[7]*Strana Sovetov za 50 let* (Moskva: Statistika, 1967), p. 116.

process, reported to be in the neighborhood of five million peasants, the destruction of animal herds created a devastation such that, for some types of animals, pre-collectivization levels were not again achieved until the 1950s.[8]

The standard western interpretation of these events suggests that the costs associated with the collectivization experience were very high, and, in turn, the rewards rather low. Any such judgment, however, must distinguish carefully between the methods utilized in the collectivization process, and the utilization of a cooperative form of production organization and the successes and failures associated with each aspect of the development program. The costs and benefits of the collectivization process will not be considered in this study.[9] Rather, the focus will be upon the collective farm as an organizational mechanism, attempting to assess its positive and negative features as a fundamental component of the successful Soviet industrialization effort.

The collective farm was intended to provide, at one and the same time, a mechanism for political control in the countryside,[10] and a mechanism for the extraction of an agricultural surplus.[11] The burden of creating such a surplus, however, was in large measure to be placed upon the peasants, for the mechanism of income distribution within the collective farm guaranteed that the state would be first claimant to the output of the farm, leaving the peasant as a secondary claimant to an annually fluctuating residual product.

Most importantly, however, it is not clear that the kolkhoz has proven to be a viable mechanism for the long term development of the agricultural sector. Indeed the performance of the collective farm sector of Soviet agriculture has been the subject of continuing criticism from Soviet political leaders, economists and planners. The list of possible causal factors is long: poor farm management (a theme constantly stressed by Khrushchev); inadequate levels of capital investment and especially neglect by the state in this sphere; low levels of mechaniza-

---

[8]This figure, mostly attributable to famine, is given by Lazar Volin, *A Century of Russian Agriculture: From Alexander II to Khrushchev* (Cambridge: Harvard University Press, 1970), p. 234.

[9]The costs and benefits that we normally attribute to collectivization may be, at least in part, those attributable to industrialization per se, and indeed quite apart from the nature of institutional arrangements and political mechanisms chosen. For an argument along these lines, see Charles K. Wilber, *The Soviet Model and Underdeveloped Countries* (Chapel Hill: University of North Carolina Press, 1969), Ch. VI.

[10]Whether such control was in fact necessary (or desirable) or could not have been better provided by some alternative mechanism is beyond the present study though a crucial aspect in any overall appraisal of the kolkhoz as an element of the Soviet industrialization model. We take as given the fact that Soviet leaders *thought* such control necessary and viewed the kolkhoz as an appropriate mechanism for its implementation.

[11]The question of an agricultural surplus, and in particular the source and utilization of such a surplus in the Soviet case has been the subject of recent debate. For a general background view, see Jerzy F. Karcz, "From Stalin to Brezhnev: Soviet Agricultural Policy in Historical Perspective" in James R. Millar (ed.), *The Soviet Rural Community* (Urbana: University of Illinois Press, 1971), pp. 36-70. For initial contributions to the debate, see James R. Millar, "Soviet Rapid Development and The Agricultural Surplus Hypothesis" *Soviet Studies*, Vol. XXII, No. 1 (July 1970), pp. 77-93, and Alec Nove, "The Agricultural Surplus Hypothesis: A Comment on James R. Millar's Article" *Soviet Studies*, Vol. XXII, No. 3 (January 1971), pp. 394-401.

tion; absence of appropriate chemical fertilizers; absence of material incentives for peasants and managers; and so on. All of these shortcomings of Soviet agriculture cannot, of course, be laid at the feet of the collective farm system; and yet it may be that the Soviet perception of the kolkhoz as ideologically and economically inferior to the sovkhoz is grounded in fact.[12]

An additional criticism which might be aimed at Soviet collective agriculture is the extent to which private production has been necessary. Although ideologically unpalatable, the private sector has provided a significant proportion of certain agricultural products with a very much smaller proportion of total agricultural inputs.[13]

In spite of the importance of the kolkhoz in the overall Soviet development experience, relatively little is known about its organizational and operational characteristics. Analyses of Soviet agricultural performance have tended to focus upon aggregative performance indicators in a macro-economic framework.[14] The present study is concerned primarily with micro-economic variables, and, in particular, the kolkhoz as a special mechanism for the organization of agricultural production during the process of economic development and change.

The kolkhoz as an institution has undergone considerable change over time. The most fundamental changes have been those instigated in the post-World War II period and those in line with a changing strategy of agricultural development. The Soviet record in agriculture since the inception of economic planning (in both state and collective farms) suggests an early development strategy basically *extensive* in character. Thus the expansion of agricultural output has been sought primarily through expansion of inputs, especially sown area (the only input for which there is no direct competition with industry) rather than expansion of factor productivity. The extensive strategy was probably relevant for the

[12]The broad picture of Soviet agricultural development presented thus far is somewhat paradoxical. By most standards, overall Soviet economic performance has been impressive. And yet, the agricultural sector which we theorize contributes to the development process has performed rather poorly. The agricultural surplus that we talk about is, of course, a *product* surplus. Certainly the Soviet rural sector released labor rather quickly to the industrial sector, and this is an important contribution. More important for our purposes, however, are the possible long-run aspects of the collective farm system. Jerzy Karcz, in a penetrating article, has suggested that while the costs may have been high in the sense of suppressing peasant living standards more than necessary, the real damage may have been the solidification of negative features of the collective farm system which served to hold down the product contribution of agriculture in the *long run*. See Jerzy F. Karcz, "From Stalin To Brezhnev: Soviet Agricultural Policy in Historical Perspective" in James R. Millar (ed.), *The Soviet Rural Community* (Urbana: University of Illinois Press, 1971), pp. 36-70. See especially pp. 67 ff.

[13]The most comprehensive treatment of the private sector is Karl-Eugen Wädekin, *Privatproduzenten in der Sowjetischen Landwirtschaft* (Cologne: Wissenshaft und Politik, 1967), to appear in translation from the University of California Press.

[14]This is a dubious distinction shared by most of the cooperative types of organization. In the case of the Israeli kibbutz, for example, with the possible exception of the monograph by Eliyahu Kanovsky *(The Economy of the Israeli Kibbutz)*, very little attention has been devoted to economic analysis of this organizational form. This is in sharp contrast to the large volume of literature on almost all other aspects of the kibbutzim and their role in *Israeli* development.

early years of Soviet development especially given the then existing resource endowments, policy goals and the prevailing level of development.

In the long run, however, the character of production must necessarily change. Planners must focus increasing attention on the efficiency of production as the margin of useful land cultivation approaches, as the labor supply in rural areas dwindles in favor of more rewarding industrial occupations and as the rural sector faces continuing competition from the industrial sector for available capital funds. Such is the path common to agricultural development in most countries, even under varying institutional arrangements and differing natural resource endowments.

Efficiency increases are very difficult to generate. They depend upon the manipulation of a relatively unknown and unmeasurable input—namely organization and management. There is, however, evidence to suggest that Soviet leaders have recognized the need for greater efficiency in the production of agricultural commodities, although solutions have not always been readily apparent. The period since 1953 is, however, a turning point in the Soviet experience. There was a tendency to shift gradually away from continual reliance upon extensive methods and a limited start along the path of *intensification*, as the Soviets have named the search for greater efficiency.[15]

Since the early 1950s, two general trends can be observed in Soviet agricultural policy. First, there was a tendency to continue the policies of the Stalin era. Thus under Khrushchev's leadership, a number of grandiose schemes, mostly extensive in character, were conceived and executed. The virgin lands program, the corn program and the plow-up campaign all displayed similar characteristics. They were typically extensive in nature (especially the virgin lands program), of short run relevance (for example the plow-up campaign) and frequently without a sound theoretical basis.[16]

In the immediate post-Stalin era, these campaigns may have, in effect, bought time at a crucial period in Soviet history, a period when, after a number of years of relative neglect (in terms of capital investment, mechanization, fertilization and so on), the Soviet agricultural sector was the focus for much criticism from Soviet economists and political leaders.[17] But what was Premier Khrushchev waiting for?

[15]The September 1953 Party Plenum of the Communist Party was devoted extensively to the question of performance in the agricultural sector. The rather frank discussions held at that time represented a break with the preceding Stalinist attitudes, and although many Stalinist policies were continued, there were also new policies associated with a drive for intensification or greater efficiency of resource use. Cf. Volin, *Century of Russian Agriculture*.

[16]For a good survey of these campaigns see Joseph W. Willett, "The Recent Record in Agricultural Production" United States Congress, Joint Economic Committee, *Dimensions of Soviet Economic Power* (Washington: U.S. Government Printing Office, 1962), pp. 91-113.

[17]In the absence of immediate payback from fundamental economic change and adjustment in Soviet agriculture, these extensive measures might be viewed as insurance against food shortages and/or massive imports. The insurance idea has been suggested by Erich Strauss, *Soviet Agriculture in Perspective*, p. 172.

Although the flamboyance of the Khrushchev personality and the prevailing *modus operandi* tended in many cases to overshadow a number of more subtle changes in Soviet agriculture directed towards improved efficiency of production, the latter were in fact very important during the Khrushchev years and deserve our attention.

In the post-Stalin era, the Soviet collective farm sector has been undergoing fundamental changes which we might loosely categorize as *structural, economic* and *managerial*. Structural change refers to significant change in the nature of the collective farm as an organization largely through amalgamation—the combining of several small farms to form one large farm—in a sense a continuation of the "gigantomania" theme of the 1930s and reflecting the continuing soviet view that large scale operations are inherently more efficient than small scale operations. In addition to sharply increased farm size, the internal production organizations of the kolkhozy (the production brigades) have also grown in size and have changed in both organization and function.

In addition to the amalgamation process which sharply enhanced the size of the typical kolkhoz, the framework within which managerial personnel operate and make decisions has changed. The economic changes represent, in broad form, the introduction of money as an important variable into the kolkhoz. Thus the sharp increases in prices paid to the collectives for their products, the enhancement of income incentives (especially in monetary form) and the implementation of the *khozraschet* system of economic management all represent a substantially changed environment in which managerial decisions are to be made.[18]

Finally, within a new framework, managerial adjustment can be characterized as a new emphasis upon the quality of managerial personnel themselves—greater emphasis upon both formal and informal educational experiences, new patterns of recruitment and placement and increasing length of tenure in farm management positions.

These changes have substantially altered both the form and function of the Soviet collective farm and indeed its present and probable future role in the Soviet agricultural schema. They are, in most instances, highly desirable for the long run enhancement of productivity in the agricultural sector, for the emphasis is increasingly upon *intensive* production (increasing production efficiency), or in Soviet terminology, the process of "intensification."

In a real sense, the process of developing intensive agricultural production is of much greater interest for Soviet long run agricultural development than the much discussed campaigns of the Khrushchev era. However, the process of in-

---

[18]The term *khozraschet*, usually translated as economic accounting, is the Soviet term for the system of management utilized in agricultural and industrial enterprises. It implies a system in which the enterprise is encouraged to be financially responsible—in a sense the balancing of revenues and expenditures—and to have a measure of financial independence through ties with other organizations, notably the banking system.

tensification will not achieve immediate results, especially in the Soviet case where agricultural policies (especially under Khrushchev) have not been consistently applied.

The process of adjustment from extensive to intensive agricultural production is a routine pattern of the economic development experience. In this sense, the ability of the Soviet rural sector to meet this challenge will bear heavily upon any evaluation of the Soviet economic experience as a model for the presently less developed nations. Indeed it can be argued that in the future, the Soviet experience will be the focus for increased attention by underdeveloped nations, and this quite apart from prevailing or future ideological commitments, but with a significant change of emphasis. Thus while our past analysis of the Soviet development experience has been primarily in terms of aggregate performance indicators, notably economic growth, our future approach is less likely to be in terms of a simplistic "Soviet model" and more in terms of the important components of that model and the relevance of each component under differing environmental circumstances. In this very fundamental sense, the kolkhoz has been a cornerstone of the Soviet development experience, of which both the successes and failures deserve our attention.

The future of the kolkhoz in the Soviet agricultural system is not of direct concern in the present study, although the question is far from academic. Many basic tenets of Soviet agricultural policy point towards the elimination, or, at a minimum, the major modification of the collective farm as an organizational form. Indeed, the present study reveals patterns of change making the kolkhoz increasingly similar to the sovkhoz in both structure and operation.

In recent years, there has been a pervasive tendency to convert collective farms to state farms.[19] Soviet leaders in varying degrees over time have tended to view the conversion process as contributing to the alleviation of agricultural problems. This view, in large measure, is based upon the perceived superiority of the state farm as opposed to the collective farm. From an ideological standpoint, the state farm is a "full partner" while the kolkhoz form of property holding ("kolkhoz-cooperative" property) is viewed as inferior. In short, the kolkhoz must be raised to the same level of competence as that of the sovkhoz, a process to be carried out by state guidance after which both may be merged into a new form of organization appropriate to the then existing demands of Soviet (Communist) society.

Whether the collective farm disappears (in form or substance) or whether it remains as a declining part of the Soviet agricultural system, surely an important

---

[19] Although varying regionally and over time, the general trend has been quite dramatic. Between 1940 and 1960, for example, the number of state farms roughly doubled, while the agricultural land under the control of state farms increased almost fivefold. For the same period, the number of collective farms declined more than fivefold, while the agricultural land under the control of collectives increased only slightly over the period and was, in the 1960s below the level of 1940. The conversion campaign has not been important in the 1960s, however.

test of its utility as an organizational form under varying (non-Soviet) circumstances is the ability of the collective to serve economic development when efficiency rather than confiscation is paramount.

Plan of the Study

The present study is an in-depth analysis of the structural and operational characteristics of the Soviet collective farm as a mechanism for the organization of economic activity in the countryside. The post-1950 period has been chosen since it most appropriately represents the kolkhoz in transition—a period in which we can examine both the kolkhoz of the past and the ability of this organization to adjust to the demands of the future.

In Chapter 2 the formal organizational structure of the kolkhoz will be examined. The focus will be upon those features which distinguish the kolkhoz from other forms of organization utilized in the Soviet economy and, especially, recent changes in this form of organization.

Chapter 3 will focus upon the theory and the reality of the kolkhoz; the theory of the kolkhoz as a semi-independent cooperative organization (and accordingly the relevance of non-Marxian economic theorizing on cooperatives); the reality of what is essentially a non-cooperative organizational form operating within an elaborate net of state and Party controls.

In Chapter 4, direct attention will be given to recent changes in the collective farm sector, notably the amalgamation campaign, the resultant increase in the size of the typical collective and the changing internal organs.

Chapter 5 will focus upon the reward structure of the collective farm system and the extent to which it may motivate decision makers to pursue and achieve the goals of the system. In particular, managerial rewards will be outlined and evaluated in terms of both form and magnitude.

Chapter 6 will be devoted to isolation and examination of the decision making process within the kolkhoz: who makes the decisions as to what will be produced and with what combinations of inputs; the bases upon which such decisions are made; and the decision making tools and techniques being utilized.

Chapter 7 will concentrate upon a single but most important issue—price formation in the agricultural sector and most important, the nature of price-cost relationships as they bear upon managerial motivation and decision making within the kolkhoz.

Finally, Chapter 8 will focus upon the managers themselves: their selection, placement and promotion within the system and, most important, the changing nature of managerial personnel (at all levels within the farm) in recent years.

This study is based upon several distinct though interrelated sources. First, the large volume of Russian language materials in the form of books, articles, newspapers and the specialized publications of Soviet academic and research institutions can provide a formal, if not always realistic, picture of the Soviet rural sector. Within this collection would be included the increasingly large and valuable output of the Soviet Central Statistical Administration.

Second, the Soviet daily press can, in part, serve to spell out operational reality on a day-to-day basis and thus to assist in the creation of a less formal and rather more realistic picture of the farm and its operations.

Finally, interviews and observations carried out by the author during an academic year of residence in the Soviet union have assisted in answering those questions not generally or fully treated in the available Soviet source material.

2

The Formal Organizational Structure of the Kolkhoz

General Principles

The Soviet collective farm or kolkhoz is formally a producer cooperative whose existence has always depended upon the policies of the Soviet government and the Communist Party apparatus.[1] As an agricultural artel, the means of production of the kolkhoz are owned by the state although said to be held in perpetuity by the farm itself.[2] The artel as an organizational form came to prominence during the collectivization drive of the early 1930s.

Though subject to important changes, to be examined in due course, the affairs of the kolkhoz were, until recently, governed by the basic charter *(ustav)* as affirmed on February 17, 1935.[3] After an extended period of discussion and debate, the Third All-Union Congress of kolkhoz members was finally held in November, 1969, and a new charter affirmed on November 28, 1969.[4] In effect, this new charter serves to formalize changes already existing in kolkhozy, changes brought about by local initiative or central directives during the past thirty-five years.

In addition to elaborating the basic organizational and operational features of the kolkhoz, the charter also contains certain principles of administration which in sum are said to guide the kolkhoz along the path of "kolkhoz democracy."

The guiding principle of kolkhoz democracy is said to operate on two levels:

---

[1] The absence of local spontaneity as a force in the formation of Soviet collectives distinguishes them from many other ventures in cooperative forms of organization, especially the kibbutzim of Israel. Throughout the present study, the term kolkhoz, unless otherwise specified, refers only to agricultural artels. Thus we do not consider explicitly the small numbers of farms of the kolkhoz type specializing in the raising of fur-bearing animals, fish etc. Throughout the remaining chapters we use the term *kolkhoz* (plural kolkhozy) to refer to the collective farms, and the term *sovkhoz* (plural sovkhozy) to refer to the state farms. The sovkhozy, organized along the lines of industrial establishments, will receive only limited attention. Library of Congress transliteration is utilized throughout.

[2] The kolkhoz consists of two parts—the public or socialized sector and the private sector. The format is spelled out in the kolkhoz charter to be considered in detail in this chapter. Under these regulations, each peasant household is entitled to specified land and animal holdings (varying regionally and over time). The private plot is approximately one-quarter hectare in size (one hectare equals 2.47 acres). Though very small relative to the sown area of the kolkhoz, we have noted that the private sector has been important in the production of certain products—notably meat, milk, eggs and vegetables. Prior to 1958, peasant households were required to meet compulsory delivery targets from their plots at low fixed prices. The most comprehensive treatment of the private sector is Karl-Eugen Wädekin, *Privatproduzenten. . . .* Description of the kolkhoz as an *artel* has been dropped from the new charter.

[3] An English translation of the 1935 charter can be found in Appendix A.

[4] An English translation of the new (1969) charter can be found in Appendix B.

first, there is immediate democracy, where questions are resolved by the kolkhoz members themselves; second, there is representative democracy, where questions are resolved through elected administrative organs. Both forms of democracy operate within the general laws of Soviet society and, in particular, under the close guidance of central and local state and Party organs. In practice, the concept of kolkhoz democracy is executed as a combination of collegiality *(kollegial'nost')*, or decision making by a board or committee, and one man management, or decision making by an individual *(edinonachalie)*. Those questions deemed to be important (as defined by the charter) will be decided collegially. The execution of these decisions and the total handling of lesser matters will be in the hands of elected or appointed officials in whom will be vested both authority and responsibility.[5]

In addition to the horizontal delineation of the decision making process, there is also a vertical stratification. At each of several levels, there are elected or appointed officials who act as a group and vote on important questions, while on questions of lesser importance, these officials act as individual decision makers.[6] The latter are in effect sub-decisions of the former and hence can be considered operational decisions as part of policy execution.

Although the concept of *democratic centralism* is normally applied to the state sector of the Soviet economy, the fundamental content of this concept is found in the operation of the kolkhoz. Thus, where questions of importance are decided by majority vote following group discussion, the resolution of such questions creates policy, the execution of which (including the appropriate sub-decisions) becomes the prerogative of a single manager.

There is, however, an important theoretical distinction between the Soviet concepts of kolkhoz democracy and democratic centralism. In the state enterprises, whether industrial or agricultural, the executive personnel are directly appointed by the state, since it is the state which grants their authority and to which they are, in theory, responsible. In contradistinction, the kolkhoz is, in Soviet theory, a voluntary cooperative organization in which peasants unite voluntarily to till the soil. As such, the kolkhoz is said to be governed by executive personnel elected by the kolkhoz members themselves. These elected officials are to come from among the kolkhoz membership and to be representative of this body.[7]

[5]It is difficult to define in any precise manner the term "importance" as it is used by Soviet authors. How does one draw the line between important and unimportant questions? In theory, the powers of the kolkhoz general meeting are wide, ranging from the election of senior managerial personnel to the ratification of plan documents and accounts. Thus the kolkhoz members can question a wide range of issues. In practice, however, the meetings are infrequent and the issues are complex making the ratification procedures little more than a formality. We shall see that in the past, the electoral process within the kolkhoz has had little significance.

[6]Although partly true, it would be an oversimplification to suggest that line personnel are elected while staff personnel are appointed. Thus in the past, chairmen have been elected, specialists appointed. But, brigade leaders have been appointed (the new charter makes the position of brigadier elective).

[7]In practice, many kolkhoz chairmen at the time of their selection do not come from the farm in which they will serve. In such cases they are automatically inducted as members.

The first fundamental characteristic separating the kolkhoz from other organizational forms in the Soviet economy is its independence as theoretically demonstrated by the electoral system. The important consideration is the extent to which kolkhoz democracy is realized in practice.

The managerial selection process will be examined in detail in Chapter 8. As an element of kolkhoz democracy, however, the electoral process has had little significance. In this respect, there has been a continuing divergence of theory and practice, amply documented in the Soviet press. The following comment from a recent publication of the Institute of Economics of the Soviet Academy of Sciences is representative:

However in practice basic kolkhoz democracy is everywhere breached: kolkhoz chairmen are appointed from above and removed without a decision of the general meeting of kolkhozniks, leadership of kolkhozy is changed to administration.[8]

The selection and removal of the kolkhoz chairman has been and remains a function of the Communist Party. While it is possible that a Party nominee will be rejected by the kolkhoz (normally resulting in the presentation of a new nominee), these occurrences are apparently rare.[9]

The Charter

The kolkhoz charter *(ustav)* is the basic document governing the structure and operation of the kolkhoz and defines the unique feature of the kolkhoz form of organization. This document outlines the goals of the kolkhoz, the means of production to be employed, the organizational structure and operational procedures to be followed in the achievement of stated goals. Soviet writers constantly emphasize the importance of this document for the guidance of kolkhoz activity.

The historical circumstances surrounding the formation of kolkhozy and development of the original charter need not detain us in the present study. It is important to note that between 1935 and 1969, the charter of 1935 prevailed in spite of continuous change in the nature and operation of the typical kolkhoz. Although many changes were the result of official policy rather than local initiative, recognition was partially forthcoming in a decree of 1956.[10] This decree

[8]I.A. Gladkova (ed.), *Razvitie sotsialisticheskoi ekonomiki SSSR v poslevoennyi period* (Moskva: Nauka, 1965), p. 325.

[9]During discussions at the Oblast Administration of Agriculture in Leningrad during the summer of 1966, the writer was told on several occasions about a kolkhoz in Leningrad Oblast which had five times rejected the Party nominee for the position of chairman. Finally the Party agreed with the reasons for rejection and a new nominee was put forth. Such instances seem to be rare although it would be incorrect to say that kolkhoz members have no voice whatsoever.

[10]"Ob ustave sel'skokhoziaistvennoi arteli i dal'neishem initsiativy kolkhoznikov v organizatsii kolkhoznogo proizvodstva i upravlenii delami arteli," in *Direktivy KPSS i Sovetskogo pravitel'stva po khoziaistvennym voprosam* (Moskva: Gospolitizdat, 1958), Vol. 4, pp. 605-611. (Hereinafter cited as *Direktivy KPSS*.)

(to be examined in detail in subsequent sections) was restrictive in terms of the private plots, but it did emphasize expansion of decision making powers within the kolkhoz. In the latter connection, the decree recognized the significantly expanded size of the typical kolkhoz, and, accordingly, the need to abandon in whole or in part the general meeting. Thus the general meeting could be replaced by a number of meetings of "elected representatives" *(upolnomochennyi).*

In addition to changes in elective procedures, each kolkhoz was to write its own charter, utilizing the format of the main charter (and regional model charters), thus preserving central wishes but with a degree of local flexibility.

The differences between the present and the earlier charters, since they bear directly upon the present Soviet conception of the kolkhoz and its future in Soviet agriculture, must be examined. However, since the new charter in effect codifies the changes of the past, and since these changes will be examined in detail in the remaining chapters, each issue will be dealt with separately.[11]

If it is appropriate to view the charter as a distinct and important feature of the kolkhoz as opposed to other forms of organization in the Soviet economy, certain questions must be answered. First, to what extent does the charter actually serve as an instrument for the resolution of important questions within the kolkhoz? Second, to what extent does the individual kolkhoz possess the powers necessary for the formulation of an individual charter differing substantially from the central charter?

Like the central charter, the individual charter is less an aspect of the ongoing operation of the kolkhoz than it is a formal reflection of those characteristics of the particular kolkhoz which have found expression in reality through operation over time.

The individual kolkhoz charter is prepared (possibly as frequently as every two years) by a project organization composed of leading kolkhoz personnel (the chairman, specialists, etc.). Conformity of the individual charter to the general charter and the various laws pertaining to change is guaranteed in two ways. First, the krai or oblast administration will normally prepare a model charter for the region and one upon which the individual kolkhoz charters will be based. Second, the kolkhoz charter will be submitted to the general meeting of the kolkhoz (or the meeting of representatives where this has replaced the general meeting), after which it will be submitted to the Raiispolkom for ratification.

There may be a new element of freedom where certain rights have been granted and restricted as opposed to a situation where such rights have never been granted. In this sense, the existence of individual kolkhoz charters (since 1956) and official encouragement for the expression of local conditions in these charters is evidence of greater flexibility at local levels. However, to the extent

[11]For a discussion of the new Charter, see Peter B. Maggs, "The Law of Farm-Farmer Relations," in James R. Millar (ed.), *The Soviet Rural Community* (Urbana: University of Illinois Press, 1971), pp. 139-156; Robert F. Miller, "Changes in The Model Kolkhoz Charter: Some Observations," paper presented at the North-East Slavic Conference, Montreal, May 1971.

that changes have been generated by state and Party policy external to the individual kolkhoz, there seems to be little freedom for the individual kolkhoz to alter its basic structure. Furthermore, the relative complexity of the formulation and verification procedures suggests the likelihood of infrequent change.

The individual kolkhoz charters examined by the writer (in the Krasnodar region) were a blueprint of the general charter or a formal recognition of the changes authorized by state and Party decrees.[12] Differentials do exist in such variables as the size of the private plots, the minimum number of required labor days, etc.

The General Meeting

As every Soviet textbook on the organization of agriculture asserts, the general meeting is the highest organ of administration in the kolkhoz. Its functions are basically twofold. First, it elects (in theory) the chairman, members of the management board *(pravlenie)* and the auditing commission *(revizionnaia komissiia)*. Second, the general meeting discusses and approves certain kolkhoz documents, such as the annual plan, annual accounts, etc. For most questions, majority vote with one-half of the kolkhoz membership present will suffice.[13] For some questions, the election of the chairman and members of the management board, determination of the size of certain monetary and other funds, in particular, two-thirds of the general membership must be present.

The frequency of the general meeting is established in the kolkhoz charter and each meeting is governed by an agenda drawn up by the chairman. Though normally called by the chairman, certain other bodies and Party organs may call a general meeting.[14] The irregularity of these meetings is a frequent complaint in the Soviet press, although, in more than a formal sense, the consequences must be minimal. Much of the business conducted by a general meeting (for example approval of plan documents) can be little more than a formality, given the complexity of these documents. At the same time, these meetings may well play a positive role in motivating kolkhoz peasants.

In recent years, the typical kolkhoz has been characterized by increasing physical size, relatively backward internal transportation facilities and, in many regions, a widely dispersed population.[15] Given these features, the convening of

[12] A case in point is the charter of the kolkhoz "Michurin" (Slaviansk Raion, Krasnodarskii Krai). This charter was registered by the Raiispolkom on June 15, 1966 and seen by the writer August 16, 1966.

[13] Though probably not widespread, the tendency has been to introduce a secret ballot.

[14] In particular, the auditing commission may call a general meeting to bring irregularities to the membership of the kolkhoz, or for that matter, the management board may do the same.

[15] In some regions, for example the Baltic area and in Belorussia, there has been an effort to shift the rural population into settlements and thus lessen the problem of transportation to work and also avoid duplication of services. See, for example, V. Kamensky, "Better Organization in Resettlement From Farmsteads," *Sovetskaia Belorussia*, (June 25, 1957), p. 3, translated and reprinted in *Current Digest of The Soviet Press*, Vol. IX, No. 27 (August 14, 1957), pp. 24-25. (Hereinafter cited as *CDSP*.)

a general meeting became increasingly difficult. Thus a new organ, the meeting of representatives *(upolnomochennyi)*, was established in 1956.[16] The meeting of representatives serves as a partial or complete replacement for the general meeting. In the former case, the representatives (one representative per 5-to-15 kolkhoz members, varying by locality) are elected at a general meeting, while, in the latter case, the representatives will be elected through the brigade meeting. Term of office varies from one to three years.

As with the general meeting, a meeting of the representatives is called by the chairman, normally more frequently than the general meeting—possibly once per month or less. To be binding, a decision of the meeting of representatives must be ratified by a two-thirds majority vote of the kolkhoz membership. This vote will take place at the brigade level (where the brigade has been the mechanism for selecting the representatives in the first instance). In theory, this sort of mechanism should strengthen the voice of kolkhoz members although, operating within a sharply expanded brigade size, it may serve only to maintain previously existing patterns.

The Brigade Meeting

Meetings have always been held in brigades and other production units of the kolkhoz. However, while brigade management remains subordinate to the overall manager of the kolkhoz, there is evidence to suggest that decision making at the brigade level is of greater importance than in the past. We have noted that it is the brigade structure through which the representatives are elected and through which they report back to the membership. In addition, the brigade meeting must perform certain tasks such as plan ratification, estimation of work norms and the proper handling of those members who do not participate according to established regulations.[17]

For the complex production brigade, for example, there is an annual plan *(godovoe proizvodstvennoe zadanie)* prepared according to a format prescribed by the Ministry of Agriculture. This plan or outline of annual tasks is examined by the brigade meeting and thereafter affirmed by the administration of the kolkhoz and the general meeting. This document, in addition to recording the means of production on hand at the particular brigade, also sets forth the basic tasks for the year, broken down on a quarterly basis and expressed in both physical and value terms. Utilization of equipment is outlined in detail and, for all inputs, expenditure limits are given.

It is important to note that it is the brigade level at which the daily distribu-

---

[16]*Direktivy KPSS,* Vol. IV, p. 611.

[17]For those not participating in the socialized sector of the kolkhoz, the new charter spells out certain penalties, among which are: reprimand, severe reprimand, transfer to a lower paying job within the kolkhoz or deprivation of supplementary payments.

tion of labor tasks takes place and where the completion of these tasks is recorded. The assignment of work tasks is carried out daily by the brigadier. Although not fully clear, it would seem likely that in conjunction with the assignment and completion of work tasks, entries will be made (at the brigade level) in the labor booklet of each kolkhoz member, a document introduced by the new 1969 charter.

There is little doubt that in both theory and practice, the period since 1956 has witnessed growth in both the number and importance of the functions performed by brigade organs of administration. However, it would be premature to characterize these changes as a *net* expansion of authority and responsibility at the brigade level since the changes are, in effect, only a recognition of the changing size and structure of the brigade.

The Management Board

The management board *(pravlenie)* is an executive-administrative organ elected by the general meeting, or, in its absence, the brigade meeting or meeting of representatives. Although procedural details are not known, it appears that a new chairman after selection by the Party will exercise a good deal of power, in conjunction with local Party officials, over the selection of those who will serve on the management board.

Theoretically, the management board is the central decision making organ of the kolkhoz, deriving wide powers from the general and the individual kolkhoz charters. These powers include planning (formulation, verification and matters of execution) as well as more general matters: routine operation of the farm, membership matters and so on.

In the past, the mangement board has consisted of from five to nine persons serving for a two-year period, although the kolkhoz now has the power to decide this question itself. The decree of 1956 formally recognized a prevailing trend of placing more members on the board and, at the same time, increasing the length of service without re-election. These changes have been incorporated into the new 1969 charter.

The chairman of the kolkhoz is also the chairman of the management board and must convene the meetings of this body in addition to preparing an agenda. While procedures can vary significantly, those farms observed by the writer were usually holding meetings of the management board from one to four times per month, with each meeting lasting from two to four hours. Within the management board, majority vote on any question is said to be decisive.

To achieve what is termed "operational leadership," there normally exists a division of authority and responsibility among members of the management board. Thus the chairman in addition to general duties may be immediately responsible for a specific branch (typically field crops) while the vice-chairman will be responsible for another branch (typically animal breeding).[18]

In recent years, there has been a tendency to form advisory bodies attached to the decision making organs of the kolkhoz. A technical or economic council *(soviet)* may be created to serve, in effect, as a staff advisory body. This pattern applies for the management board and also at the brigade level.

The Council (Soviet) of the Brigade

The council, or soviet, of the brigade is a relatively recent phenomenon not envisaged in the general charter nor, for that matter, in the adjustments thereto made in 1956. According to recent Soviet legal publications, this organ is composed of from five to twenty of the best kolkhoz members at the brigade level. The Soviet notion of "best" normally includes the leadership personnel, staff specialists and those termed the "aktiv." This pattern also applies within other production units (animal fermy, subsidiary enterprises, etc.).

In a broad sense, the function of the council is to render help to the brigadier (and the management board) in the introduction of all measures in the sphere of economic leadership and mass political work. It is, therefore, basically an organ of communication and serves to channel information from the kolkhoz membership to the leadership and vice versa.

One would not expect the brigade council to be an organ of significant criticism since the brigadier is normally the chairman, and the brigade bookkeeper *(schetovod)* is its secretary. Meetings are normally held two or three times per month and may be convened by the brigadier or by the management board of the kolkhoz.

The power of the management board to convene a brigade meeting would seem to extend the powers of kolkhoz leaders thus permitting them to communicate directly with kolkhoz members but bypassing the administrative structure at the brigade level. However, there is no evidence to suggest that this power is of practical significance. Decisions made by the brigade council take the form of a recommendation and become generally obligatory only after ratification by the management board.

Although substantive material on the brigade council is scant, the emergence of this organ must be weighed as evidence in our assessment of decision making powers at the brigade level. Thus while it does allow the improvement of communication between the kolkhoz chairman and the membership at large, as we have suggested, the main transmission of information seems to be between leaders and kolkhoz members within the brigade structure.

---

[18]The fact that the chairman normally bears responsibility for the field crop sector may say something about the state priorities in this regard. As we shall see in Chapter 8, the number of farms served by an assistant chairman has fluctuated both over time and regionally. In the 1960s, however, there seems to be a greater likelihood that this position will exist and be occupied. Indeed the new 1969 charter provides for the election of one or *two* such persons.

It is difficult to conclude that the presence of the brigade council means the decentralization to its level of decisions formerly made at higher levels. However, as we shall see in a subsequent section, the recommendation is, in Soviet legal theory, a more powerful concept than its English translation would imply. In the past, however, the brigade council has apparently focused upon what are termed "cultural-personal" matters. Questions of labor discipline, socialist competition and the examination of complaints by members might be considered. It is in this light that we view this organ as basically a transmitter of information and as an outlet for frustrations of kolkhoz members, thus increasing their motivation to contribute.

The Auditing Commission

The formal organ of internal control in the kolkhoz is the auditing commission *(revizionnaia komissiia)*. This organ serves both as a source of information and as a control over managerial personnel, and reports to the kolkhoz membership. Like other organs of the kolkhoz, the structural and operational details are established in the general charter, the individual kolkhoz charter, and, since 1960, a union-republican decree.[19] Normally the members (from three to ten in number) are elected at a general meeting or meeting of representatives and serve for a period of from two to three years.[20] All members of the auditing commission (from among whom the chairman is chosen) must be approved by the raiispolkom.

In theory, the powers of the auditing commission are wide. Thus it is required to carry out a complete financial-economic review (including physical balances) four times per year or more frequently if deemed necessary.[21] Members of the commission are freed from their other duties during the period of review and are paid according to their average earnings (of the previous year) in their usual work. The chairman of the commission is paid at the same rate as the chairman of the kolkhoz. During the review procedure, the commission has the power to call witnesses for both written and oral testimony and, where necessary, to utilize the services of outside specialists. Throughout the year, intermediate acts of review are prepared and subsequently summarized and presented to the general meeting of the kolkhoz.

[19] "Primernoe polozhenie o rezivionnoi komissii sel'skokhoziaistvennoi arteli," as cited in *Sbornik reshenii po sel'skomu khoziaistvu* (Moskva: Izdatel'stvo sel'skokhoziaistvennoi literatury, 1963), pp. 400-402. (Hereinafter cited as *Sbornik*.)

[20] Originally the auditing commission was to have three to nine members serving for a period of two years. Recently the tendency has been to increase the size and lengthen the term of office. This decision falls within the competence of the individual kolkhoz and will be spelled out in its charter. In this regard, there appear to be no rules to guide the kolkhoz, though suggestions have been made advocating commission membership based upon the size of the kolkhoz as measured by total membership or number of brigades.

[21] At the discretion of the auditing commission and in the light of suspected illegal practices or irregular behavior. There is no evidence to suggest that this right is of practical importance.

In practice, the auditing commission is one of the weakest and most ineffective kolkhoz organs. It is the subject of continual attack in the Soviet press, and this along two basic lines. First, the required review operations are frequently not performed, and, where they are, members settle for a partial or incomplete result. The following example is typical: in the Kirgiz republic there were a total of 295 kolkhozy in 1961.[22] Of these, 48 carried out only one quarterly review, 104 carried out only two quarterly reviews and seven carried out no review whatsoever.[23] Indeed, the press frequently reports monetary and other violations, the control of which fall within the purview of this body.[24]

Second, where review work is in fact performed, its quality is generally poor. This is partly a function of the basic structure of the review mechanism, but, in large measure, it is a function of the inadequate preparation of the personnel involved. As an organ of review, rules prohibit the participation within this function of any person holding a leadership position in the kolkhoz. According to Soviet commentary on the matter, members of the review group are typically ignorant of basic principles of accounting, finance, etc. and indeed lack general competence.[25]

Though nominally accountable to the general meeting of the kolkhoz, the auditing commission is asked to perform duties which normally would be a function of internal control of the accounting system and which, in practice, bring the members of the commission into close and undesirable contact with the management board. Thus as one Soviet author has pointed out, the commission becomes not an organ of control, but rather an adjunct of the administration, and its helper on economic questions.[26]

Apparently the auditing commission frequently seeks redress of grievances through the management board, in spite of the fact that the former is said to control the latter. In this sense, the report to kolkhoz members becomes little more than a formality. It is true that the commission can convene a general meeting, though there is no evidence to suggest that this power is utilized.

Finally, it would seem difficult for members of the commission to seek assistance from the procurator if those in command of the kolkhoz are hostile to the action. The evidence suggests that where illegal acts are uncovered and publicized, there frequently have been long delays and representations to several

[22]Tsentral'noe Statisticheskoe Upravlenie, *Narodnoe Khoziaistvo SSSR v 1961 godu* (Moskva: Gosstatizdat, 1962), p. 440. (Hereinafter cited as *Narkhoz-1961*).

[23]A. Evseev, "Uluchshit' rabotu revizionnykh komissii v kolkhozakh," *Kolkhozno-Sovkhoznoe Proizvodstvo Kirgizii*, No. 1 (January, 1963), p. 11.

[24]See, for example, L. Dzhaidakbaeva, "Revizionaia komissiia kolkhoza," *Sel'skoe Khoziaistvo Uzbekistana*, No. 5 (May, 1965), pp. 59-61.

[25]Evseev, op. cit., p. 10.

[26]Ibid. For further discussion of these problems, see, for example, G. Abramov, "Revizionnye komissii-organy kontrolia," *Kolkhozno-Sovkhoznoe Proizvodstvo Moldavii*, No. 12 (December 1964), pp. 11-13; Belov, op. cit., pp. 46-47.

levels above the kolkohz before appropriate action is taken.[27] It must be difficult for a rank and file member of a kolkhoz to carry such an action to its conclusion.

There is an interesting paradox in our picture of the auditing commission. This body has been pictured as basically weak and ineffective. But, would we not expect the control function to be an important one in Soviet planning, and, in particular, is not affirmation of commission members by the raiispolkom evidence of this importance?

In addition to the aspects of control that we have already examined (relatively low quality of personnel, possible conflict of interest, etc.), there remains the question of the powers of outside supervision and especially the role of the Communist Party in this sphere.

Prior to their abolition in 1958, the Machine Tractor Stations (MTS) were the external organs directly responsible for the supervision of auditing procedures. Subsequently, this task fell to the Raion Inspection for Agriculture. It might be suggested that the proximity of, and extent of general supervision by, these external organs facilitated the upward flow of information by channels relatively more efficient than the auditing commission.[28] As we shall see in subsequent sections of the present study, the early 1950s witnessed a significant strengthening in the potential capabilities of the MTS vis-a-vis the kolkhoz. In addition, we shall also consider the rather significant growth of the Party in this period.

There is no evidence to suggest that the quality of control operations improved either during or following the era of the MTS. We have already cited complaints directed at the structure and membership policies of the auditing commission. In recent years, there has been a tendency to focus upon the low numbers of agricultural specialists at the raion level vis-a-vis the large number of kolkhozy as a causal factor of poor control. Nevertheless, the significant reduction in the number of kolkhozy in recent years has had no noticeable effect (although reduction of numbers per se may not be the relevant variable), if frequency of complaints can be taken as a reliable indicator.

Soviet efforts to disseminate new ideas in this sphere have met with mixed

---

[27]There are frequent reports in the Soviet press indicating that such activities as padding, false reporting, speculation, etc. are frequently brought to the surface by the Party or organs other than the auditing commission. One such case, brought to the oblast level by a dismissed agricultural specialist is reported in P. Polynsky, "Why are Frauds Shielded in Chernovtsy?", *Sel'skoe Khoziaistvo* (September 12, 1957), p. 3, translated and reprinted in *CDSP*, Vol. IX, No. 42 (November 27, 1957), pp. 20-21. Discussing various shortcomings in the operation of a collective farm, A. Yeremin suggests that "officially we have an inspection committee, but it does no work." See A. Yeremin, "Do Not Violate Collective Farm Democracy," *Pravda*, February 21, 1961, p. 2, translated and reprinted in *CDSP*, Vol. XIII, No. 8 (March 22, 1961), pp. 36-37.

[28]As we have suggested, the Party has a significant role in this respect. In addition, we shall see that the MTS was in a position to act as a channel of communication upwards. Also, to the extent accounting practices were supervised by external organs, manipulation would be more difficult.

success. Thus in a rather typical case occurring in the early 1960s, the kolkhozy of Kolushkoi Oblast were given a pamphlet describing the patterns of auditing work on advanced farms in the hope of spreading these techniques (a very typical Soviet procedure for the dissemination of information). After one year, thirty kolkhozy were checked. Many were not carrying out review procedures at all, and those that were frequently did so on a partial basis, for example a simple check of cash balances and nothing more.[29]

It may well be that in addition to the inadequate preparation of auditing personnel, Soviet leaders have underestimated the complexity of the task involved, and have used a mechanism unable to meet the challenge.[30]

The Party Committee

The Party organization is probably one of the most important though, at the same time, most incomprehensible organs of the Soviet kolkhoz. The function of the Party in the kolkhoz is one of organizing and leading the masses toward the fulfillment of state goals. This activity focuses upon the decision making centers and especially the information inputs and personnel matters. Beyond the Party status of leadership personnel (which we examine later) substantive data on the Party is very limited. Let us turn initially to some indicators of Party *growth* for Kazakhstan and Tadzhikistan, both of which might suggest useful general insights. The analyst of the Soviet economic system must always be mindful of significant regional differentials. In the present case, Tadzhikistan is thought to be broadly representative of Central Asia, while Kazakhstan is thought to be broadly representative of other important agricultural areas. Also, to the extent that Party expansion can be considered a function of central wishes, one would expect regional differentials to be less significant.

If we examine Tables 2-1 and 2-2, it will be apparent that while both the numbers and the socialized sown area of kolkhozy have declined markedly, Party membership has declined insignificantly in Kazakhstan, and on the contrary, grown significantly in Tadzhikistan. In this section we are concerned with the Party Committee as an organ in the kolkhoz. In addition, we are concerned

[29]N.A. Panin, "Revizionnym komissiiam nuzhna pomoshch'," *Uchet i Finansy v Kolkhozakh i Sovkhozakh*, No. 2 (February 1963), p. 37.

[30]The frequent complaints about the auditing commission have not resulted in significant action to improve this organ. It may be that in the past, this organ has not been important, given the rather crude physical planning and the great importance of Party and state organs external to the kolkhoz. Nevertheless, it might also be suggested that as "monetization" of the collective farm sector proceeds, the functions of this commission will become increasingly important as will the improvement of accounting procedures. In the absence of external audit purchased as a service and required by law as is frequently the case in the U.S., these services will be performed internally or at best by an organ above the kolkhoz. Given that the organs at the raion level, for example, also have targets to be met, the possibility of collusion may be increased. In sum, the formulation of an appropriate system of checks may well prove a difficult task.

Table 2-1

Growth of the CPSU in Kolkhozy of Kazakhstan, 1953-1960 (1953 = 100)

	1953	1956	1960
Number of kolkhozy[a]	100	88	44
Sown area–total socialized in kolkhozy[b]	100	141[f]	64
Kolkhoz households[c]	100	101	77
Average annual labor force in kolkhozy[d]	100	107	77
Party membership in kolkhozy[e]	100	100	97

Sources: [a]*Sel'khoz-1960*, p. 51; *Narkhoz-1960*, p. 500.
[b]*Sel'khoz-1960*, p. 145; *Narkhoz-1960*, p. 501.
[c]*Sel'khoz-1960*, p. 52; *Narkhoz-1960*, p. 500.
[d]*Sel'khoz-1960*, p. 459; *Narkhoz-1960*, p. 522, includes workers of tractor brigades and those in construction, subsidiary enterprises and cultural-personal organizations.
[e]*Kommunisticheskaia partiia kazakhstana v dokumentakh i tsifrakh* (Alma-Ata: Kazakhskoe gosudarstvennoe izdatel'stvo, 1960), pp. 325, 354, 361. Party membership includes full and candidate members, but apparently does not include members of the Komsomol.
[f]1957.

Table 2-2

Growth of the CPSU in Kolkhozy of Tadzhikistan, 1953-1960 (1953 = 100)

	1953	1956	1960
Number of kolkhozy[a]	100	66	60
Sown area–total socialized in kolkhozy[b]	100	98[f]	85
Kolkhoz households[c]	100	106	118
Average annual labor force in kolkhozy[d]	100	95	87
Party membership in kolkhozy[e]	100	101	163

Sources: [a]*Sel'khoz-1960*, p. 51; *Narkhoz-1960*, p. 500.
[b]*Sel'khoz-1960*, p. 145; *Narkhoz-1960*, p. 501.
[c]*Sel'khoz-1960*, p. 52; *Narkhoz-1960*, p. 500.
[d]*Sel'khoz-1960*, p. 459; *Narkhoz-1960*, p. 522, includes workers of tractor brigades and those in construction, subsidiary enterprises and cultural-personal organizations.
[e]*Kommunisticheskaia partiia Tadzhikistana v dokumentakh i tsifrakh* (Dushanbe: Izdatel'stvo Irfon, 1965), pp. 167, 220, 224. Party membership includes full and candidate members, but apparently does not include members of the Komsomol.
[f]1957.

with the presence of the Party, not only in terms of Party membership as a portion of kolkhoz membership, but also in terms of the organizational structure of the Party within the kolkhoz and the extent to which this structure has been brought closer to non-Party personnel through formal expansion in various parts of the kolkhoz. We shall examine in due course the types of decisions influenced by the Party and the manner in which this influence is brought to bear upon the kolkhoz. It might be suggested however, that the success of the party in bringing its message to the peasants is in part a function of (1) the proportion of the peasants who are Party members and who actively promote the Party line among non-Party personnel, and (2) the "strength" of the Party structure, which we suggest can be measured, in part, by the depth to which the organizational structure extends, and the *formal* strength given to those Party organs at the extremities. Thus the prevalence of Party membership in the collective farm population has increased, and one would think that Party influence would also tend to increase though not necessarily at a similar rate.

In addition, the growth of the Communist Party in the collective farm sector of these republics has been accompanied by an increase in the size of the kolkhoz Party organization and the creation of formal Party organizations where none previously existed. In the latter connection, a decree of 1960 formally recognized the possibility of Party expansion (with more than one Party organization) within the kolkhoz, and notably at the brigade level.[31] The formal strengthening of the Party at lower levels in the kolkhoz can be seen in our data for Kazakhstan and Tadzhikistan which, in part, reflect the results of the 1960 decree referred to above.

Prior to 1955 in both Kazakhstan and Tadzhikistan, Party members of collective farms were organized, for the most part, in the form of a kolkhoz Party organization. In both cases, though with varying patterns, the size of the kolkhoz Party organization(s) grew throughout the decade 1950-1960. In the second half of the decade moreover, *in addition to* the maintenance of these full kolkhoz Party organizations (though the ratio of full Party organizations to kolkhozy increased in Tadzhikistan and declined in Kazakhstan), there was a most significant increase in the number of formally organized Party organizations. Furthermore, these newly recognized Party organizations, though of lesser stature than a full Party organization (typically a Party-Komsomol group, candidate group or department organization), were organized not in the kolkhozy in general, but in the brigades, fermy and subsidiary enterprises in particular. Also (as noted in note 1 to Table 2-3), after 1959, a kolkhoz with a party organization numbering 50 or more members (previously 100 or more members) could create these subsidiary Party groups and most important, grant them the rights of a local *(pervichnye)* Party organization. Thus it would appear that Party membership in the kolkhozy has grown rather faster than other indicators, such as num-

---

[31] *Kommunisticheskai a partiia Sovetskogo Soiuza v rezoliutsiiakh i resheniiakh* (Moskva: Gospolitizdat, 1960), Part IV, p. 501. (Hereinafter cited as *KPSS v rezoliutsiiakh.*)

25

Table 2-3

CPSU Structure in Kolkhozy of Kazakhstan, 1950-1960: Selected Indicators

	Artels	No. of Communists	No. of Kolkhoz Party Orgs.	No. of Candidate Groups	No. of Party-Komsomol Groups
1950	3,670	65,984	6,226	79	59
1951		62,996	3,765	19	35
1952		58,770	3,178	10	34
1953	2,966	56,210	3,100	6	4
1954		51,951	3,015	5	6
1955		51,845	2,915	1	2,061[a]
1956	2,611	56,172	2,803	1	2,107
1960	1,291	54,529	1,459	1,001	–

Sources: *Sel'khoz-1960*, p. 51; *Narkhoz-1960*, p. 500. All remaining data from *Kommunisticheskaia partiia Kazakhstana v dokumentakh i tsifrakh* (Alma-Ata: Kazakhskoe gosudarstvennoe izdatel'stvo, 1960), pp. 314, 317, 321, 325, 328, 351, 354, 361. (Page numbers coincide with the data by years, starting with 1950 on page 314).

[a]From 1955 onward, the term "Party group" is used rather than "Party-Komsomol." According to the charter of the Communist Party as of 1952, a local (pervichnye) Party organization can be formed in a kolkhoz where there are not less than three Party members. Where less than three exist, a candidate or Party-Komsomol group is formed. Further, where the Party organization has more than 100 members (and candidate members), a Party organization can be created in sub-sections of the kolkhoz. Where less than 100 members are present, a Party group will be formed. See *KPSS v rezoliutsiiakh*, pp. 590-591. Since the numbers of Party groups did not expand sharply until 1955, increased Party pressure to form such groups in conjunction with the Virgin Lands Program may have been influential. From 1959 onward, a kolkhoz with a Party organization numbering 50 to more members could create in brigades, fermy and departments, Party Committees having the rights of a local (pervichnye) Party organization. See *KPSS v rezoliutsiiakh*, Part IV, p. 501.

bers of households, average annual labor force, etc. (or, in Kazakhatan, maintained its position in the face of a decline in these other indicators). At the same time, the Party structure has been formally diffused into lower levels of the kolkhoz, and the rights of these lower level groups increased.

The Party organization has a section devoted to cadres, and in combination with Party organs external to the kolkhoz will have a powerful voice in the selection, training and placement of personnel. A typical Party structure for a large economically advanced kolkhoz is given in Figure 2-1.

It is difficult to be precise when speaking about the influence of the Party in kolkhoz affairs. We have touched upon the matter of personnel selection and indeed will do so at greater length in a subsequent section. Also, we shall comment upon the Party as the purveyor of policy in the collective farm sector. In this latter aspect, it is important to note that both the formulation and execution of Party policy is facilitated to the extent that virtually all top managerial personnel are Party members. Indeed the chairman and the secretary of the

26

Table 2-4
CPSU Structure in Kolkhozy of Tadzhikistan, 1950-1960: Selected Indicators

	No. of Artels	No. of Communists	No. of Kolkhoz Party Orgs.	No. of Candidate Groups	No. of Party-Komsomol Groups
1950	1,314	8,299	968	49	34
1951		8,917	791	29	8
1952	589	9,236	683	16	7
1953		9,398	683	12	6
1954		9,020	511	3	4
1955		9,022	468	2	132[a]
1956	388	9,480	435	34[b]	150
1960	353	15,294	392	697	73

Sources: *Sel'khoz-1960*, p. 51; *Narkhoz-1960*, p. 500. All remaining data from *Kommunis-ticheskaia partiia Tadzhikistana v dokumentakh i tsifrakh* (Dushanbe: Izdatel'stvo Irfon, 1965), pp. 164, 165, 166, 167, 218, 219, 220, 224. (Page numbers coincide with the data by years, starting with 1950 on page 164).
[a]From 1955 onward, the category "Party-Komsomol Groups" changed to "Party Groups."
[b]It should be noted that in 1956, there existed only *one* Party Group. However, in 1956, a new category of department Party organization (tsekhovaia partorganizatsiia) was formed and this with *thirty-three* such organizations. Hence the sum of the two forms is given for the year 1956. It should also be noted that the term "Party Group" was dropped in 1957, and hence the entire sum of 697 represents department Party organizations. Given that the term department (tsekh) is normally applied to the industrial sector, it may be that these department Party organizations fall within the subsidiary enterprises of the kolkhozy. For a general note on Party structure, see Footnote a to Table 2-3.

Party organization seem to be in close contact, facilitated in part by the close physical proximity of their office facilities.[32]

If their Party is to lead the masses, it must disseminate the policy formulated within the Party structure. In this respect, the Party organization is a vital organ of kolkhoz affairs. In addition to regular Party meetings at which kolkhoz officials will report on the progress of the farm, "agitators" will transmit the Party line at the local level (brigade, ferma, etc.) through the organization of seminars, discussion groups and meetings. In this connection, it is the responsibility of the Party organization to operate small libraries which may exist down to brigade level. In addition to semi-technical material, they display in prominence a wide range of state and Party publications both for consumption on the spot, and for home reading. Finally, the Party organizes competition between farms, and fre-

[32]In those cases examined by the writer, Party offices were normally in the main administration building of the kolkhoz. In addition, the Party secretary was typically accommodated in physical proximity to the chairman, and both had meeting facilities in their offices. Indeed it was apparent that the Party secretary is a person of position and competence, enjoying a close working relationship with the kolkhoz chairman.

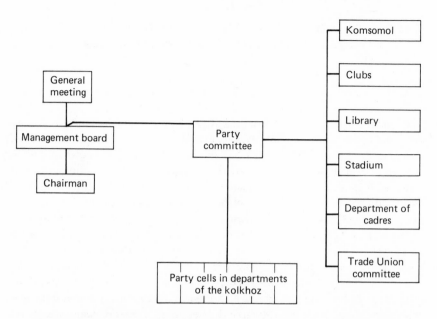

Figure 2-1. Organization of the Communist Party in the Kolkhoz "Nasha Rodina", Kavkazskii Raion, Krasnodarskii Krai. Source: Personal communication.

quently will promote the exchange of visits of groups of peasants between farms. These techniques are thought to increase motivation and assist in the spread of new techniques and methods of production.

Soviet writers point out that in theory, the Party is an organ of "control from below," and as such is obliged to discuss at Party gatherings all important questions of kolkhoz life.[33] Its role is that of "recommendation" and, in theory, to exercise persuasion *through* the organs of administration within the kolkhoz.

Finally, the Party has the right of control *(pravo kontroliia)* over the management board. The precise meaning of this concept has never been clarified, though western writers seem to limit it to checking or verification, rather than any broader concept, possibly including the power to direct the activity of the kolkhoz.[34] One writer has pointed out, however, that where the manager is

[33]For an incisive discussion of the rural Party mileu and reference to the discussion in Soviet Literature, see Alec Nove, "Soviet Agriculture Marks Time," *Foreign Affairs*, Vol. 40, No. 4 (July, 1962), pp. 576-594 and especially pp. 589-590; Alec Nove, "Peasants and Officials," in Jerzy F. Karcz (ed.), *Soviet and East European Agriculture* (Berkeley and Los Angeles: University of California Press, 1967), pp. 57-72.

[34]See, for example, Jerry F. Hough, "The Soviet Concept of the Relationship Between the Lower Party Organs and the State Administration," *Slavic Review*, Vol. XXIV, No. 2 (June, 1965), pp. 223-224.

faced with the making of a decision not elaborated in the plan, the Party may play a role in policy formulation before the actual decision is made.[35]

Summary

The kolkhoz as an organizational form, though in theory a semi-independent co-operative organization, in fact owes its existence to the directives of the Soviet state and the Communist Party. While the body of principles known as kolkhoz law serves to delineate the nature of the kolkhoz and its interaction with other forms of organization in Soviet society, the basic structure of the kolkhoz and its operational characteristics are elaborated in the main kolkhoz *charter*, and, patterned directly after this document, a charter for each individual kolkhoz.

Between the years 1935 and 1969, structural and operational details of kol-khozy were spelled out in the original 1935 charter. During this period, kol-khozy underwent significant changes making the original charter less and less meaningful. These changes, discussed elsewhere in this study, were brought into being through both central directive and local initiative. Many found immediate expression in various state and Party decrees, and, in essence, were finally codi-fied in 1969 with the writing of a new charter.

The fundamental organizational structure of the kolkhoz remains intact: a chairman presiding over a management board; revision commission for the in-spection function; various organs of administration at the brigade level; and so on. Of significant note, however, is the expansion of decision organs at the bri-gade level in line with the sharply increased size and expanded functions of the typical brigade or department. Thus a meeting of representatives can replace the general meeting of the kolkhoz where the representatives are elected through the brigade structure. The increased size of the typical kolkhoz has also been recog-nized by removal of a limit on the number of members who may serve on the management board, formal provision for more than one assistant chairman and the formalization of administrative organs at the brigade level: an elected briga-dier; brigade meetings; a council of the brigade; and so on.

Although we know relatively little about the operational details of the Party structure within the kolkhoz, its presence seems to be pervasive not only as a general purveyor of guidance as to state and Party goals and priorities, but also as a participant in the daily activities of the farm.

The data presented for Kazakhstan and Tadzhikistan would suggest that the Party has adapted rather well to operating within the larger kolkhozy of recent years. This adaptation has taken place through expansion of membership (rela-tive to other indicators of kolkhoz expansion) for both peasants and managerial personnel (the latter to be examined in Chapter 8), and through a "deepening" of the Party apparatus such that Party members and the cells through which they operate penetrate to the lowest organizational levels of the kolkhoz.

[35] Hough, op. cit., p. 226.

These changes should be borne in mind as we examine the changing structure of the kolkhoz in Chapter 4. It will be evident that, as the typical kolkhoz has grown in size and its internal production units have assumed new and more complex tasks, the administrative apparatus of the kolkhoz including the Party structure has, in a sense, also expanded and has penetrated more deeply into the kolkhoz in what seems to be an effort to maintain at a minimum the same administrative "presence" in the average kolkhoz.

3

The Kolkhoz in the Planned Economy

The General View

This study focuses upon the organization of economic activity *within* the kolkhoz. To the extent, however, that the kolkhoz is something less than a wholly self governing cooperative organization, it has fallen within the purview of certain external organs, for example, Agricultural Inspectorates of the Raion Executive Committee, the Machine Tractor Stations and the Territorial Production Administrations.[1]

The structure and operating principles of this external administrative network have shifted over time. It is not our purpose to spell out in detail the nature of administrative changes, nor shall we give specific attention to the operational details of the many external organs which in greater or lesser degree interact with the kolkhoz. Our goal in the present section is twofold.

First, the kolkhoz is an integral part of the Soviet system of economic planning, and, as such, decisions relevant to the kolkhoz are made at all levels of the economic and political hierarchy and result in a continuous flow (vertically and horizontally) of information.[2] When examining decision making wihin the kol-

---

[1] Our treatment of state and Party organs external to the kolkhoz is very limited. The reader is referred to the following sources: Jerzy F. Karcz, "Seven Years on The Farm: Retrospect and Prospects," in United States Congress, Joint Economic Committee, *New Directions in The Soviet Economy* (Washington: U.S. Government Printing Office, 1966), pp. 383-450; Jerzy F. Karcz and Vladimir P. Timoshenko, "Soviet Agricultural Policy, 1953-1962," *Food Research Institute Studies*, vol. IV, no. 2 (1964), pp. 123-163; Roy D. Laird, "Khrushchev's Administrative Reforms in Agriculture," in Roy D. Laird (ed.), *Soviet Agricultural and Peasant Affairs* (Lawrence: University of Kansas Press, 1963), pp. 269-286; Robert F. Miller, "Continuity and Change in The Administration of Soviet Agriculture Since Stalin," in James R. Millar (ed.), *The Soviet Rural Community* (Urbana: University of Illinois Press, 1971), pp. 73-102; Robert F. Miller. *One Hundred Thousand Tractors* (Cambridge: Harvard University Press, 1970); Alec Nove, "Some Thoughts on Soviet Agricultural Administration," in Roy D. Laird and Edward L. Crowley (eds.), *Soviet Agriculture: The Permanent Crisis* (New York: Frederick A. Praeger, 1965), pp. 1-12; Sidney I. Ploss, *Conflict and Decision Making in Soviet Russia: A Case Study in Agricultural Policy 1953-1963* (Princeton: Princeton University Press, 1965); Howard R. Swearer, "Agricultural Administration Under Khrushchev," in Roy D. Laird (ed.), *Soviet Agricultural and Peasant Affairs* (Lawrence: University of Kansas Press, 1963), pp. 9-40; Lazar Volin, *A Century of Russian Agriculture: From Alexander II to Khrushchev* (Cambridge: Harvard University Press, 1970), Ch. 21.

[2] The kolkhoz as a *khozraschet* organization must by law maintain appropriate connections with the state banking system. In addition, the kolkhoz is likely to have dealings with various inter-kolkhoz organizations, subsidiary enterprises, educational institutions and experimental centers, various agents and inspectors (accounting, insurance, etc.) and trade union organizations.

khoz, it will be necessary to know, for each decision examined, what portions of those decisions are in fact made externally or, at a minimum, what external information has influenced the nature of the given decisions. To do so, it is necessary to examine the *forms* in which information flows from external organs into the decision making process of the individual kolkhoz. We can then examine in detail the nature of planning within the kolkhoz, while at the same time understanding how internal planning operates in conjunction with external plan directives.

Specific attention to the matters outlined above is essential, given the peculiar nature of the kolkhoz vis-a-vis other forms of production organization in the Soviet economic system. The entire range of questions pertaining to the kolkhoz and its external relationship is subsumed in Soviet writing under the heading "state leadership of kolkhozy." The methodology of operation and its formal impact upon the kolkhoz is elaborated in the specialized branch of Soviet legal theory known as "kolkhoz law."

Second, brief consideration will be given to the nature and operation of the Machine Tractor Stations.[3] Separate discussion of the MTS is necessary on several grounds: first, to a degree in excess of other organs external to the kolkhoz, the personnel of the MTS were intimately connected with the planning and operation of the internal affairs of the kolkhoz. This intimacy arose not simply through directives, but rather through active participation. Second, as opposed to other external organs, the MTS were directly responsible for the utilization of a major input in agricultural production: machinery and equipment. Third, while we shall attempt to demonstrate a growing internal strength (politically and economically) of the MTS especially in the early 1950s, it is not clear that this strength was passed on to the kolkhozy or indeed to organs external to the kolkhoz following the dissolution of the MTS in 1958. Thus to understand the powers of decision making which reside within the kolkhoz, it is necessary to examine the powers of the MTS and the distribution of those powers following the dissolution of the MTS.

The Nature of State Leadership

What is state leadership and what does it attempt to accomplish?[4] In a most

---

[3]For an excellent discussion of the role of the MTS in Soviet agriculture, see Robert F. Miller, *One Hundred Thousand Tractors* (Cambridge: Harvard University Press, 1970).

[4]Questions relating to the kolkhoz in Soviet society, legal status, kolkhoz property, etc., are widely discussed by Soviet writers. See, for example, Z.S. Beliaev and I.F. Pankratov, *Gosudarstvennoe rukovodstvo kolkhozami v period razvernutogo stroitel'stva kommunizma v SSSR* (Moskva: Gosiurizdat, 1961); E.D. Damanina (ed.), *Kolkhoznoe pravo* (Moskva: Vsesoiuznyi iuridicheskii zaochnyi institut, 1965); V.N. Dem'ianinko, *Formy i metody rukovodstva kolkhozami so storony raiispolkoma* (Moskva: Gosiurizdat, 1960); I.V. Pavlov (ed.), *Pravovoe polozhenie kolkhozov v SSSR* (Moskva: Gosiurizdat, 1961); I.V. Pavlov (ed.), *Pravovye voprosy sblizheniia kolkhoznoi i obshchenarodnoi sobstvennosti* (Moskva: Gosiurizdat, 1963); I.V. Pavlov, *Razvitie kolkhoznoi demokratii v period razvernutogo kommunizma* (Moskva: Gosiurizdat, 1962); V.G. Venzher, *Kolkhoznyi stroi na sovremennom etape* (Moskva: Ekonomika, 1966); A.I. Volkov (ed.), *Osnovy kolkhoznogo prava* (Moskva: Izd. "Iuridicheskaia literatura," 1963).

general sense, state leadership is the body of doctrine and associated activities concerned with the construction of a Communist society. Though they find expression only in generalizations, these cannot simply be dismissed.

Thus in Communist doctrine, kolkhoz property is presently viewed as an inferior form of ownership, and as such, will be replaced by a new single form of Communist property, presumably combining the best features of the present state *(sovkhoz)* and kolkhoz-cooperative *(kolkhoz)* forms of ownership. This new form is said to be directed towards the fulfillment of three basic goals.

First, economic and other differences between the working class and the peasants will be eliminated and the present situation, where the former exercise leadership over the latter, will become obsolete. At present, the state is said to represent the working class, and in addition, to possess superior leadership strength and thus find justification for state leadership of peasants.

Second, it is said that the differences between agricultural and industrial labor will be eliminated in a Communist society, and, presumably, questions such as longer hours of work and lower pay per hour in the agricultural vis-a-vis the industrial sector will be resolved on some basis other than the fact that work is agricultural per se. In a broad sense, the differences in levels of living between the urban and the rural areas will be eliminated in a Communist society.

If the kolkhoz is in any sense a self governing cooperative organization, how is external leadership justified even if it does arise from a "superior" force? The Soviet answer to this question is twofold: first, the goals and tasks of state leadership are said to be identical with those of the kolkhoz and its members, so there is no contradiction. Second, the raising of the kolkhoz sector to its appropriate role in the future Soviet (Communist) society is said to result from the natural forces of development in the agricultural sector, subject only to the application of "appropriate guidance." Such guidance is said not to conflict with the concept of kolkhoz democracy since the state does not direct *(upravliat')* the kolkhoz, but rather is said to lead it *(rukovodit')* through kolkhoz administrative organs.

The Legal Content of State Leadership

The kolkhoz operates in, and is governed by, the laws *(zakony)* of Soviet society. Thus the kolkhoz may be guided by a resolution *(postanovleniia)* of the supreme court, or more likely, from state and Party organs. Edicts *(ukazy)* and resolutions are issued by the Presidium of the Supreme Soviet of the USSR and the presidiums of the supreme Soviets of the union republics and autonomous republics. Resolutions and regulations *(rasporiazhenie)* of the Soviet Ministers of the USSR along with joint resolutions of the state and Party authorize policy from the highest level.

Relevant ministries, for example the Ministry of Agriculture, may issue commands and instructions *(prikazy)*, statements *(vedomosti)*, direction *(upravlenii)*, decisions *(resheniia)* and regulations. Thus there is an impressive array of instruments to which the kolkhoz must pay attention. In practice, however, there is a considerable volume of communication directed to kolkhozy by external organs which does not bear the formal significance of a law. To understand the nature of this communication as it pertains to the freedom of decision making enjoyed within the kolkhoz, we must consider the different forms of communication, the anticipated response in each case and grievance procedure where response is not forthcoming.

Possibly the simplest form of relationship between an external organ and the kolkhoz is the *imperative norm.* For example, the kolkhoz is required to pay certain taxes, it is required to hold specified sums of insurance on crops and livestock, the amounts of which will be specified in the appropriate norms. These norms are legally binding, though, in some cases, their general outline will be formulated at the highest levels, while the specific content vis-a-vis a given kolkhoz will be elaborated locally. Thus the actions of local insurance agents are spelled out by a decree *(polozhenie).* In some cases, the general regulations will be elaborated in a normative act *(normativnyi akt),* while the details for a specific case will be contained in an agreement *(dogovor).* Finally, there may exist a sample or model contract *(tipovoi dogovor)* from which a specific agreement suitable for a given situation will be drawn.

Normally a hierarchical structure of administration is preserved. Thus leadership from the oblast level will be of a general character while specific details will be elaborated at the raion level. In addition to the legally binding norms elaborated locally, the state may regulate the internal affairs of the kolkhoz on an all-union basis. Thus in the case of accounting and auditing procedures, one finds centralized decrees spelling out specific procedures in detail. Planning and accounting documents are centrally formulated. Further, the roles of key personnel, for example the accountant, may be specifically elaborated in a decree. These are areas which are said not to depend upon local conditions and hence are capable of fully centralized direction.

A second and widely utilized form of communication is the *recommendation.* Since the theory of kolkhoz democracy implies self-government of the kolkhoz by elected organs of administration, a recommendation is frequently used to specify the *policy* or direction in which a certain activity is to be executed. However, while a legally binding order is fully elaborated by an organ external to the kolkhoz and thus binding upon the kolkhoz without change, the recommendation is elaborated *within* the kolkhoz and with appropriate guidance from the Party. Of course to the extent that external organs close to the kolkhoz issue such a recommendation, the distinction between this and a legally binding order of some type may be meaningless.

The recommendation is not, therefore, a legally obligatory form of directive, but rather is described as *authoritative advice*. The recommendation is viewed as assistance so that a kolkhoz can correctly (that is in accordance with state wishes, which theoretically do not differ from those of the kolkhoz or its members) decide questions falling within its competence.[5] Nevertheless, the *direction* is obligatory. Thus two Soviet legal scholars suggest that the 1956 decree of the CPSU and Soviet Ministers with regard to changing the kolkhoz charter gave to kolkhozy the direction *(napravlenie)* which they must have in mind when making these adjustments. They state further:

This direction is obligatory for kolkhozy, in it is represented a command (velenie), and not the advice (sovet) of the state to kolkhozy.[6]

As with legally binding directives which take the form of acts of individual significance, the execution of a recommendation is under the control of state and Party organs.

A third form of communication is the case where decisions formulated internally by a kolkhoz require external approval prior to their implementation. Thus, the charter of the kolkhoz becomes operative only after it is approved by the raiispolkom.

The practical application of the approval technique will become apparent later when we examine the manner in which specific important decisions are made. If one considers this mode of communication in conjunction with others already examined, it will become apparent that the potential for external control over kolkhoz decision making is very great. As a case in point, consider the annual plan. The format of this document is prepared centrally, while the specific content pertaining to a given kolkhoz will be subjected to confirmation by external organs prior to execution by the kolkhoz. In addition to much of the specific content of the plan being generated externally, at the time of confirmation, recommended changes will find expression in a binding contract, for example to deliver output.

The notion of a decision being recommended or requiring subsequent approval does imply a definable sphere (however limited) in which the kolkhoz is freely able to make decisions. Soviet writers talk about those areas in which the kolkhoz has competence.[7] Competence is, of course, a matter of degree. Thus for example, Soviet writers suggest that the formulation of a charter is within the competence of the individual kolkhoz. While formally correct, the extent to which the charter reflects discussion and dissent within the kolkhoz is minimal given the existence of a model charter for the republic specifying the format in detail and, the requirement that external approval be obtained for all decisions made within the kolkhoz. Nevertheless, to the extent that the individual kolkhoz

[5] Beliaev and Pankratov, op. cit., pp. 150-151.

[6] Ibid., p. 151 (literal translation).

[7] Ibid., p. 152.

has any say in the formulation of a charter (which it did not have prior to 1956) the degree of competence for freedom of decision making by the kolkhoz has increased. It remains however to ask by how much and in what directions.

Soviet writers generally suggest that the area of competence of the individual kolkhoz has increased in recent years.[8] A kolkhoz may be empowered to make decisions in an area previously handled partly or entirely by an external directive. Also, a decision previously made externally might be delegated to internal kolkhoz organs subject to subsequent confirmation from without. In sum, increased freedom of decision making for the kolkhoz can arise from many different combinations and shifts in the administrative structure.

The external organizational structure with which the kolkhoz must interact has undergone marked change in recent years. For the pre-1958 period the decisive instrument of state control in the countryside was the Machine Tractor Station. Their abolition (in 1958) and sale of machinery and equipment to kolkhozy led to the establishment of Agricultural Inspectorates under the Raion Executive Committees. This structure remained essentially intact until the year 1962 when new organs, the Territorial Production Administrations, were established as organs of local control.[9] These Administrations, though not formally abolished, faded into the raion organizations which presently administer agriculture at the local level. Let us turn to a consideration of the MTS.

The Machine Tractor Stations

The MTS were budget financed state organizations performing two basic services in the countryside. First, most machinery and equipment was owned by the MTS and thus much of the kolkhoz work requiring the use of such inputs was contained in an annual agreement *(dogovor)* between the two institutions.[10] Given the vital importance of the machinery input (especially in field crop operations), a close relationship between the MTS and the kolkhoz was essential. Second, the MTS served as an important organ of planning and control, and played a decisive role in both plan formulation and execution within the kolkhozy, and indeed were held responsible for the successful completion of kolkhoz tasks.[11] Further, the Party apparatus functioned within as well as external to the MTS.

Given the vital and unique functions performed by the MTS in the execution of economic activity within the kolkhoz, it would seem that any examination of decision making powers within the farms must initially consider the extent to

[8]Ibid., pp. 30-31.

[9]For a discussion of the Territorial production Administrations, see Alec Nove, op. cit., pp. 9-12 and Howard R. Swearer, op. cit., pp. 28-37.

[10]I.F. Pokrovskii, *MTS-Opornyi punkt gosudarstvennogo rukovodstva kolkhozami* (Moskva: Gosiurizdat, 1957), pp. 16-17.

[11] Ibid.

which (if any) decision making powers of the MTS vis-a-vis the kolkhoz may have increased up to 1958, and where these powers resided after 1958.

The *potential* ability of the MTS to control the kolkhozy might be assessed, in part, by the following indicators:

1. The physical presence of the MTS vis-a-vis the kolkhozy: the MTS/kolkhozy ratio and the MTS/sown area ratio.
2. The ability of the MTS to service the kolkhozy effectively in terms of (a) the availability of agricultural specialists, and (b) the availability of equipment.
3. The internal strength of the MTS and its ability to exercise strong control over the kolkhozy as indicated by (a) the quality of the leadership personnel in the MTS and (b) the position of the Party organization in the MTS.

It might be suggested that reduction of the span of control in an organization facilitates the control of a subordinate organ by a superior organ.[12] In terms of the interaction between the MTS and the appropriate management organs of the kolkhozy, the span of control became more favorable between 1953 and 1957, since the number of kolkhozy declined markedly throughout the Soviet Union (with the exception of Armenia), while the number of MTS also declined, though at a lesser rate. In some regions, the number of MTS increased. The net result left the MTS with a greater potential to control kolkhoz activity, and to do so more effectively given a decreased span of control.

The kolkhozy/MTS ratio can be defended as an indicator of potential MTS ability to control the kolkhozy if we accept the notion that the fewer kolkhozy each MTS is called upon to supervise, the closer and more effective will be the supervision.[13] On these grounds and in spite of significant regional differentials, the data in Table 3-1 suggests a substantially increased ability of the MTS to control the kolkhozy. However, planning and control are only part of the MTS role. Given the importance of mechanization in the field crop sector and the responsibility of the MTS for its proper execution, a more useful indicator of potential MTS presence might be the sown area/MTS ratio.[14]

[12]Herbert A. Simon, *Administrative Behavior* (2d ed. rev.; New York: The Free Press, 1965), pp. 26-28.

[13]Such an argument would seem plausible since the relationship between the MTS and the kolkhoz was close, and both were operating in a sphere of production characterized by instability and time pressures on a seasonal basis. Also, to the extent that the kolkhozy became more highly specialized, the task of coordination may have been increasingly difficult, at least insofar as a single MTS might control several kolkhozy of different directions of specialization. For a discussion of theoretical questions pertaining to span of control, coordination, etc., see Joseph A. Litterer, *The Analysis of Organizations* (New York: John Wiley & Sons, Inc., 1965), pp. 308-316.

[14]Since the MTS was a supplier of major machinery and equipment to the kolkhozy, the sown area/MTS ratio might be more relevant than the kolkhoz/MTS ratio. If sown area serviced by a single MTS declines, service to each kolkhoz should improve, especially given the concentration of service requirements at peak periods. Also, the sown area/MTS ratio is especially relevant for the 1950s, a period when decline in the number of kolkhozy was primarily a product of amalgamation, thus leaving a similar production capacity (sown area, cattle) to be serviced by a single MTS.

Table 3-1
Relative Growth of Kolkhozy, Sown Area and Cattle per MTS, 1953 and 1957

	MTS[a] (1953=100)	Kol.[b] MTS	Sown Area MTS	Cattle MTS
USSR	94	67	106	106
RSFSR	91	70	108	111
North	104	85	83	82
Northwest	89	91	100	103
Center	104	74	94	98
Volga-Viatka	99	72	101	93
Cen. Black Earth	96	63	108	116
Volga	86	66	109	119
North Caucasus	86	62	101	121
Urals	91	65	107	115
West Siberia	77	60	131	131
East Siberia	97	56	122	100
Far East	91	81	148	121
Ukraine	101	75	99	105
Belorussia	89	48	108	115
Lithuania	114	39	84	83
Latvia	97	73	84	78
Estonia	107	37	69	71
Georgia	135	66	61	60
Azerbaidzhan	135	67	81	68
Armenia	113	114	73	82
Kazakhstan	87	53	162	108
Uzbekistan	77	57	118	136
Kirghizistan	110	53	103	90
Tadzhikistan	108	31	91	89
Turkmenistan	124	49	87	77
Moldavia	70	69	141	173

Source: Computed from *Sel-khoz-1960*, pp. 51, 74, 145, 274.

[a]We neglect adjustments to existing MTS and examine only the changing *number* of stations.

[b]For each indicator, we use the following formula: $\dfrac{\text{Kol. } 1957/1953}{\text{MTS } 1957/1953}$.

Turning again to Table 3-1, one can observe marked regional differences in the sown area/MTS ratio. For the country as a whole the ratio has increased slightly, although for some republics notably Georgia, Azerbaidzhan, Armenia, Turkmenistan and the Baltic region, the ratio decreased significantly.

The ratio of number of cattle to MTS is a less useful indicator given the relative unimportance of mechanization in this sector. For the country as a whole, this ratio increased slightly. As was the case with the sown area/MTS ratio however, there are significant regional differentials. In particular, the ratio decreased significantly in the Baltic region, Georgia, Armenia, Azerbaidzhan and Turkmenistan, the same regions in which the sown area/MTS ratio decreased.

The ability of the MTS to plan and execute economic activity within the kolkhozy was in part determined by the personnel available to perform these functions and the nature of the equipment available for utilization on the farms. From Table 3-2, it is apparent that while the number of personnel attached to the MTS increased sharply up to 1957, these increases were restricted to certain groups. In particular, there was a tendency for the average annual numbers of workers to increase substantially, with rather smaller increases in service and other personnel and a notable decline in engineering-technical personnel. The matter of MTS personnel cannot, however, be handled simply in terms of numbers. The administrative structure of the MTS, especially after 1953, bears closely upon this question.

At the September, 1953 Party Plenum, the MTS were the subject of criticism for their weakness vis-a-vis the kolkhozy. Several measures were adopted in an effort to eradicate this situation. First, the execution of tractor work was to be improved by the formation in the MTS of constant tractor brigades.[15] Thus the

Table 3-2
Machine Tractor Stations: Selected Indicators (1953 = 100)

	1953	1956	1957
Number of MTS	100	97	88
All Personnel–MTS-RTS (Average Annual)	100	267	225
Of Which:			
Workers (rabochie)	100	317	278
Engineer-Tech. Workers	100	99	93
White-Collar Workers (sluzhash-chie)	100	128	122
Junior Service Personnel	100	160	151
Workers in Housing and Amenities, Capital Repair of Buildings and Fixtures	100	149	145

Source: *Sel'khoz-1960*, pp. 74, 458.

[15]The tractor brigade was the basic form of organization within the MTS, for the provision of tractor and equipment services to the kolkhozy. Prior to 1953, these brigades were formed on a temporary basis using kolkhoz members as workers only for the period of field work. The basic change in 1953, designed to increase the productive usage of machinery, involved the creation of constant brigades with workers transferred from the kolkhozy to be used in the brigades and *employed* by the MTS. See I.F. Pokrovskii, op. cit., p. 21. One might suspect a degree of underutilization of labor in the winter with the constant brigade system. Broad training and other techniques may have partially alleviated the problem.

notion of a seasonal brigade, or one formed spontaneously for the fulfillment of a particular task, was to be replaced by permanently organized brigades available for service at all times. In addition, however, the workers of these brigades, coming from the kolkhozy as had been the case with the temporary brigades, would be employed by the MTS, and would be paid according to scales operative in the MTS and presumably rather better than their alternative employment in the kolkhozy.

In the sphere of technical personnel, Party organs were obliged to direct engineer-mechanics into leadership positions. In addition, 6500 engineer-mechanics were to be directed into the MTS during 1954-1955, of which, in 1954, 2500 were to be young engineers from various institutes for the mechanization of agriculture.[16]

At the September, 1953 Plenum, Khrushchev pointed out that while there were a total of 350,000 agricultural specialists with higher and secondary education engaged in the system of agricultural organs, there were only 18,500 such specialists working directly in kolkhozy and 50,000 working in the MTS.[17] To improve what was perceived as an adverse balance and to bring the services of the specialists closer to the kolkhozy, the September, 1953 Plenum established the goal of placing specialists *in the MTS* such that each kolkhoz would be continuously served by one or two specialists. To achieve this goal, government organs were obliged to send, by the spring of 1954, 100,000 agronomists and zoötechnicians for attachment to the MTS.[18] These specialists were to be obtained by a reorganization of the Ministry of Agriculture and its local organs. While employed by the MTS, their basic function was that of servicing the kolkhozy, and emphasis was placed upon the need for their physical presence in the kolkhozy on a continual basis.

To what extent was Khrushchev successful in his efforts to expand the volume of specialists on the local level? The evidence (Table 3-3) suggests that the dispatch of specialists to the local level was, in fact, achieved. In addition, it would seem that the rapid timetable was met, for on February 23, 1954 Khrushchev was able to declare that more than 100,000 agronomists and zoötechnicians were working spontaneously in kolkhozy.[19]

If the increased presence of agricultural specialists on the kolkhozy, though employed by the MTS, increased the degree to which the latter could potentially service the former, what of the machinery and equipment held by the MTS?[20]

One possible indicator of service capacity is horsepower per hectare of sown

[16]"O merakh dal'neishego razvitiia sel'skogo khoziaistva SSSR," *Kirektivy KPSS*, vol. 4, p. 48.
[17]*Direktivy KPSS*, vol. 4, p. 24.
[18]Ibid., p. 54.
[19]N.S. Khrushchev, "O dal'neishem uvelichenii proizvodstva zerna v strane i ob osvoenii tselinnykh i salezhnykh zemei'," in N.S. Khrushchev, *Stroitel'stvo kommunizma v SSSR i razvitie sel'skogo khoziaistva* (Moskva: Gospolitizdat, 1962), vol. 1, p. 229.
[20]It should be noted that small equipment could be held on the kolkhozy themselves. Indeed, the movement towards self-purchase of equipment by the kolkhozy started prior to the abolition of the MTS.

41

Table 3-3
Agronomists, Zoötechnicians, Veterinary Workers and Forestry Experts with Higher and Secondary Specialized Education: Selected Years

	1953 July 1	1955 July 1	1956 Dec. 1	1957 Dec. 1
Kolkhozy	18,500	n.a.	n.a.	n.a.
MTS	64,500	n.a.	n.a.	n.a.
MTS and kolkhozy	69,000	204,000	220,000	211,000

Sources: *Narkhoz-1957*, p. 151, *Narkhoz-1958*, p. 528, V.G. Venzher, *Voprosy kompleksnoi mekhanizatsii kolkhoznogo proizvodstva* (Moskva: Akademiia Nauk SSSR, 1955), p. 319. The categories are most likely inexact given the non-additive nature of the data for the year 1953.

Note: This table is only broadly comparable with Table 3-2 since the bases of classification are different. In particular, the expansion of specialists shown above should not be compared with the decline of engineering-technical personnel (Table 3-2) since the latter are not agricultural specialists.

area (Table 3-4). Such an indicator of energy capacity of equipment held by the MTS is not ideal insofar as shifts in the structure of the machinery park, for example a trend away from higher horsepower units to lower horsepower units or vice-versa, might be hidden. Assuming, however, that such shifts are not likely to have been especially important, our data would suggest limited expansion of machinery and equipment vis-a-vis sown area during the 1950s. The case of automobiles is an exception. Also, given the relatively stable nature of the Soviet automobile in terms of body styles and size of motor, horsepower is probably a good indicator of availability. The trend is not unusual given the significantly

Table 3-4
Energy Capacity of MTS-Kolkhozy by Horsepower per Hectare of Sown Area: Selected Machinery, 1954-1960

	1954[a]	1957	1958	1959	1960
Horsepower per hectare (sown area–all crops)					
Tractors	.19	.23	.22	.23	.24
Motor Combines	.09	.09	.11	.12	.11
Automobiles	.22	.33	.33	.35	.38

Source: *Sel'khoz-1960*, pp. 145, 399, 405.

Note: Since energy capacity of different forms of equipment is not given for MTS-kolkhozy, we assume this to be equal to the difference between energy capacity for the entire agricultural sector and that for sovkhozy.

[a]Sown area is for the year 1953 for all forms of equipment.

increased size of the average kolkhoz and the need to improve internal transportation.[21]

Thus far attention has been focused upon the physical presence of the MTS in the countryside and its ability to service the kolkhozy as indicated by availability of personnel and equipment. However, the MTS was more than simply a service organ supplying machinery and equipment. The ability of the MTS to be effective in its second role as a planner and controller of kolkhoz activity must have been partially determined by the quality of the leadership personnel in the MTS and the position of the Party organization.

The record of raising educational levels of leadership personnel in the MTS has been impressive (Table 3-5) and should have assisted the MTS in strengthening their role in the planning and operation of kolkhozy. In addition to raising educational levels, however, steps were also taken, especially in the early 1950s, to strengthen the position of the Party within the MTS.

In 1953, the Raion department of agriculture was abolished and the functions divided between the MTS and the ispolkom of the raion soviet. The function of inspection, previously carried out by the state inspector for the supervision of the quality of MTS work (who was the chief agronomist of the raion agricultural department), was now assumed by the chief agronomist of the MTS. Thus there existed a potentially unhealthy relationship between the inspection and administration sections of the MTS similar to that in kolkhozy.

Primarily the raion retained the formal functions such as registering charters and agreements. As one Soviet writer has pointed out, most raiispolkoms did

Table 3-5
Educational Levels of Selected MTS Personnel (in percentages)

	Higher Education			Secondary Spec. Education		Lower Level and Practical	
	Sept. 1953	Early 1954	Jan. 1955	Sept. 1953	Early 1954	Sept. 1953	Early 1954
Director	22.6	39.3	59.3	47.0	40.0	30.4	20.7
Chief Engineer	14.8	78.5	80.0	20.8	10.0	64.4	16.5
Chief, Repair Shop	1.3	28.5	29.0	8.8	40.6	89.9	30.9

Sources: Compiled from N.S. Khrushchev, *Stroitel'stvo kommunizma v SSSR i razvitie sel'skogo khoziaistva* (Moskva: Gosudarstvennoe izdatel'stvo politicheskoi literatury, 1962), Vol. I, p. 56; Robert F. Miller, *One Hundred Thousand Tractors* (Cambridge: Harvard University Press, 1970), p. 122. V.G. Venzher, *Voprosy kompleksnoi mechanizatsii kolkhoznogo proizvodstva* (Moskva: Akademiia Nauk SSSR, 1955), p. 318.

[21] In terms of arable land being tilled, the average kolkhoz grew in size from 1,706 hectares in 1953, to 3,606 hectares in 1959. In terms of agricultural land in general *(sel'skokhoziaistvennaia ugod'ia)*, the average kolkhoz grew from 4,211 hectares in 1953, to 5,538 hectares in 1959. See *Sel'khoz-1960*, pp. 58-59, 62.

not have special departments concerned with agriculture and hence they were purveyors of general state leadership.[22]

Within the MTS, the position of deputy director for political affairs was abolished and instructor groups were formed to carry out Party work in zones serviced by MTS. Each group was headed by a raikom secretary, reporting to the first secretary of the raikom Party, the latter serving as a general leader of their activities. This served, as Alec Nove has suggested, to streamline the Party apparatus. However, the immediate success of this structure was limited, and both the raion Party and the instructor groups were subjected to severe criticism for the inadequacies of their work—criticism forthcoming at the March, 1954 Party Plenum.

The instructor groups apparently remained largely ineffective. Khrushchev, at the January, 1955 Party Plenum, again criticized them for never having left the "organization period."[23]

In 1958, the MTS were abolished and their planning and control functions shifted to other organs. In particular, the task of supervision passed to agriculture inspectorates under the raion executive committee. The use of the raion as the organ of immediate control did not last. It should be noted that while these changes were taking place, the Ministry of Agriculture was also being downgraded. In 1955, in a decree that we shall examine later, the kolkhozy were granted increased powers in the determination of sown area. Second, in 1959, the Ministry planning functions were transferred to Gosplan. Finally, in 1961, the Ministry was reduced to an organ supervising research and education.

The March, 1962 Party Plenum authorized the creation of a new unit of control over the agricultural sector: the Territorial Production Administrations (TPA). Each TPA, with wide powers over agricultural matters, was to operate in one or more raions, and would have an inspector-organizer who would represent the state on the kolkhozy. In addition, each Administration had a Party organizer from the oblast Party committee and, with assistants, was authorized to supervise all local agricultural matters. The Party organizer reported upward through the Party structure rather than that of the TPA.

Although statistical material on the composition of the TPA's is limited, Table 3-6 gives us a picture of this structure in the Ukraine for the year 1962. Considering the composition of the chairmen of the TPA's, it would appear that there was no intention of lessening the Party role in agriculture simply because the MTS had been abolished. Further, to the extent that the structure in the Ukraine can be considered as representative of the country as a whole, there seems to have been an attempt to preserve the external technical control of the MTS by supplying agricultural specialists for the position of inspector-organizer. Further evidence of the effort to maintain a strong control of agriculture at the

---

[22]I.F. Pokrovskii, op. cit., p. 31.

[23]N.S. Khrushchev, "O rukovodstve sel'skim khoziaistvom i Partiino-politicheskoi rabote v derevne," op. cit., vol. 1, p. 491.

Table 3-6

Structure of the (Sovkhoz-Kolkhoz) Territorial Production Administrations in the Ukrainian SSR, 1962

Total number of Production Administrations	190
Chairmen of which were:	
1st Secretaries of Raikom and Gorkom Party	85
Chairmen of Raiispolkom	43
Heads of Oblast Directorates of agriculture, sovkhozy or procurement organs	49
Chiefs of Departments of Oblast Party Committees or Deputy Chairmen of Oblast Executive Committees	13
Inspector-Organizers	2,338
Of which:	
Agronomists, zoötechnicians and other specialists of agriculture	2,034
Non-specialists	304

Source: N. Podgorny, "Neustanno uluchshat' rukovodstvo sel'skim khoziaistovom," *Pravda* (July 8, 1962), pp. 2-3.

raion level came at the November, 1962 Party Plenum, when the number of TPA's was to be increased from 960 to 1,500. Thus the Production Administration came closer to representing a single raion. As Howard Swearer has pointed out, to the extent that jurisdictional battles arose between the Territorial Production Administration and the raion authorities, it was made clear in 1962 that the former would prevail when dealing with agricultural matters in the given area.[24]

In the period after the abolition of the MTS, machinery and equipment was sold to the kolkhozy. In addition, in 1961, an organization was formed *(soiuzsel' khoztekhnika)* for the purpose of supplying new equipment, spare parts and fertilizer. The range of issues associated with the supply and utilization of machinery and equipment in the post-MTS era are interesting, though beyond the present study. However, Douglas Diamond has observed that both the quantity and quality of machine operators (average numbers per unit of power equipment) has declined in recent years.[25] In addition, Diamond notes that between 1960 and 1964, the average use of tractors per day of operation (acreage plowed) declined by 21 percent, in addition to a decline in the number of daily shifts (1960-1963).[26] Diamond concludes that the abolition of the MTS ". . . had a negative impact on factor productivity.", and in addition to the problems already cited, notes the low level and quality of equipment repairs in the post-

[24] Howard R. Swearer, op. cit., pp. 30-32.

[25] Douglas B. Diamond, op. cit., p. 363.

[26] Ibid.

MTS period.[27] In addition to suggesting the existence of serious inefficiencies in the MTS during their final years (1955-1957), Jerzy Karcz has also drawn attention to the issues related to payment for the equipment, and indeed, the quality of the equipment transferred from the MTS.[28] Finally, Lazar Volin, also noting some of the above difficulties, suggests that the strengthening of the rural Party made possible the abolition of the MTS as an organ of control.[29] Volin concludes, however, that the abolition of the MTS did eliminate dual management, served to restrict duplication of procurement organs, and, ultimately, facilitated the purchase of equipment by kolkhozy as the income of the latter increased in the late 1950s and early 1960s.[30]

Summary

The kolkhoz is an integral part of the Soviet economy and its planning apparatus and as such differs substantially from the theoretical construct of a producer cooperative. It is important to realize, however, that the mechanisms utilized to integrate the kolkhoz into the planned economy have differed from those utilized for other organizational forms in the Soviet economy.

One of the basic control mechanisms of the pre-1958 era was the Machine Tractor Stations. On several grounds, MTS internal strength (and thus potentially as a control mechanism vis-a-vis the kolkhozy) seems to have increased during the early 1950s. Some of this strength, as a control mechanism, must have been transferred to other organizations after the demise of the MTS. Indeed, the Party structure within the kolkhozy has been adjusted to recognize changes such as the abolition of the MTS and the changing size and structure of the kolkhoz itself. In spite of these readjustments, however, surely the dissolution of the MTS must be seen as a relaxation of external control over kolkhoz affairs, for few would dispute the very great extent to which the MTS was involved directly in the internal affairs of the kolkhoz on a day to day basis. In a sense, the abolition of the MTS might be viewed as an effort by the state to enhance the stock of both physical and human capital in the countryside, and, especially, to improve the utilization of this capital. Such a move could have been of direct benefit to the kolkhoz system, but was undoubtedly viewed as dependent upon large scale state assistance. The latter was in fact forthcoming when kolkhoz debts for the purchase of MTS machinery and equipment were cancelled.

During the years of Khrushchev's leadership, there were continual organizational shifts of those organs external to the kolkhoz system. The post-Khrushchev era has seen many of the original changes dismantled: the downgrading and

---

[27] Ibid., p. 364.

[28] Jerzy Karcz, op. cit., pp. 402-410.

[29] Lazar Volin, op. cit., p. 299.

[30] Ibid.

re-location of the Ministry of Agriculture has been reversed; the division of the Communist Party into industrial and agricultural branches has been abandoned. Indeed, Brezhnev and Kosygin have been much less prone to undertake organizational shuffling of the type so common in the 1950s.

4 Structural Change in the Kolkhoz Sector

Background and Approach

Throughout the period under study, there has been a continuing process of *structural change* in the collectivized sector of Soviet agriculture having a significant impact upon the nature of the kolkhoz as an economic organization. Structural change is defined as changing size of the kolkhoz, (as measured by land labor and capital), and the component production units of the kolkhoz and the accompanying re-definition of the roles played by each production unit within the kolkhoz.

For the period 1950 through 1968, the number of kolkhozy in the Soviet Union declined from 121,400 to 35,600.[1] For the same period, the socialized sown area per kolkhoz grew from 997 to 2,874 hectares, and the number of households per kolkhoz grew from 165 to 240 although total sown area in the collective sector declined from roughly 121 million hectares in 1950 to 102 million hectares in 1968.[2] These changes have been the result of four distinct though interrelated programs:

1. Amalgamation of small kolkhozy to form larger units
2. Conversion—kolkhozy attached to an existing sovkhoz
3. Conversion—kolkhozy combined to form a new sovkhoz
4. Land taken from the agricultural sector

The impact of structural change has varied regionally and over time. A summary of important organizational changes is presented in Table 4-1.

The present study is concerned primarily with amalgamation since it is only this process which ultimately results in or diminishes the number of kolkhozy. In particular, the focus here will be changes in the absolute size of the kolkhoz; the brigade and ferma within the kolkhoz; and also, the shifts in the size of the brigade and ferma vis-a-vis the kolkhoz. The time pattern of these changes, in addition to regional variations, will be considered. The latter emphasis upon regional variations of structural change is essential given the possibility of initially different production structures and decision making patterns based upon crop differences, climatic differences, and historically different patterns of regional investment.

---

[1] *Narkhoz-1958*, p. 313; *Narkhoz-1968*, p. 349.

[2] Computed from *Narkhoz-1958*, pp. 313, 338; *Narkhoz-1968*, pp. 349, 394.

Table 4-1
USSR State and Collective Farms: Organizational Adjustments, 1950-1968

	1953[a]	1956	1957	1958	1959	1960	1961	1962	1963	1964	1965	1966	1967	1968
1. Kolkhozy (decline)	30,200	8,200	6,486	8,854	14,245	9,455	3,487	761	1,156	1,106	1,340	224	313	587
2. Sovkhozy (increase)	(−131)	241	807	97	494	879	906	289	606	902	1,603	508	594	615
3. Kolkhozy[b] (newly org)	...	...	109	30	26	0	7	7	4	...	...	...	...	...
4. Kolkhozy (dismantled)	...	...	1,031	368	101	163	504	317	343	...	...	...	...	...
5. Kolkhozy (amalgamated)	...	1,866	8,010	12,271	4,550	1,092	683	1,037		...	...	...	...	...
6. Kolkhozy (converted)	...	5,730	1,256	2,074	5,068	2,906	402	271		...	...	...	...	...

Sources: Data for the years 1957 through 1963 from V.G. Venzher, *Ispol'zovanie zakona stoimosti v kolkhoznom proizvodstve* (2nd ed. rev.; Moskva: Nauka, 1965), p. 113. Remaining data from selected volumes of *Narkhoz-SSSR*.

[a]Changes are between column years, the base year being 1950. For the years 1953, 1956 and 1966, the number of kolkhozy are to be the nearest hundred and, accordingly, year to year changes are approximate.

[b]Data on amalgamation and conversion should be considered as approximate due to possible double counting. For example, in any given year, several kolkhozy may be newly formed but later amalgamated or even converted.

Examination of size will focus upon sown land area, labor force and capital investment, since the question of amalgamation is closely related to internal decision making and the effective utilization of these inputs. While the trend towards fewer numbers of larger farms might be construed as a trend towards centralization, it is important to consider the changing nature of the brigade and its role in the internal decision making process before such a conclusion is attempted.

To the extent that the brigade has grown vis-a-vis the kolkhoz (and thus there are fewer brigades per kolkhoz), the administrative task facing top level kolkhoz management might be simplified and thus managerial performance improved. Such an argument would proceed along the lines presented in Chapter 3 where the MTS/kolkhozy ratio was considered. On the other hand, it could be argued that insofar as the size of the brigade has increased absolutely, potential gains from the smaller numbers of brigades might be offset. In this latter respect, changes in the nature of the brigade, resulting, in part, from increased absolute size, have created in many cases a brigade whose operation is similar to that of a whole kolkhoz of the past. In this respect, the brigade has become an increasingly important center of focus for an examination of decision making activity within the kolkhoz. Thus the final section of this chapter will be devoted to a consideration of the different types of brigades and their temporal and regional patterns of development.

Amalgamation

Although contraction in the numbers of kolkhozy is not strictly a recent phenomenon, there was a spurt of this activity in 1950-1951 as the result of a decree of the Council of Ministers dated July 17, 1950.[3] On the basis of this decree, amalgamation was to be carried out only with the permission of the membership concerned, and certain benefits were to be extended. These benefits related primarily to the payment of bank loans and the matter of deductions into the indivisible fund *(nedelimyi fond)*, and, in essence, took the form of time delays.[4] It was decreed, however, that the obligatory deliveries of the new larger kolkhozy would be the sum of those applicable to the previously existing farms.[5]

There were undoubtedly many factors, both political and economic, which led to the continuing amalgamation of collective farms throughout the 1950s. Lazar Volin has suggested that ". . . confusion of the largest with the optimum size has long dominated Soviet policy under Khrushchev as under Stalin."[6]

[3]"O meropriiatiiakh v sviazi s ukrupneniem melkikh kolkhozov," as cited in *Sbornik*, pp. 47-48.

[4]Ibid., p. 48.

[5]Ibid., p. 47.

[6]Lazar Volin, "Khrushchev and The Agricultural Scene," in Jerzy F. Karcz (ed.), *Soviet and East European Agriculture* (Berkeley and Los Angeles: University of California Press, 1967), pp. 1-21. See especially p. 16.

Further, Volin suggests that given a managerial group largely recruited externally, an increasing gap between management and the peasants may have facilitated the control of the latter by the former, though he concludes that the impact of amalgamation was largely negative.[7] Alec Nove has pointed out that "The sheer size of a kolkhoz makes close human contact impossible."[8] He concludes, however, that the impact of this minimal degree of contact depends in large measure upon the personality of the farm chairman.[9]

R.E.F. Smith, writing prior to the dissolution of the Machine Tractor Stations, suggested that "technical reorganization of the land" was the basic factor in the amalgamation campaign.[10] Smith suggests that with increased Party influence in the farms and ". . . increased importance of the MTS and their closer integration with the collective farms . . ." larger production units will permit improved crop rotation, and ". . . the rational disposition of livestock farms. . . ."[11]

He concludes that the movement is in essence, ". . . an attempt to extend planning to the sphere where it is weakest."[12]

It has been suggested by Soviet writers and in part demonstrated by western observers that weak kolkhozy were the ones most frequently amalgamated or converted.[13] Given the goal of wanting to increase the economic strength of weak farms, and the perceived superiority of large scale as opposed to small scale production units, pressure for the amalgamation of weak farms is understandable.[14] Further, to the extent that such a program could be demonstrated to be potentially effective, collective farm members, especially on weak farms, would most likely voice approval. From the point of view of raion officials, amalgamation must have been viewed favorably to the extent that it might in any degree facilitate the achievement of delivery targets.

Ignoring for the moment changes within the kolkhoz and the nature of re-

[7]Ibid.

[8]Alec Nove, "Peasants and Officials," in Jerzy F. Karcz (ed.), *Soviet and East European Agriculture* (Berkeley and Los Angeles: University of California Press, 1967), pp. 57-72. See especially p. 62.

[9]Ibid., pp. 62-65.

[10]R.E.F. Smith, "The Amalgamation of Collective Farms: Some Technical Aspects," *Soviet Studies*, vol. VI, no. 1 (July 1954), p. 30.

[11]Ibid., pp. 30-31.

[12]Ibid., p. 31.

[13]See, for example, A. Dryden, "A Note on the Conversion of Collective Farms Into State Farms," *The ASTE Bulletin*, vol. VII, no. 3 (Winter 1965), pp. 17-19, and the comments thereafter by Robert C. Stuart, "Conversion of Collective Farms Into State Farms: Further Note I," *The ASTE Bulletin*, vol. IX, no. 1 (Spring 1967), pp. 14-16, and Arthur W. Wright, "Conversion of Collective Farms Into State Farms: Further Note II," *The ASTE Bulletin*, vol. IX, no. 1 (Spring 1967), pp. 12-14. On the general theme, see Allen B. Ballard, "An End to Collective Farms?," *Problems of Communism*, vol. X, no. 4 (July-August 1961), pp. 9-16. Soviet writers have also suggested that it is the weak *(slabyi)* kolkhozy that are amalgamated and converted. See, for example, V.P. Rozhin, *Nekotorye voprosy pod'ema ekonomiki slabykh kolkhozov* (Moskva: Ekonomizdat, 1961), pp. 98-102; V.G. Venzher, *Ispol'zovanie zakona stoimosti v kolkhoznom proizvodstve* (2d ed. rev.; Moskva: Nauka, 1965), p. 112.

[14]Erich Strauss has suggested that this pattern changed over time, and in fact during the early years it was the relatively better off kolkhozy which were converted. See his *Soviet Agriculture in Perspective* (London: George Allen and Unwin, Ltd., 1969), p. 183.

gional differentials, Table 4-2 presents a broad picture of collective farm development for the period 1950-1968 in terms of land, labor and capital inputs.

While the numbers of kolkhozy have declined significantly, socialized sown area was, by 1968, not significantly less than that of 1950, indicating a marked increase in the average sown area per collective farm. At the same time, the labor input has declined steadily (with the exception of 1955). This decline is to be explained almost wholly in terms of a reduction in the numbers engaged in the collective farm labor force, rather than a decrease in the length of the working day, or the number of days worked per year. Finally, capital investment has increased significantly, though with a slight downturn in the post 1959 period.[15]

In the absence of complete data for the brigade level, the examination of these units is restricted to the relatively short period 1957 to 1961. Turning to the results presented in Table 4-3, it is apparent that while kolkhozy and their

Table 4-2

The Development of Collective Farms in the Soviet Union, 1950-1968 (1950=100)

	1950	1953	1955	1959	1962	1965	1968
Number of farms[a]	100	75	71	44	33	30	30
Sown area[b]	100	109	123	107	95	87	85
Number of cattle[c]	100[f]	99[g]	96	114	131	132	143
Capital investment[d]	100	157	282	469	436	575	1,087
Average annual man-days of employment[e]	100	87	94	81	66	60	...

Sources: Employment data from U.S. Department of Commerce, *Measures of Agricultural Employment in the U.S.S.R.: 1950-1966* International Population Reports Series P-95, No. 65, October, 1968, p. 32. All other data from selected volumes of *Narkhoz*.

[a]Refers to agricultural artels only.

[b]Sown area refers to the socialized sector—all crops.

[c]Number of cattle refers to long horned cattle only, in socialized sectors of kolkhozy.

[d]Capital investment is the official Soviet series. This series does not include investment in herds or capital repairs. Expenditures by kolkhozy for the purchase of machinery and equipment from the MTS in 1958 and thereafter are not included.

[e]This series is the product of the average annual employment in collective farms (agricultural and non-agricultural) and the number of man-days worked per average annual collective farmer.

[f]1951

[g]1954

[15]For the period 1959-1965, total planned investment in the agricultural sector was 50.0 billion rubles (constant 1955 prices), while actual investment was 55.2 billion rubles. Of this planned total investment, 34.5 billion rubles was to be collective farm investment. In fact, collective farm investment was 24.9 billion rubles. See Keith Bush, "Agricultural Reforms Since Khrushchev," in United States Congress, Joint Economic Committee, *New Directions in the Soviet Economy* (Washington, D.C.: U.S. Government Printing Office, 1966), p. 462.

Table 4-3

The Development of Collective Farms in the Soviet Union, 1957-1961 (1957=100)

	1957	1958	1959	1960	1961
Number of farms[a]	100	88	70	57	53
Number of brigades[b]	100	86	75	62	56
Sown area[c]	100	99	98	93	84
Average annual man-days of employment[d]	100	96	96	88	81
Capital investment[e]	100	129	160	144	143

Sources: Employment data from U.S. Department of Commerce, *Measures of Agricultural Employment in the U.S.S.R.: 1950-1966* International Population Reports Series P-95, No. 65, October, 1968, p. 32. Data on brigades from G.I. Shmelev, *Raspredelenie i ispol'zovanie truda v kolkhozakh* (Moskva: Mysl', 1964), p. 55, and I.I. Sigov, *Razdelenie truda v sel'skom khoziaistve pri perekhode k kommunizmu* (Moskva: Ekonomizdat, 1963), p. 139. All other data from *Sel'khoz-1960* and selected volumes of *Narkhoz*.

[a]Refers to agricultural artels only.

[b]The limited time span is dictated by the absence of comprehensive data on production brigades. This series is the sum of all types of brigades. We ignore the possibility of double counting on the grounds that most production brigades in the post-1957 period were of a permanent rather than a temporary character.

[c]Sown area refers to socialized sector—all crops.

[d]This series is the product of the average annual employment in collective farms (agricultural and non-agricultural) and the number of man-days worked per average annual collective farmer.

[e]Capital investment is the official Soviet series. This series does not include investment in herds or capital repairs. Expenditures by kolkhozy for the purchase of machinery and equipment from the MTS in 1958 and thereafter are not included.

brigades grew in absolute size (in terms of inputs available), the rate of decline in the numbers of kolkhozy and brigades was almost identical, thus indicating no change in the size of the brigade *relative to* the kolkhoz.

Structural Change—Regional and Temporal Patterns

Thus far we have concentrated upon amalgamation, examining only aggregative data pertaining to certain selected years. In the present section, a broader approach will be pursued, though data limitations will force us to lose a degree of depth. Adequate data on brigades are not available even for the country as a whole, not to mention the various regions. Also, as one examines the mid-1950s when brigades were formed on a temporary basis, the problem of defining a brigade for measurement purposes (sown area, labor force) becomes acute. We will consider the spatial and temporal patterns of amalgamation and conversion for the period 1959 through 1965, and the interrelationship of variables crucial to decision making, namely: the number of kolkhozy, number of sovkhozy, and (pertaining to kolkhozy only) number of brigades,[16] labor force,[17] and capital investment.[18]

The spatial and temporal patterns of structural change may be characterized by a tripartite classification: simple amalgamation, complex amalgamation and simple conversion.

Simple Amalgamation

The pattern of simple amalgamation portrays that situation where, as the number of kolkhozy declines over time (regardless of the rate of decline), the number of brigades and the inputs thereto remain constant. Given that only amalgamation is occurring, the number of sovkhozy would also remain constant. To the extent the median is considered, we assume that amalgamation is not peculiar to those kolkhozy with an abnormally high or low number of brigades and/or sown area, capital investment and labor force. Thus the number of brigades per kolkhoz, and the quantity of other inputs per kolkhoz are increasing, while, on a per brigade basis, they remain constant. In essence we have a simple regional combination of kolkhozy to form larger kolkhozy. To the extent that each kolkhoz administers a greater number of brigades, the task may grow more complex as the kolkhoz grows vis-a-vis the brigade. At the brigade level however, the structure remains unchanged.

Complex Amalgamation

With sown area and other inputs remaining constant, the number of kolkhozy and the number of brigades decline at the same rate, hence the quantity of inputs per brigade and per kolkhoz increase at the same rate. Both the kolkhoz and the brigade leaders face the task of administering units that have grown ab-

[16]For the period 1957-1960, data on the number and type of brigades in kolkhozy has been published by Soviet authors as gathered from collective farm accounts. For the period 1961-1965, we rely upon the series from *Narkhoz* pertaining to the number of brigadiers of production brigades. Insofar as the latter series overlaps the former for two years (1959 and 1960), a check upon the accuracy of our proxy is possible. Such a check reveals our proxy to be 11 percent understated for both years, and accordingly, we have adjusted upward by 11 percent for each year from 1961 to 1965. Since we generate indices for all series, there is no need to consider further adjustment to other data. The understatement of the series "brigadiers of production brigades" may arise from exclusion of brigades devoted to other than production activity. However, if the series in fact measures *person* rather than organizational *position*, one would expect an overstatement of number of brigades, unless there is virtually no turnover of brigadiers.

[17]Measurement of the labor force is by the official Soviet series of the average annual number of kolkhoz members participating in kolkhoz work. For our purposes, this series is a sufficiently accurate representation of the labor input.

[18]Official Soviet series.

54

solutely (measured by a growth of inputs) but which have not grown relative to each other. It is entirely possible that the rate of decline of brigades and kolkhozy will not be equal; in which case there will develop a shift in the size of brigades relative to kolkhozy, as one grows absolutely at a more rapid rate than the other.

Simple Conversion

The final illustration is that of simple conversion. In this case, kolkhozy are converted to sovkhozy, and, at an equal rate, inputs are removed from the collective sector.

The patterns outlined above have been utilized for the examination of structural change in agriculture of the Soviet Union as a whole and for the Kazakh, Belorussian, Turkmen and Lithuanian Republics, with the results presented in Figures 4-1 through 4-5.[19] The regions selected best illustrate the different patterns of structural change, although these figures portray only general trends.

Turning to Figure 4-1, the patterns for the country as a whole are those generally anticipated from the data. Of interest, however, is the persistent decline of kolkhozy in the post-1961 period though at a slower pace than the period prior to 1961. Also of note is the significant decline of kolkhoz sown area in the period 1959-1961 vis-a-vis the period after 1961. The changing pattern of sown area could indicate that, for the earlier period, the number of kolkhozy converted was relatively greater than for the latter period, or, alternatively, during the earlier period those kolkhozy converted were large in terms of sown area.[20]

The pattern of structural change for Kazakhstan is illustrated in Figure 4-2 and closely represents simple conversion. The decline in the number and sown area of kolkhozy is almost a mirror image of the increase in number and sown area of sovkhozy. Conversion is especially apparent for the period 1960-1961 during which time the relatively more rapid decline of kolkhoz sown area vis-a-vis number of kolkhozy would indicate the conversion of large kolkhozy. There appears to have been amalgamation during 1959-1960. It may well have been these large amalgamated kolkhozy that were converted to sovkhozy during 1960-1961. The explanation for the trends in Kazakhstan is the creation of large sovkhozy for the purpose of grain specialization.[21]

[19]These republics are chosen for graphic presentation solely on the grounds that they approximately represent the regional diversity postulated in our theoretical models.

[20]The relatively sharper decline of kolkhoz sown area in the pre-1961 period vis-a-vis the post-1961 period is most likely a function of the numbers of kolkhozy converted. There was a sharp decline in the number of conversions after 1961.

[21]During the period 1953-1957, the sown area of all grain crops in Kazakhstan increased from 5,853 to 8,189 for kolkhozy (all figures in thousands of hectares), and from 1,006 to 14,321 for sovkhozy. After a period of relatively stable sown area (1957-1959), there was a shift from kolkhozy to sovkhozy. Thus between 1959 and 1962, sown area (all grain crops) of kolkhozy declined from 7,728 to 3,640, while that of sovkhozy increased from 13,802 to 21,234. Karl-Eugen Wädekin has calculated that the share of state farms and other state agricultural enterprises in the total cultivated area of Kazakhstan has increased from just under 30 percent in 1954 to approximately 75 percent in 1962. See Karl-Eugen Wädekin, "Soviet Agriculture and Agricultural Policy, Some Regional Features," in Roy D. Laird (ed.), *Soviet Agriculture: The Permanent Crisis* (New York: Frederick A. Praeger, 1965), pp. 57, 75.

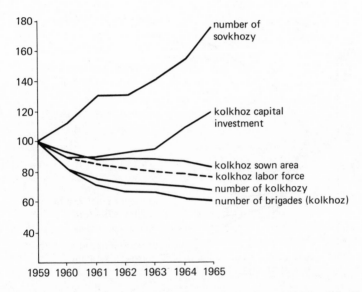

Figure 4-1. Structural Change in Soviet Agriculture: Selected Indicators, 1959–1965 (1959 = 100). Source: *Narkhoz*, selected volumes.

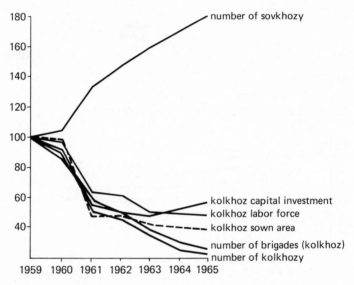

Figure 4–2. Structural Change in Agriculture of the Kazakh SSR, 1959–1965 (1959 = 100). Source: *Narkhoz*, selected volumes.

Figure 4-3 for the Belorussian Republic indicates that there has been a minimal amount of structural change in the collective farm sector and with only very minor temporal differentials. During 1959-1960, there was both amalgamation and conversion, the former producing increases in the sown area per brigade and per kolkhoz at approximately the same rate as indicated by the almost identical decline in the number of brigades and kolkhozy. Thereafter, there was a significant upturn in capital investment (after 1962), and, after 1963, a moderate downturn in the number of brigades vis-a-vis the other series. This could indicate an attempt in the Belorussian Republic to increase the size of the brigade vis-a-vis the kolkhoz, and indeed this trend would be in line with what we know about attempts at population resettlement in this area.[22]

The case of simple amalgamation is illustrated in the Turkmen Republic (Figure 4-4). For the period after 1962 however, the sown area per kolkhoz has tended to increase more rapidly than the sown area per brigade, indicating ex-

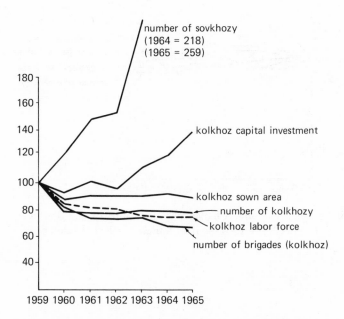

Figure 4-3. Structural Change in Agriculture of the Belorussian SSR, 1959-1965 (1959 = 100). Source: *Narkhoz*, selected volumes.

[22] In the post-1956 period there was a campaign, especially in Western Belorussia, to move peasants from homesteads to collective farm settlements and thus reduce the dispersion of the population. Certain financial and other benefits were made to those participating. The goal was a concentrated population to reduce the cost of providing services and also to bring the labor force closer to work. See, for example, V. Kamensky, "Better Organization in Resettlement from Farmsteads," *Sovetskaia Belorussia* (June 25, 1957), p. 3, translated and reprinted in *CDSP*, vol. IX, no. 27 (August 14, 1957), pp. 24-25.

58

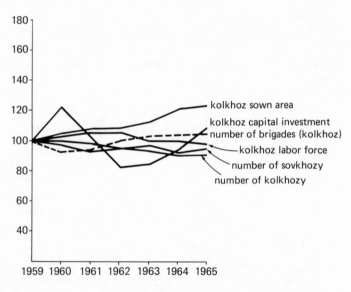

Figure 4–4. Structural Change in Agriculture of the Turkmen SSR, 1959–1965 (1959 = 100). Source: *Narkhoz*, selected volumes.

pansion of the number of brigades to allow only minimal increases in the sown area per brigade. There also has been notable shifts in the level of capital investment in kolkhozy of the Turkmen Republic.

Finally, structural change in the Lithuanian Republic is illustrated in Figure 4-5. There are two interesting trends. First, it would appear that, for a relatively short period (1960-1961), there was a serious attempt to increase the size of the brigade vis-a-vis the kolkhoz. This trend was halted in 1961 as simple amalgamation at a relatively slow pace took over. Second, during 1964-1965, the decline in the number of kolkhozy along with sown area and number of brigades vis-a-vis the increase in number of sovkhozy suggests conversion, though at a relatively slow pace.

Data limitations have restricted consideration of regional and temporal changes to a relatively short period of time. Nevertheless, diversity is apparent, suggesting that, with only limited exceptions (for example, Lithuania, 1960-1961), the size of the brigade (as measured by inputs) has not grown *relative* to the size of the kolkhoz. In absolute terms, however, both have grown, especially in respect to sown area and capital investment (the latter with significant temporal fluctuations). Generally speaking, labor force has declined at the same rate as the declining number of kolkhozy.[23]

The Brigade Structure

Thus far we have assumed that the brigade is a homogeneous unit and as such can be compared with the kolkhoz. Unfortunately, this is not the case. To examine the nature of the brigade as a production unit, let us consider two time periods, the dividing line being the year 1957. This division, though somewhat arbitrary, will prove convenient for two reasons: first, the abolition of the MTS in 1958 marked a trend towards change in the brigade structure; second, while there is virtually no statistical material for the pre-1957 period, we do have useful if limited data for the post-1957 years.

---

[23] In some cases (Lithuania) the decline of labor force and number of kolkhozy has been almost identical, while for other regions, the former has generally declined somewhat more slowly than the latter. The general pattern of our indices (labor force declining and capital investment increasing) is an understanding pattern of input substitution that we would expect in the agricultural sector during the process of economic development. In the present case, however, the rather similar behavior of the indices for number of kolkhozy and labor force may provide a partial and dynamic explanation for the amalgamation process. If we assume that for a given region (i.e. Kazakhstan) the size distribution (in terms of labor force per kolkhoz) of kolkhozy has little variability, and further, that Soviet leaders feel they know what optimal size is for that particular region (again on the basis of labor force per kolkhoz), amalgamation might be viewed as a mechanism for the maintenance of this optimal size in terms of labor force per kolkhoz. The decline in labor force vis-a-vis sown area and capital investment can, as we have suggested, be viewed as input substitution.

60

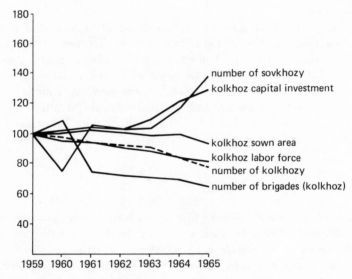

Figure 4-5. Structural Change in Agriculture of the Lithuanian SSR, 1959–1965 (1959 = 100). Source: *Narkhoz*, selected volumes.

Classification of Brigades (pre-1957)

To some extent, the system for classifying brigade structure depends upon the source considered.[24] However, the differences are more illusory than real. For the period 1953-1957, the types of brigades may be classified according to the *time period* for which the brigade is to be in existence, and the *number of different tasks* which it is to perform. Accordingly, the following types of brigades can be distinguished:

Time: 1. Temporary *(vremennyi)* brigades
2. Seasonal *(sezonnyi)* brigades
3. Constant *(postoiannyi)* brigades
Task: 1. Specialized *(spetsializirovannyi)* brigades
2. Combined *(kombinirovannyi)* brigades

By time of classification, the short term or temporary brigade was formed to carry out a single and particular function. It might, for example, perform a single repair task, or be responsible for the reclamation of a piece of land. To the extent that the temporary brigade performed a single task, it was also a specialized brigade. However, in this classification, the specialized brigade was one concerned with a particular *production* task. The distinction here seemed to be direct production activity for the specialized brigade as opposed to subsidiary activities for the temporary brigade.

The seasonal brigade has been used widely in those areas where the production process was of a seasonal nature, while the constant brigade was used where seasonality was not a factor. Accordingly, the seasonal brigades found greater acceptance in the field crop sector, while the constant brigades were utilized in animal breeding, subsidiary enterprises and inter-kolkhoz organizations.

Finally, the combined brigade was a popular form for so-called multi-purpose activities. Such a brigade could be formed on a seasonal or non-seasonal basis depending upon the nature of the activity. Also, there were tractor brigades, though these were attached to the MTS.

The temporary nature of the brigade as an organizational force during the pre-1957 period makes the assembly of meaningful statistical material most difficult. It is possible, however, to identify certain trends based upon the commentary of Soviet writers.[25] First, continuous, as opposed to temporary, forms

---

[24]The combined brigade, is essentially the precursor of the complex brigade, insofar as the former was formed for the purpose of performing more than a single task.

[25]There are a number of useful sources discussing the brigade system of the collective farm. See, for example, V.A. Abramov (ed.), *Ekonomika sel'skokhoziaistvennykh predpriiatii* (Moskva: Gospolitizdat, 1962), 112-125; D.F. Kozyreva (ed.), *Organizatsiia i planirovani proizvodstva v kolkhozakh i sovkhozakh* (Moskva: Kolos, 1965), pp. 118-129; K.P. Obolenskii, G.G. Kotov and G.K. Rusakov (eds.), *Voprosy ratsional'noi organizatsii i ekonomiki sel'skokhoziaistvennogo proizvodstva* (Moskva: Ekonomiki, 1964), pp. 206-236; K.L. Olefir (ed.), *Ekonomika i organizatsiia proizvodstva v sotsialisticheskikh sel'skokhoziaistvennykh predpriiatiiakh* (Moskva: Kolos, 1966), pp. 220-233.

of organization were increasingly favored on the basis of improving work performance through continuity of contact between the job and the worker.[26] Second, there has been a tendency, especially marked in recent years, to broaden rather than restrict the input-output structure of each brigade. Thus the combined form (having more than one form of output) tended to be favored with a penchant for attaching small machinery and equipment to the brigade on a continuous basis. The ultimate expression of this trend came with the abolition of the MTS in 1958.

Third, although the temporary nature of the brigade and the absence of data on same for the early 1950s makes useful analysis difficult, it must be recognized that the amalgamation campaign itself was in large part motivated by the desire to bring many small pieces of land together and also to decrease the number of small fields through which the crop rotation schemes were operating, both within single farms and also as among farms. There was, therefore, a tendency to amalgamate small pieces of land within each kolkhoz, and, at the same time, to increase the size of the field brigades (as measured by labor force) to handle these larger fields and, in addition, to facilitate the joint operation of the kolkhoz field brigades and the tractor brigades from the MTS. There were long-term motives directed towards a basic restructuring of the kolkhoz and short-term motives directed towards better immediate utilization of labor and a partial resolution of seasonal difficulties. For the early 1950s, field brigades normally averaged 80-100 peasants in the South, 60-80 in regions other than the Black Earth (about 30), Leningrad region about 27, and finally Smolensk about 42.[27]

Classification of Brigades (Post-1957)

The brigade as a form of organization used in the period after 1957 can best be described in terms of the following classification, based upon the method of handling mechanization and the structure of output:

1. The complex brigade (crop and animal production)
2. The branch brigade (field brigades, tractor-field brigades, potato brigades, etc.)
3. The specialized brigade (single product)[28]

---

[26]Thus in recent years the classification of brigades by time is no longer used, since all brigades are basically of a continuous nature. Since brigades have been growing in absolute size, it might be suggested that in recent years the brigade has become similar in structure and function to a small kolkhoz of the past, while the link has taken over as the immediate organizational form at the lowest level. However, this argument is weakened by the tenuous nature of the link in recent years. On this point, see Dimitry Pospielovsky, "The 'Link System' in Soviet Agriculture," *Soviet Studies*, vol. 21, no. 4 (April 1970), pp. 411-435.

[27]R.E.F. Smith, op. cit., p. 22.

[28]For a recent discussion of this system of classification, see A.I. Zakharov and V.N. Perekrestov, *Organizatsiia i oplata truda v mekhanizirovannykh brigadakh i zven'iakh sovkhozov i kolkhozov* (Moskva: Rossel'khozizdat, 1969), pp. 5-11.

The term complex normally describes that situation where a group of kolkhoz members serves several different branches, and several products (field and animal) are produced. The complex brigade is basically a result of amalgamation, in that many such brigades were formed on the base of a single small kolkhoz which was then attached to a larger kolkhoz.[29] It is difficult to estimate the extent to which complex brigades have been formed on those kolkhozy *not* subjected to amalgamation. However, the brigade structure for 1957, the first year for which disaggregated data is available, suggests that the number of kolkhozy amalgamated in that year (1,866),[30] could not "account" for the number of complex brigades (59,010),[31] unless many such brigades were formed in each kolkhoz. This assumption is unreasonable and indeed need not be made, for complex brigades did exist prior to 1957 though to what extent, we do not know. Considering the annual rate of amalgamation (see Table 4-1) and the rate of growth of complex brigades (see Table 4-4) there is a possibility that the former could "support" the latter. That is, complex brigades would be formed for the most part on the base of a single small kolkhoz at the time of amalgamation.

Soviet writers frequently suggest that the complex, and especially the tractor-complex brigade, is the most appropriate form of organization. While the abso-

Table 4-4
The Development of Complex and Tractor-Complex Brigades, USSR

	1957	1958	1959	1960	1961
Total brigades (all types)	416,033	357,666	314,049	256,991	232,365
Of which:					
Complex brigades	59,010	67,909	77,012	73,925	68,190
Of which:					
Tractor-complex brigades	...	11,940	16,892	18,189	...

Sources: Data for the years 1957-1960 from I.I. Sigov, *Razdelenie truda v sel'skom khoziaistve pri perekhode k kommunizmu* (Moskva: Ekonomizdat, 1963), p. 139. Data for the year 1961 from G.I. Shmelev, *Raspredelenie i ispol'zovanie truda v kolkhozakh* (Moskva: Mysl', 1964), p. 55.

Note: The tractor-complex brigade is a complex brigade that is mechanized in the sense that machinery and equipment is held at the brigade level. These are basically an outgrowth of the abolition of the MTS in 1958.

[29]K.P. Obolenskii, G.G. Kotov and G.K. Rusakov (eds.), op. cit., p. 218; K.I. Olefir (ed.), op. cit., p. 225.

[30]I.I. Signov, *Razdelenie truda v sel'kkom khoziaistve pri perekhode k kommunizmu* (Moskva: Ekonomizdat, 1963), p. 139.

[31]The point is in fact more general. Thus the most advanced type of brigade is one that is mechanized. For a discussion of this point and the general strategy of structuring kolkhoz brigades along the lines of those in sovkhozy see K.P. Obolenskii, G.G. Kotov and G.K. Rusakov (eds.), op. cit., pp. 213-218, and especially p. 214.

lute number of complex brigades has declined in the period 1959-1961 (Table
4-4), they grew relatively more important during these years. Thus complex production brigades accounted for slightly over 14 percent of all brigades in 1957,
and, at the beginning of 1962, they had grown to 34 percent of all brigades for
the Soviet Union as a whole.[32] By the late 1960s, roughly one-third of all kolkhoz brigades in the RSFSR were of the complex type.[33] During the period
1958-1960, the average number of kolkhoz members per complex brigade grew
from 105 to 135.[34] Finally, the number of kolkhoz members engaged in complex brigades as a portion of those engaged in all brigades grew from 25 percent
in 1958 to 39 percent in 1960.[35]

If the importance of the complex brigade has increased for the country as a
whole, there is considerable regional variability, both in terms of the number of
complex brigades vis-a-vis other types, and in terms of their size as measured by
hectares of plowland (see Tables 4-5 and 4-6).

What factors might account for the observed regional and temporal patterns
of development of the complex brigade? Basically, this form of brigade has been
utilized where production is *not* highly specialized, and where both the field
crop and animal breeding sectors are relatively highly developed. Thus in Table
4-5, we observe that in Central Asia only 2.3 percent of all production brigades

Table 4-5

Complex Production Brigades in Selected Regions of the USSR (Early 1962)

Region	Complex Production Brigades As a Proportion of All Production Brigades
U.S.S.R.	34.2%
R.S.F.S.R.	53.4
Moscow Oblast	23.1
Vladimir Oblast	19.4
Riazan Oblast	12.7
Belorussia and the Baltic Republics -	26.3
Central Asia	2.3
Kalinin Oblast	75.8
Smolensk Oblast	78.1
Kirov Oblast	90.0

Source: K.P. Obolenskyi, G.G. Kotov and G.K. Rusakov, (eds.), *Voprosy ratsional'noi
organizatsii i ekonomiki sel'skokhoziaistvennogo proizvodstva* (Moskva: Ekonomika, 1964),
pp. 218-219.

[32] Ibid., p. 218; I.I. Sigov, op. cit., pp. 138-139.

[33] A.I. Zakharov and V.N. Perekrestov, op. cit., p. 7.

[34] Computed from I.I. Sigov, loc. cit.

[35] Ibid.

Table 4-6

Regional Size Differentials of Complex and Tractor-Complex Brigades, 1961
(Hectares of Plowland/Brigade)

	Complex	Tractor-Complex
U.S.S.R.	953.2	1,737.2
R.S.F.S.R.	907.1	1,817.1
North-West	264.0	406.2
Center	284.0	470.1
Volga-Viatka	913.6	1,592.7
Central Chernozem	1,233.5	1,550.8
Volga	1,706.4	2,300.5
Northern Caucasus	2,260.6	2,368.6
Urals	1,195.2	1,595.4
Eastern Siberia	1,902.4	2,052.1
Western Siberia	1,240.6	1,509.3
Far East	1,930.1	2,316.6
Kazakhstan	3,006.9	2,821.8
Central Asia	387.7	1,263.0
Ukraine and Moldavia	988.0	1,362.0
Belorussia and the Baltic Republics	361.8	403.9

Source: K.P. Obolenskyi, G.G. Kotov and G.K. Rusakov (eds.), *Voprosy ratsional'noi organizatsii i ekonomiki sel'skokhoziaistvennogo proizvodstva* (Moskva: Ekonomika, 1964), p. 230.

are of the complex form. The high concentration of cotton growing in this region is the most likely explanation for this pattern.[36]

The pattern observed in Table 4-6 is basically a function of the historical development of land usage in the various regions. In the North-West and Center for example, complex brigades, to the extent they are used, are smaller and less specialized because the kolkhozy on which they are formed are also of a similar pattern. For example, in the North-West and Center regions, each kolkhoz on the average had 1,215 and 1,954 hectares of sown areas respectively for the year 1961.[37] In Kazakhstan and the Northern Caucasus however, the average kolkhoz had 12,128 and 3,742 hectares of sown areas respectively for the year 1961.[38] Thus in Kazakhstan and the Northern Caucasus one finds, as would be expected, that complex brigades are significantly larger as measured by land

[36]The complex brigade is a multi-product organization and thus would not be utilized where there is a high degree of specialization in a single product. A priori, one would expect greater seasonal fluctuations in the participation of kolkhoz members in the socialized sector under such conditions. In an absolute sense, however, this problem may be partially resolved by a high degree of mechanization and irrigation in addition to the development of secondary processing industries.

[37]Computed from *Narkhoz-1961*, pp. 318-319, 440-441.

[38]Ibid.

input.[39] Also, in the North-West and Center, useable land areas are frequently small being broken up by unuseable hills, bogs and marshes. In addition, there tend to be greater numbers of population points creating labor supply difficulties where administrative units are concentrated. Finally, the level of mechanization is lower in these areas, and as we can observe from Table 4-6, complex-mechanized brigades are, under most conditions, significantly larger than the complex brigades from which they arise.[40]

The complex brigade is found in what Soviet writers see as its most advanced form in the South and South-East. In these areas, the complex brigade, even though it does not differ from other complex brigades, may be called a department *(otdelenie)*.[41] The department is basically the pattern of organization prevailing in the sovkhoz and represents in essence a complete farm as a subunit of the kolkhoz.[42] This type of structure represents a significant departure from the traditional brigade and ferma arrangements of earlier years.

The kolkhoz *"Nasha Rodina,"* (Kavkazskii Raion, Krasnodarskii Krai) may be taken as an example of an organization utilizing the otdelenie or department. An organization chart for the entire kolkhoz is presented in Figure 4-6, and for a single department in Figure 4-7. This particular kolkhoz is large, with 10, 429 hectares of plowland or approximately 2,000 hectares per department. The organizational structure is essentially comparable to that outlined in Chapter 2, although in this case the brigade is called a department, the latter performing various functions, including animal breeding. This structure can be contrasted with that of a smaller kolkhoz (2,627 hectares of plowland) also utilizing a complex brigade structure. Figure 4-8 illustrates the structure of the kolkhoz *"im. XXI s'ezda KPSS"* located in Berezovskii Raion of Odessa Oblast.[43] Finally, for comparison, Figure 4-9 presents an organizational structure typical of the late 1940s and early 1950s.[44]

The leader of the otdelenie (the brigadier) will normally have specialists and helpers. The specialists will lead the branches within their area of specialization—thus the ferma will be lead by a zoötechnician, and the field crop sector by an agronomist. If the otdelenie is especially small (as would be the case in the North and North-West) there may be a single leader for the entire operation. The distribution of daily work tasks to kolkhoz members takes place at the depart-

[39]See Table 4-6.

[40]This fact can be seen from Table 4-4. The only exception is Kazakhstan, where the tractor-complex brigades were, in 1961, slightly smaller than the complex brigades, though in an absolute sense both were larger than for any other region in the Soviet Union.

[41]See, for example, K.P. Obolenskii, G.G. Kotov and G.K. Rusakov (eds.), op. cit., p. 219. The authors point out that in some parts of the country, notably the south, southeast and east, the complex brigade and the department are in fact identical, and thus the complex brigade in a kolkhoz can be identified as a department.

[42]See, for example, V.A. Abramov, *Ekonomika sel'skokhoziaistvennykh predpriiatii* (Moskva: Gospolitizdat, 1962), pp. 106-125.

[43]For details on this kolkhoz, see M.V. Mikhailov (ed.), *Planirovanie i rezhim ekonomiki v kolkhozakh* (Moskva: Ekonomika, 1965), pp. 129ff.

[44]From Fedor Belov, *The History of a Soviet Collective Farm* (New York: Frederick A. Praeger, 1955), p. 39.

67

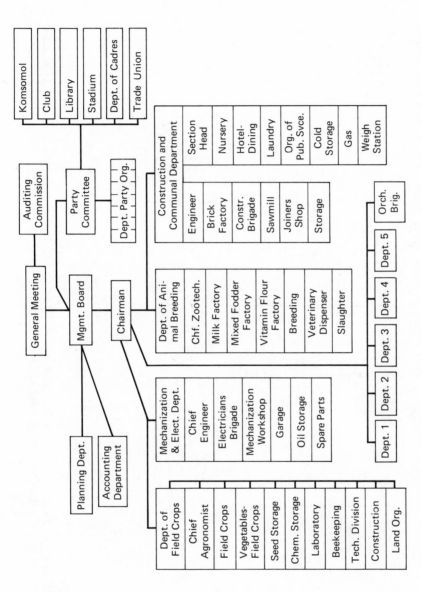

Figure 4-6. Organization of Kolkhoz "Nasha Rodina", Kavkazskii Raion, Krasnodarskii Krai (August 1966). Source: Personal communication.

68

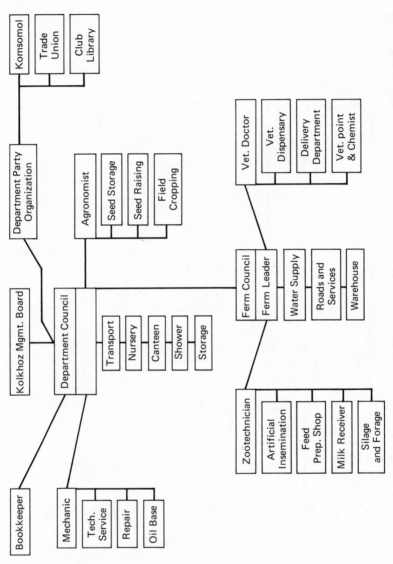

Figure 4–7. Organization of a Department in Kolkhoz "Nasha Rodina", Kavkazskii Raion, Krasnodarskii Krai (August 1966). Source: Personal communication.

69

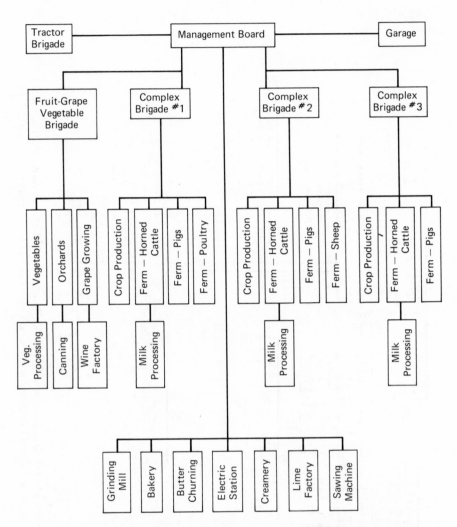

Figure 4-8. Organization of Kolkhoz "im. XXI s'ezda KPSS", Berezovskii Raion, Odessa Oblast (1957). Source: M. V. Mikhailov (ed.),
Planirovanie i rezhim ekonomiki v. kolkhozakh (Moskva: Ekonomika,
1965), p. 130.

70

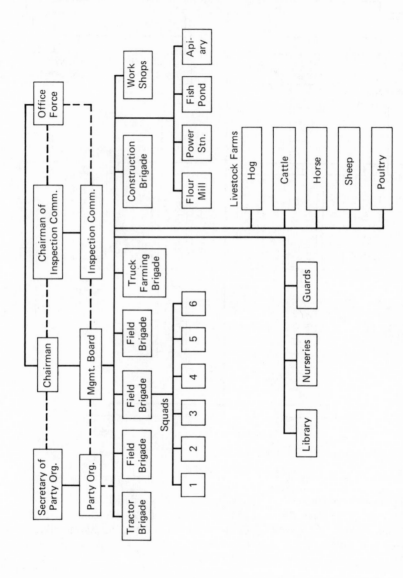

Figure 4-9. Organizational Structure of a Soviet Kolkhoz, late 1940's and early 1950's. Source: Feodor Below, *The History of a Soviet Collective Farm* (New York: Frederick A. Praeger, 1955), p. 39.

ment level. Normally, these workers will remain within a single department, and within the department, a single section such as field crops. There is naturally a tendency for one branch to assist another by provision of labor services, especially given a high degree of seasonality.

It might be noted, however, that where the departmental form of organization is most highly developed (in the South and South-East), there is probably not a significant imbalance between the supply of and demand for labor among different seasons and agricultural campaigns.[45]

The development of the complex brigade has been the combined result of many forces. However, the tendency has been to increase the absolute size of the brigade such that it closely resembles an entire collective farm of the late 1940s. This trend might be characterized as a desire to reap the perceived benefits of large scale production units, while at the same time bringing to bear upon the pattern a high degree of scepticism as to the possible benefits of specialization.[46] Thus, with regard to output, the short-term and specialized brigades of the early 1950s have been gradually replaced by large, constant, complex types of brigades in which several crops will be grown, and, indeed, crop rotation will be possible *within* a single brigade. On the input side, the trend has been to bring machinery and equipment into each brigade, but, at the same time, make both the brigade and the kolkhoz sufficiently large such that product specialization will be handled by sub-units *within* the brigade.

The labor input has been a continuing organizational problem. Thus, while training has been designed to create specialization to a relatively high degree, the seasonality of the production process suggests a need to increase flexibility such that workers can be moved from one task to another as the seasonal pattern dictates. In this sense, the short-term form of brigade must have provided greater flexibility, though apparently at a price of lower productivity because of the continual movement from one position to another. One might expect this sort of problem to be less severe as mechanization of agriculture increases. The Soviet response, however, has been one of creating constant organizational attachment, but at the same time enlarging the unit to which workers are attached such that the seasonal problem is reduced by the broadening of the output structure.[47]

---

[45]The collective farms which utilize the mechanized complex production brigade seem to be those that are the most highly developed. Also, according to Obolenskii et al., this form of brigade organization is designed to assist rather than hinder the transfer of labor from one brigade to another as production conditions dictate. See K.P. Obolenskii, G.G. Kotov and G.K. Rusakov (eds.), op. cit., p. 223.

[46]Soviet leaders have tended to promote agricultural gigantonmania. Where this has resulted from amalgamation, the trend has been that of forming a single brigade on the base of a previously independent collective farm. At the same time however, each brigade (with some exceptions such as the specialized cotton growing brigades), has maintained a multi-product (both plant and animal products) status.

[47]Thus within a single brigade, several crops with varying seasonal growth patterns can be raised and in addition, basically non-seasonal activities such as animal breeding can be established. In addition, there has been emphasis upon the training of specialists with a so-called "wide profile." Finally, one would suspect that the transfer of labor from one brigade to another within a given kolkhoz would be relatively more simple than the transfer among kolkhozy as would have been the case under the pre-amalgamation structure.

To some extent, it has also been possible to combine animal breeding (a non-seasonal activity) with field crop growing (a seasonal activity), and place both under one organizational unit such as the complex brigade. In this sense, it may be possible to more fully utilize the available labor force. As we have suggested, however, it is difficult to know to what extent labor services are in fact transferrable as between these two sectors. Given the Soviet pattern of narrowly specialized training, one would suspect that transfer is minimal. On the other hand, it may be that in actuality educational specialization is taken less seriously, and those trained for one task may in fact perform a different or possibly related task. In recent years, there has been increased emphasis upon the training of specialists with a so-called "wide profile."

Increased scale at the brigade level has other advantages, especially in the Soviet case. There is, for example, the problem of indivisibility of certain inputs. In the absence of organizations from which small amounts of accounting services can be hired, it may be necessary to hire one accountant on a full time basis. There is an advantage to that scale of organization capable of totally exhausting the services of this single employee. Soviet leaders seem to be constructing an organization such that there will be greater work volume for each specialist within his own sphere, avoiding indivisibilities, and the nature of the output will be such that the less specialized workers (in terms of training) can be shifted according to seasonal needs. Soviet economists have suggested that by restructuring the organization along the lines indicated, the number of "non-productive" (basically administrative) personnel can be reduced as a portion of the labor force. There is continual pressure towards the goal of reducing the number of administrative personnel.[48] It is very difficult to assess the extent to which large scale agricultural organizations are necessarily characterized by fewer (relatively) numbers of administrative personnel than smaller organizations.[49]

[48]This pressure takes the form of state norms specifying appropriate numbers of various types of administrative personnel that should be employed on different collective farms. The basis of classification is typically some indicator of farm size, for example, land area or money income. There is also emphasis upon the need to reduce that portion of total labor expenditure going to administrative-service personnel. For a discussion of the reduction of administrative-service personnel in one case from one in ten kolkhoz members to one in eight, see M. Dzhakypov, "Uporiadochivaem shtaty v kolkhozakh," *Kolkhozno-sovkhoznoe proizvodstva Kirgizii*, No. 7 (July 1963), p. 19. For a discussion of regional differentials and appropriate norms, see V.P. Kulakov, "Sokrashchenie upravlencheskogo personals v kolkhozakh" (opyt rostovskoi oblasti), *Uchet i finansy v kolkhozakh i sovkhozakh*, No. 3 (March 1963), pp. 22-24; I. Ramaev, "O chislennosti administrativno-khoziaistvennogo personala v kolkhozakh," *Vestnik statistiki*, No. 6 (May 1961), pp. 67-69; "Rekomendatsii o primernykh shtatnykh normativakh administrativno-upravlencheskogo i obsluzhivaiushchego personala kolkhozov Turkmenskoi SSR," *Kolkhozno-sovkhoznoe proizvodstvo Turkmenistana*, No. 5 (May, 1963), pp. 3-7; M. Ia. Tseitlin, "Sokrashchaem upravlencheskii apparat (opyt kolkhozov Ukrainskoi SSR)," *Uchet i finansy v kolkhozakh i sovkhozakh*, No. 12 (December 1963), pp. 18-20.

[49]The writer is not aware of any study pertaining to variation in the size of administrative structure vis-a-vis different forms of agricultural organization under capitalism. One might anticipate, however, that managerial scale effects would exist, at least for smaller organizations. This is suggested to be the case for industrial organizations with certain reservations and depending upon the manner in which the organization expands. See, for example, Joseph A. Litterer, *The Analysis of Organizations* (New York: John Wiley & Sons, Inc., 1965), pp. 408-410. One is tempted to argue that in the Soviet case, administrative inputs are seen as basically unproductive, and in many instances "padded" by illegal behavior.

Thus far the focus has been the development of the complex brigade. While this type of organization is seen as the most appropriate for future development, what remains of the traditional forms of brigades? The various types of branch and specialized brigades remain in wide, though declining, usage (Table 4-7). This absolute decline must be interpreted with some caution, however, for it represents, in the main, the process of amalgamation and less a changing role for different types of brigades within the general number of brigades. In the late 1950s, as in the late 1960s, the proportion of complex among all brigades remained at roughly one-third. At the same time, the numerically important field brigades have declined only marginally faster (for the period 1957-1961) than the declining number of kolkhozy.

As with the complex brigades, the field, tractor and other types of brigades show considerable regional size variation (Table 4-8). These variations are basically a function of patterns of crop specialization, geographic and regional considerations and the degree of mechanization. The number of complex brigades as a portion of all brigades, the number of kolkhoz members in these brigades as a portion of all kolkhoz members in brigades, and finally the absolute number of kolkhoz members per brigade grew significantly in the late 1950s.

For the period 1958-1960, field brigades, as a portion of all brigades, declined from 51.4 to 41.0 percent, while kolkhoz members engaged in these brigades, as a portion of those in all brigades, declined from 60.3 to 45.5 percent.[50] Thus while the number of field brigades shrunk, the net result was a very small change in average absolute size from 94 kolkhoz members per brigade (1958) to 89 per brigade (1960)[51] Tractor brigades as a portion of all brigades have declined, while tractor-field brigades have increased. However, both types together repre-

Table 4-7
Brigade Structure of Kolkhozy: USSR, 1957-1960

	1957	1958	1959	1960	1961
Total brigades	416,033	357,666	314,049	256,991	232,365
Of which:					
Field brigades	213,495	183,980	139,000	105,353	97,583
Tractor brigades	94,201	55,423	50,123	37,114	33,266
Tractor-Field brigades	5,562	12,614	15,178	14,507	11,721
Vegetable brigades	26,043	21,870	17,329	14,370	12,838
Fruit brigades	10,515	9,546	9,153	10,460	8,767
Other brigades	7,207	6,324	6,164	1,262	...

Sources: Data for the years 1957-1960 from I.I. Sigov, *Razdelenie truda v sel'skom khoziaistve pre perekhode k kommunizmu* (Moskva: Ekonomizdat, 1963), p. 139. Data for the year 1960 from G.I. Shmelev, *Raspredelenie i ispol'zovanie truda v kolkhozakh* (Moskva: Mysl', 1964), p. 55.

[50] I.I. Sigov, op. cit., p. 139.

[51] Computed from ibid.

Table 4-8

Regional Size Differentials of Various Types of Brigades, 1961 (Hectares of Plowland/Brigade)

	Field	Tractor-Field	Vegetable (sowing)	Orchard (planting)
U.S.S.R.	390.8	1,120.0	58.5	107.7
R.S.F.S.R.	539.3	1,895.7	62.4	106.4
North-West	194.7	n.a.	17.7	34.0
Center	241.8	445.1	53.4	70.0
Volga-Viatka	490.3	1,025.3	24.1	32.6
Central Chernozem	992.5	1,611.0	50.7	126.5
Volga	1,137.3	2,493.9	69.3	49.7
Northern Caucasus	2,742.4	1,671.3	110.3	139.0
Urals	834.3	2,056.2	24.6	49.7
Eastern Siberia	984.7	1,874.9	59.3	31.9
Western Siberia	720.8	1,878.9	31.5	21.7
The Far East	793.8	1,786.6	70.7	27.9
Kazakhstan	1,628.5	2,192.1	199.3	123.6
Central Asia	148.3	163.2	71.1	37.5
Ukraine and Moldavia	633.4	1,204.0	55.8	149.6
Belorussia and the Baltic Republics	304.1	319.3	18.9	42.1

Source: K.P. Obolenskyi, G.G. Kotov and G.K. Rusakov (eds.), *Voprosy ratsional'noi organizatsii i ekonomiki sel'skokhoziaistvennogo proizvodstva* (Moskva: Ekonomika, 1964), p. 230.

sented only 20 percent of all brigades in 1960, and at that time, engaged only 9.6 percent of the labor force employed in various types of brigades.[52] Finally, there has been very little shift in vegetable brigades in terms of numbers and personnel involved, and only a slight upward shift in the importance of orchard brigades. The latter grew from 2.7 percent of all brigades (1958) to 4.1 percent of all brigades (1960) while the labor force engaged in these brigades as a portion of the entire brigade labor force grew from 1.5 to 4.2 percent.[53]

The branch and specialized brigades are utilized along with the presence of animal breeding fermy where each is administered separately. In many cases, this type of organization is used even where there is a relatively compact land mass with limited population dispersion.[54] It is important to note that brigades are not normally formed for a single crop, but rather a single brigade will grow several crops and will, if large enough, be responsible for a full crop rotation scheme within a single brigade. The important requirement is that the crops be suffi-

[52]Ibid.
[53]Ibid.
[54]K.P. Obolenskii, G.G. Kotov and G.K. Rusakov (eds.), op. cit., p. 229.

ciently similar such that similar types of equipment and other inputs can be utilized.

Organization Within The Brigade

The lowest level in the formal organizational structure of the brigade is the link *(sveno)*. The link is a small group of kolkhoz workers brought together to encourage good work habits in the completion of specific tasks where coordinated work activity is thought desirable. There is a link leader who supervises the group while at the same time performing routine duties along with the members of the link. The link leader normally receives supplementary pay for his services.

Although it has been suggested that the link as an organizationl sub-unit of the brigade has enjoyed a revival in recent years, there is in fact very little evidence to suggest to what extent the link is actually used in practice.[55] The concept of the link and the degree to which it should be utilized in Soviet agriculture has been the subject of continuing controversy in the Soviet Union.[56]

Like the brigade itself, there are various different types of links which might be identified by alternate schemes of classification. The nature of these classification schemes has been subject to great variation over time, and in fact, there is no agreement on any single scheme. The distinction among different types of links usually rests upon whether the link is mechanized, whether it is a temporary or a permanent arrangement, and, finally, whether it is formed on a single or multi-product basis. In recent years, the tendency seems to have been towards the usage of multi-product mechanized links formed on a relatively long term basis.

Organization of Animal Production

In a sense, there is little to add at this point to what we have already said about the organization of production in this sector. This is especially true given the peculiar features of this sector in the Soviet case.[57]

As we have already indicated, the basic organizational unit in the animal breeding sector is the ferma. The ferma is organized by the management board

---

[55] See Roy D. Laird, "Khrushchev's Administrative Reforms in Agriculture: An Appraisal," in Jerzy F. Karcz (ed.), *Soviet and East European Agriculture* (Berkeley and Los Angeles: University of California Press, 1967), pp. 29-50.

[56] For a detailed discussion of the link system and recent debates about its efficacy in Soviet Agriculture, see Dimitry Pospielovsky, "The 'Link System' in Soviet Agriculture," *Soviet Studies*, vol. 21, no. 4 (April 1970), pp. 411-435.

[57] In particular, the private sector plays a substantial role in the production of meat, milk and other related products. For a recent discussion of the development of the dairy economy, see E. Strauss, "The Soviet Dairy Economy," *Soviet Studies*, vol. 21, no. 3 (January 1970), pp. 269-296.

of the kolkhoz and is subject to confirmation by the general meeting. It is headed by a ferma leader or one who occupies a position similar to that of a brigadier.

A ferma may be specialized, though, more likely, each ferma will have several types of animals, possibly producing different products. In the past, the ferma would typically have been an independent organization similar in structure to the brigade. In recent years however, and especially with the growth of the complex brigade, the ferma has become a part of the brigade. In addition, there will be division of labor within the ferma.

Summary

The Soviet collective farm as an organizational form has changed significantly during the past twenty years. This change has been in two major directions. First, the typical collective of the present day is at least two to three times larger than it was in the late 1940s and early 1950s. This dramatic size increase is the direct result of a pervasive campaign of amalgamation begun in the early post-war years and continued until the early 1960s. Second, while both the kolkhoz and its internal sub-units have grown substantially, the latter are now fundamentally different than those of the pre-amalgamation era. The brigade is no longer a small, semi-permanent and non-mechanized organizational form for the production of field crops. Increasingly, the brigade (or department) is a large multi-product permanent production unit, typically with its own mechanization and encompassing both the production of field crops and animal products. From an organizational point of view, the typical kolkhoz has come to resemble the sovkhoz. More important, though, the brigade of the present day differs very little from the pre-amalgamation collective and, indeed, has come to be a farm in its own right.

Although it remains to examine decision making and the nature of information flows within the collective, the sorts of changes outlined in this chapter must be considered as a notable trend towards centralization, if in fact kolkhoz and brigade managers have the same decision making authority and responsibility today than they did in the pre-amalgamation period. The present brigade manager commands an organization differing little from that commanded by the kolkhoz manager of the pre-war years. It is essential, therefore, that any focus upon collective farm management consider not only the upper level managers, but also those at the brigade and lower levels.

5 The Nature of Rewards and Inducements

Managerial behavior is in part a function of rewards, inducements and penalties associated with different forms of action. In this chapter we examine the nature of this incentive system for the post-1950 period. The focus will be on the manager of the collective farm, the agricultural specialists and the intermediate managers, or leaders of brigades and fermy. This group collectively comprises the leadership personnel of the kolkhoz.

The investigation will center upon three distinct though interrelated questions: first, in what manner have basic and supplementary rewards been determined, and in particular, how has the basis of determination shifted during the period under study?; second, to what extent has the incentive structure been consistent with, and effective for, the achievement of stated goals?;[1] finally, how important have incentives been and how well do leadership personnel fare vis-a-vis other members of the collective farm and managerial personnel in other sectors of the economy?

Rules of the Game

Rules for the payment of collective-farm leadership personnel (base and supplementary pay) were set forth in an all-union decree of April 19, 1948.[2] While it is difficult to assess the longevity of this decree, there is evidence that it was still of great importance in the late 1950s and early 1960s, in spite of a decree of March 6, 1956 passed by the Central Committee of the CPSU recommending that kolkhozy themselves, in accordance with local conditions, establish the rules for

---

[1] The important goals of the kolkhoz are taken to be: (1) increasing output; (2) reduction of inputs; (3) increasing capacity; (4) increasing welfare of farm members. The primary focus is earned managerial incomes (basic and supplemental) in both monetary and non-monetary forms, although limited consideration will be given to the structure of peasant incomes insofar as the latter bear upon the labor supply function to be discussed in Chapter 6. This chapter is an expanded version of the author's article on managerial incentives appearing in *Soviet Studies*, vol. XXII, no. 4 (April 1971), pp. 539-555.

[2] "O merakh po uluchsheniiu organizatsii povysheniiu proizvoditel' nosti i uporiadocheniiu oplaty truda v kolkhozakh," *Direktivy KPSS*, pp. 263-283. For a general discussion of labor remuneration on Soviet collective farms during the pre-1955 period, see Henri Wronski, *Remuneration et niveau de vie dans les Kolkhozi le Troudoden* (Paris: Societe d'edition d'enseignement superieur, 1957).

supplementary payment (in money and kind) for leadership personnel.[3] In many cases, the rules of 1948 tended to persist, although the 1956 decree did represent a turning point and some farms began to work out new incentive programs. By the early 1960s, there was growing recognition among Soviet economists that one of two undesirable conditions prevailed. First, in many cases, the original rules as developed in 1948 were still being utilized, and these, under new conditions and goals, were seen by economists and political leaders as highly inappropriate.[4] Second, where adjusted or wholly new schemes had been introduced, there were no raion, republican or other guidelines to follow. The result was a conglomeration of schemes that did not necessarily differ in accordance with real (or perceived) differences among collective farms.

During the early 1960s, several steps were taken in an effort to unify the incentive schemes. In 1961-62, the union republics, krais and oblasts formulated recommendations which, on balance, must have led to greater uniformity.[5] Further, a decree of the Central Committee of the CPSU of April 12, 1962 effectively re-centralized the payment system for agricultural specialists.[6] In addition to these formal decrees, there was considerable press discussion as to the general principles which should govern the establishment of pay scales in general, and bonus systems in particular, for leadership personnel.

Collective Farm Chairmen

On the basis of the decree of 1948, the base pay of the collective farm chairman was established as a function of farm size as measured by: sown area (including orchards, vegetables and berry gardens); quantity of livestock of various types; and numbers of poultry.[7] Thus on a 7-10 point scale, the chairman would receive labor days for each of the preceding categories. Depending upon the number of hectares of sown area, the manager might receive from 27 to 54 labor days; likewise, for cows, swine and sheep from 5 to 18 labor days; for horses from 2 to 18 labor days; and for poultry from 3 to 10 labor days, all on a monthly basis.[8]

[3]For criticism of the 1948 decree, see, for example, I.A. Ivin, *Oplata truda rukovoditelei i spetsialistov v kolkhozakh* (Moskva: Ekonomizdat, 1963), p. 14; and K.A. Shaibekov, *Pravovye formy oplaty truda v kolkhozakh* (Moskva: Gosiurizdat, 1963), pp. 225-226. The new decree, "Ob ustave sel'skokhoziaistvennoi arteli i dal'neishem razvitii initsiativy kolkhoznikov organizatsii kolkhoznogo proizvodstva i upravlenii delami arteli," can be found in *Sbornik*, pp. 251-258.

[4]G. Ia. Kuznetsov, *Material'noe stimulirovanie truda v kolkhozkh* (Moskva: Mysl', 1966), p. 136.

[5]I.A. Ivin, op. cit., p. 40.

[6]"O povyshenii roli agronomov, zootekhnikov i drugikh spetsialistov sel'skogo khoziaistva i razvitii kolkhoznogo i sovkhoznogo proizvodstva," in *Sbornik*, pp. 588-595.

[7]"O merakh po uluchsheniiu organizatsii povysheniiu proizvoditel' nost i uporiadocheniiu oplaty truda v kolkhozakh," *Direktivy KPSS*, vol. 3, pp. 277-278.

[8]The number of labor days paid depended upon the number of animals in each category. Thus, in general, the greater the number of *animals* the greater the number of labor days paid to the farm manager.

In addition to payment in labor days, there was also a monthly ruble amount based upon the level of money income *(denezhnyi dokhod)*, varying from 25 to 400 old rubles on a 14 point scale. The final component of base pay was a percentage supplement to the labor day component based upon length of service: 5 percent for three years of service; up to 15 percent for five years and over.[9]

The bonus system was based upon the overfulfillment of a yield plan for crops and production in the husbandry sector. On the average, for all grain crops, a bonus (as a percentage of the base pay in labor days and rubles) could vary from a low of 15 percent for an overfulfillment up to 10 percent, up to a high of 40 percent for an overfulfillment above 25 percent. For technical crops and potatoes and vegetables, the same scale applied as for the husbandry sector. In the latter case, overfulfillment must have been achieved by two or more animal fermy in order to pay a bonus to the manager of the farm.[10]

The potential bonus earnings of collective farm chairmen were very small vis-a-vis top level industrial managers of the same era.[11] In addition, the bonuses, as outlined above, were conditional and operative in a negative as well as a positive direction. Thus in order to receive a bonus for the overfulfillment of yields, the plan for the sowing of grains, technical crops, vegetables and potatoes (assortment plan) must have been met. If the harvest plan was underfulfilled by 1 percent for a certain group of crops (all grain crops, leading technical crops, vegetables and potatoes) then for each crop in this group there would be a deduction from managerial earnings (in labor days) of 1 percent. Similarly, if the plan for the development of cattle and the plan for milk yields were underfulfilled by 1 percent, then 1 percent of the earned labor days would be deducted for each type of cattle. There was an annual limit of 25 percent deduction from earned labor days.[12] Also, the portion of earnings derived from length of service was not to be affected by such deductions. In addition to the standard bonuses as outlined, there were from time to time special bonuses for the delivery to the state of selected high priority crops.

Given the numerical importance of those collective farm chairmen directed to their posts from industry, it is worth noting that the payment system for this

---

[9]Though not specified, such bonuses are presumably paid for length of service as chairman of *any* collective farm, rather than length of service on a single farm. This supplement might be interpreted as an attempt to extend the decision-making horizon of the farm manager. Such a system is consistent with Soviet efforts in recent years to reduce the high rate of managerial turnover but inconsistent with a managerial system which seeks removal for short term "failure."

[10]In this case there appears to be a double discontinuity: first, the bonus starts with 100% fulfillment, and second, it is discontinuous at the point of plan fulfillment by two animal fermy.

[11]On the magnitude of bonuses in Soviet industry, see Joseph S. Berliner, *Factory and Manager in the U.S.S.R.* (Cambridge: Harvard University Press, 1957), pp. 29-32; David Granick, *The Red Executive* (New York: Doubleday, 1960), pp. 130-134; Barry M. Richman, *Soviet Management with Significant American Comparisons* (Englewood Cliffs, New Jersey: Prentice-Hall, Inc., 1965), pp. 134-135.

[12]The extent to which this negative sanction has in fact been utilized is not known.

group differed somewhat from that outlined above.[13] Although not spelled out in the 1948 decree, the pay for those chairmen with industrial backgrounds was to be determined by the general meeting of the kolkhoz, and was to be a monthly monetary sum (apparently with no minimum specified), the arrangement to last for three years. For this group, a 10 percent penalty could be applied for the non-fulfillment of certain basic plans and sales to the state. For the special managerial group placed in 1955, the original decree of 1948 was to apply, although state assistance to the kolkhoz was promised to finance the monetary portion of the chairman's pay over a period of three years.[14]

Formal decentralization of pay scales for collective farm leadership personnel was established in 1956, and the payment system of 1948 continued to be subjected to widespread criticism by Soviet economists. In particular, it was argued that while the early system was suitable for conditions prevailing at that time (namely the pursuit of extensive methods of cultivation and the expansion of animal herds), it only marginally recognized increases in output from improved efficiency of production.[15] In recent years the trend has been away from payment for the expansion of sown area and herds and toward payment based upon some interpretation of output and/or money income of the farm. Given existing accounting and pricing procedures, it is not clear that the latter system will be significantly better than the former. In any event, this trend has led to significant regional diversity in the nature of payment systems for farm chairmen.

In many kolkhozy of Moscow and Gorky Oblasts, the Turkmen, Uzbek and Estonian Republics base pay for the chairman is a ruble amount per unit of product of every type, varying from farm to farm.[16]

---

[13] Approximately 23% of collective farms received new chairmen in the 1955 recruitment campaign. Ultimately, 32,078 new collective-farm chairmen were designated as members of the so-called "thirty thousander" group. According to Hough (see below), turnover among this group has been surprisingly low, although managerial turnover has, in general, declined in recent years. For details of this campaign, see A.N. Karamelev, "Dvizhenie tridtsatitysiachnikov i ukreplenie kolkhozov," *Voprosy Istorii KPSS*, no. 1 (1962), pp. 115-126. For a Western discussion of the campaign, see Jerry F. Hough, "The Changing Nature of the Kolkhoz Chairman," and Robert C. Stuart, "Structural Change and the Quality of Soviet Collective-Farm Management, 1952-1966," both in James R. Millar (ed.), *The Soviet Rural Community* (Urbana: University of Illinois Press, 1971).

[14] Specifically, newly elected chairmen were to receive, from the state, and supplementary to payments from the Kolkhoz, 1500 old rubles per month in the first year, 1200 old rubles per month in the second year, and 1000 old rubles per month in the third year of service. For details of this arrangement, see *Direktivy KPSS*, vol. 4, p. 396.

[15] See for example I.A. Ivin, op. cit., p. 9; G.Ia. Kuznetsov, loc. cit.; N.I. Nizhnii, A.M. Onishchenko N.I. Romanenko and A.S. Storozhuk, *Denezhnaia oplata truda v kolkhozakh* (Moskva: Sel'khozgiz, 1961), p. 170.

[16] Thus, for example, in the Il'ianskyi raion of the Tashausskyi Oblast of the Turkmen Republic, the number of labor days per ton of grain varies as follows: Kolkhoz "Bolshevik" 1.0, Kolkhoz "Leninism" 1.9. Other differentials are greater, for example per ton of potatoes: Kolkhoz "Moskva" .36, Kolkhoz "Bolshevik" 3.0. See I.A. Ivin, op. cit., pp. 14-16. This system might be construed as a form of straight-piece rate payment. A similar system for kolkhoz members has been praised by some writers. Thus in the kolkhoz "Logvinenko" (Kirgiz Republic), payment is a percentage of the crops placed in the storage bins—if targets are not met, percentages are lowered. Thus, for grain, 12 percent is given with achievement of the yield plan, 9 percent without fulfillment. If this applies to the intramarginal units delivered, it is a stiff penalty. See V.P. Rozhin, *Nekotorye voprosy pod'ema ekonomiki slabykh kolkhozov* (Moskva: Ekonomizdat, 1961), p. 129.

In many instances, base payment of the chairman is based upon the level of money income or gross output of the farm, the latter valued at state purchase prices.[17] Such a pattern prevails on farms in the Kalinin and Volgorod Oblasts, Krasnodarskii Krai and the Tadzhik, Georgian, Armenian, Kazakh, Moldavian and Azerbaidzhan Republics.[18]

In some parts of the Ukraine, in the Volga region and Ulianov, Kuibyshev, Volgograd and Kherson Oblasts, monthly pay of the chairman varies directly with annual money income of the kolkhoz and money income per 100 hectares of land being utilized.

In still another variant, some chairmen in Voronezh, Orlov and Kherson Oblasts are paid in accordance with the level of payment of the general kolkhoz membership. Thus in Voronezh Oblast, for example, a 1960 recommendation established a pay scale based upon annual planned money income of the farm and a fourfold classification based upon money pay per man-day of work performed by the average kolkhoz member.[19]

Based upon a 1959 recommendation of the Vladimir Raion (Vladimir Oblast), the base pay of a kolkhoz chairman is a function of gross value of output in state purchase prices and the profitability of the farm. A monthly sum is established according to the gross output indicator, while for every one percent profit (loss) this amount is raised (lowered) by one percent, though by not more than 20 percent in either direction.

Quite apart from the specifics of income determination, regional variability and the distinction between base and supplemental portions (the latter is not always clear as the preceding regional examples illustrate), the notion of a guaranteed and a non-guaranteed portion of *base pay* has gained widespread acceptance in recent years. Thus, in a sense, the base pay of the chairman includes a built-in bonus component, although this part is relatively very small, whether operative in a negative or a positive direction. The precise nature of the system varies, and depends, in part, upon the manner in which base payment is calculated. Assume a base pay rate (determined by the prevailing tariff) of 200 rubles per month. As the example in Table 5-1 illustrates, base pay consists of two portions—a guaranteed minimum (140 rubles in this case) and a non-guaranteed portion. The former is independent of farm performance, while the latter is directly tied to monthly plan fulfillment. In the example, the base pay of the manager can range from 140 rubles per month (assuming actual output is zero), up to 200 rubles per month (assuming 100 percent plan fulfillment). Overfulfillment of the plan does not add to the total base pay of 200 rubles per month.

The question of bonus systems has received much attention in the past twenty years, although the precise distinction between base and bonus payment

---

[17]In a sense this is a partial return to the 1948 system insofar as it rewards management for the size of the farm and less for the efficiency with which that size is achieved and utilized.

[18]See I.A. Ivin, op. cit., pp. 18-27. The kolkhozy are grouped according to the size of their money income, the cotton and non-cotton growing farms being separated. A monthly ruble amount varying from 140 to 250 is specified. Better performance is expected from the cotton growing farms. Thus for the chairman to receive 170 rubles per month, a cotton growing farm must have a money income range of 600-750 (money income figures in thousands), while the non-cotton growing farm must be in the range 460-575.

[19]I.A. Ivin, op. cit., pp. 23-24.

Table 5-1

Monthly Base Payment of Soviet Collective Farm Chairmen: Methodology of Calculation

Month	Planned Output ('000 rubles)	Actual Output ('000 rubles)	Percentage Plan Fulfillment	Guaranteed Minimum Portion of Base Pay	Non-guaranteed Portion of Base Pay	Total Base Pay
1	30	27	90	140.0	54.0	194.0
2	40	36	90	140.0	54.0	194.0
3	40	34	85	140.0	51.0	191.0
4	50	46	92	140.0	55.2	192.2
5	60	63	105	140.0	60.0	200.0
6	80	82	102.5	140.0	60.0	200.0

Source: I.A. Ivin, *Oplata truda rukovoditelei i spetsialistov v kolkhozakh* (Moskva: Ekonomizdat, 1963), pp. 35-37.

Note: All monthly payment figures in new rubles.

is frequently difficult to discern. During the latter half of the 1950s, the bonus arrangements of earlier years most likely prevailed in those cases where bonus systems were utilized. The use of managerial bonuses probably declined somewhat from earlier years, partly as a response to the complexity of prescribed arrangements and partly due to the feeling that transition to regular full money payment would lessen the need for bonuses as an incentive.[20]

However, the early 1960s witnessed increased agitation for the utilization of bonus systems and the formulation of specific recommendations as to the form to be assumed by such systems in each region. The recommendations of 1961-62 were surprisingly similar for most regions, differing only with regard to the specific payment scales to be applied.[21]

[20] For an interesting discussion of this question, see for example, A. Pesin, *Garantirovaniia oplata i raspredelenie po trudu v kolkhozakh* (Minsk: Urozhai, 1969), pp. 93 ff.

[21] On the 1961-62 adjustments, see I.A. Ivin, op. cit., pp. 40-41. Without better data on the operation of bonus schemes, it is difficult to assess the extent to which they have been operative in Soviet collective farms. While bonus schemes have always existed on paper, many Soviet writers agree that in practice, they have not been utilized. K.A. Shaibekov, op. cit., p. 226, suggests that the absence of local assistance has led to abuses in the application of bonus schemes. Shaibekov cites a check of 27 kolkhozy in the Ukraine of which 16 paid the chairman 4-5 times more than the kolkhoz members on the average, thus breaching the "rule" that such differentials should not be greater than 2-3 times. It may be that a peculiar dilemma exists. Thus where there is centralization, the rules do not allow for regional variability and they are not followed in part because they are not understood on the local level. However, when there is decentralization, there are no rules and no motivation for managerial action. This sort of view is presented by V.I. Voropaev and P.F. Belichenko, *Dopolnitel' naia oplata truda v kolkhozakh* (Moskva: Ekonomizdat, 1962), pp. 167-168. It is also worth noting that during 1962 in the RSFSR, bonus payments as a portion of all pay to labor constituted 10 percent for those kolkhozy using the labor day system, and 3.11 percent for those kolkhozy having abandoned the labor day. Further, in many regions of the RSFSR and for almost all kolkhozy transferring from labor days to full money calculation, bonuses were not used. On this matter, see Akademiia Nauk SSSR, Institut Ekonomiki, *Puti povysheniia proizvoditel' nosti truda v sel'skom khoziaistve SSSR* (Moskva: Nauka, 1964), pp. 113-114.

According to these recommendations of the 1960s, the chairman was to receive a bonus amounting to 50 percent of the bonus calculated on the average for the brigadier and ferma leader. These potentially very small bonus earnings were further restricted insofar as they were conditional upon fulfillment of the production plan and fulfillment of the plan for sales to the state. In addition, for each percentage reduction of production expenditures as compared with the level envisaged in the plan, the chairman would receive a bonus in the amount of one percent of base pay.[22]

Both regionally and temporally, this format was subject to change. Thus in 1963 adjustment was made so that overfulfillment of an indicator, such as gross value of output or money income of the farm, would bring a small percentage of base pay as a bonus. In addition, the lowering of cost of production below plan would bring a bonus of 1-2 percent of the sums saved.[23]

To summarize, the Khrushchev era represents certain shifts of strategy for payment of collective farm chairmen. First, the emphasis has been upon the *results* of production, however crudely measured (for example gross value of output), rather than the expansion of inputs (sown area) or expansion of capital stock (animal herds). Second, the emphasis has switched from in-kind valuation to valuation at state purchase prices. This, in conjunction with increased emphasis upon collective farm money income as a "success indicator," places increased importance upon the appropriate measurement of farm money income and the whole range of issues associated with price formation in the agricultural sector. Third, in terms of bonus arrangements, there has been a tendency to switch from in-kind to monetary measurement and to tie bonus payments of upper level personnel to those at lower levels. Fourth, it must be noted that, throughout the 1950s and early 1960s, the value of managerial earnings depended in large measure upon the size of labor-day distributions. However, since July of 1966, the introduction of guaranteed labor payments in kolkhozy will shift the basis of managerial payment to a tariff system, as used in sovkhozy.

The Brigadier and Ferma Leaders

For the brigadier, the system of payment envisaged in 1948 was broadly similar to that for the farm chairman.[24] Base pay (in labor-days) varied in accordance with the type of product being produced and the sown area. In addition, a supplement for length in the position was paid identical to that of the farm chairman. For the complex brigade, the base pay scale was to be established by the management board of the kolkhoz and hence could vary from farm to farm.

[22] During the late 1950s and early 1960s, there appeared to be increased emphasis upon the desirability of relating bonuses of managerial personnel at higher levels to those personnel at lower levels, though there is little comment as to the actual application or effectiveness of this notion.

[23] Although cost *(sebestoimost')* is normally defined to include outlays to labor, it is not clear that this is so in the present case.

[24] "O merakh po uluchsheniiu organizatsii, povysheniiu proizvoditel'nosti uporiadocheniiu oplaty truda v kolkhozakh," *Direktivy KPSS*, vol. 3, pp. 279-281.

For overfulfillment of the planned yield, the brigadier was to receive one and one half times the average supplementary payments received by the workers of the brigade. Finally, certain bonuses could be paid for above-target deliveries to the state, especially for priority crops.

The system for payment of the ferma leader was broadly similar to that for the brigadier. In part, the manner of payment depended upon the prevailing form of organization, and this could vary from farm to farm. If there were sufficient numbers of cattle (or other animals) of a given type, a ferma would be formed and an individual would be its leader on a full time basis. Where the number of animals did not justify a separate administrative unit, a full time head of animal breeding might be appointed, or, the job might be held on a part time basis. Naturally the size of the payment varied among these alternate possibilities.

With the exception of the part time leader who received the majority of his income from other sources, base pay depended upon the type of ferma, the number of animals of the given type, and the value of the labor-day. The range varied from 30 to 50 labor-days with supplements for length of service identical to those received by the farm chairman.[25] The leader of animal breeding or the leader of a ferma received a one percent bonus (of the base pay in labor-days) for every percentage overfulfillment of the plan for growth of numbers of cattle and their productivity (produktivnost'). The upper limit on this form of bonus was to be 25 percent of the base pay.

As with the farm chairman, the 1948 rules have tended to persist even after the changes introduced in a 1956 decree, though to what extent it is very difficult to determine. Also, as with other leadership personnel, krais and oblasts have in recent years worked out recommendations which in essence suggest payment for the ferma leader in accordance with the value of gross output in the particular administrative unit.[26] The system is basically the same for the brigadier.

In some cases (for example the Altai krai), the ferma leader is to receive a base income 30 percent higher than the monthly earnings of the average worker in the farm. In many cases (for example in the recommendations of the Ministry of Agriculture of the RSFSR) bonus payments are a given percentage of the average bonus earnings of the workers in the ferma or brigade. In this case, the precise percentage varies with the type of brigade and the region.

In the RSFSR, for example, the brigadier of a complex production can receive 50 percent of the average bonus earnings (in absolute terms) of the brigade workers, while in Belorussia the comparable figure is 150 percent. Finally, in some cases, bonuses are envisaged for overfulfillment of an output plan and/or the lowering of cost in the brigade or ferma.

Since July of 1966, arrangements for the payment of brigadiers have followed

---

[25] Ibid.

[26] I.A. Ivin, op. cit., pp. 40-42.

those utilized in sovkhozy. Basically, this has meant the establishment of a tariff based upon indicators, such as number of personnel in the brigade and volume of production. In Novosibirsk Oblast of the RSFSR, for example, the brigadier of a mechanized brigade can receive from 75 to 180 rubles per month base payment, depending upon the value of gross production, ranging from under 50,000 rubles annually to over 400,000 rubles annually.[27] In this particular case, brigade members may receive bonuses: 25 percent of any savings made by lowering the cost per 100 rubles of output, and/or for above plan production (2 percent of the annual earnings of each member of the brigade for every one percent overfulfillment of the production).[28]

The Agricultural Specialists

Agricultural specialist refers, above all, to the agronomist and zoötechnician, though in many cases the engineer and possibly senior accountant will be included.

For the period prior to 1962, the system for payment of these specialists was relatively complicated. For example, the pay of an agronomist could vary depending upon how the individual was placed in the particular position, age, education, and place of work.[29]

As pointed out earlier, agricultural specialists were basically not a part of the kolkhoz leadership group until after 1955. Thus specialists working within a kolkhoz, described as "own" *(sobstvennyi)* specialists were to be paid on a different basis from those specialists reintroduced into the farm from the staff of the MTS after 1955.[30] Finally, young specialists graduating from higher educational institutions were placed in yet another category for pay purposes.

Apparently there was no single decree establishing the pay scales for these specialists at the time. However, most Soviet writers suggest that the level was in essence a certain percentage of the base and bonus pay of the chairman.[31] For the agronomist and zoötechnician, this varied from 70-90 percent for those having higher education, and from 60-80 percent for those with only secondary education.[32]

The period from 1956 to 1962 witnessed several important developments. According to the decree of March 6, 1956, the kolkhozy were themselves to establish the nature and size of bonuses, both in natural, and in money, terms.[33]

[27] A.I. Zakharov and V.N. Perekrestov, *Organizatsiia i oplata truda v mekhanizirovannykh brigadakh i zven'iakh sovkhozov i kolkhozov* (Moskva: Rossel'khozizdat, 1969), pp. 58-61.

[28] Ibid., p. 59.

[29] K.A. Shaibekov, op. cit., p. 234.

[30] Ibid.

[31] See, for example, A.T. Ashcheulov and A.T. Bocharov, *Oplata truda rukovodiashchikh rabotnikov, spetsialistov i mekhanizatorov kolkhozov* (Moskva: Gosiurizdat, 1962), pp. 29-32.

[32] Ibid.

[33] "O ezhemesiachnom avansirovanii kolkhoznikov i dopolnitel' noi oplate truda v kolkhozakh," *Direktivy KPSS*, vol. 4, pp. 603-605.

This decree was notably vague, suggesting only that these bonuses should be paid to specialists for the overfulfillment of plans for crop yields and productivity in the animal sector.[34]

In the post-1956 period, there was no general decree covering the payment of these specialists. In many cases, the general guidelines of earlier years prevailed. There was, however, a tendency for some differentiation to arise at the local level partly as a response to the growth of specialists operating within a collective, and the resulting classification along such lines as chief specialist and branch specialist.

For example, in the Ukraine, a decree of December 29, 1959, established a tariff for the senior specialists with higher education varying from 80 to 150 rubles per month and dependent upon the level of money income in the collective.[35]

In some cases, a labor-day and/or money amount would be specified depending upon the level of output in physical or value terms. Such payment could be based upon output for the farm as a whole or, for the specialist working within a single brigade or ferma, based upon the output of that single production unit. In some cases, a specific monthly amount (in rubles) was specified regardless of the new level of progress.

The post-1956 period of relative drift ended with a decree of April 12, 1962 in which the details for the payment of agricultural specialists were spelled out on an all-union basis.[36] According to this decree, a senior specialist would receive 80-90 percent of that received by the farm chairman (including all supplements and bonuses), but not less than 80 rubles per month for a specialist working as such for more than two years. Those specialists working within a brigade or ferma were to be paid according to the gross value of production generated within their unit. As a guideline, their earnings were to be in the order of 80-90 percentage points of the earnings of the senior specialist.[37] Finally, the young specialists, immediately after graduation, would receive a minimum monthly amount of 70 rubles (with higher education) and 60 rubles (with secondary education).[38]

With regard to bonus payments for specialists, the decree of 1956 was vague. It did, however, suggest that such payments should exist and that they should be based not upon sown area and number of animals, but rather upon overfulfillment of plans for crop yields and animal productivity.[39] The 1962 all-union decree pertaining to specialists said little more than the 1956 decree on the matter of bonus payments. The desirability of paying bonuses for the overfulfillment of yield plans was again emphasized. It went further, however, to suggest

[34]Ibid., p. 605.

[35]N.I. Nizhnii, A.M. Onishchenko, N.I. Romanenko and A.A. Storozhuk, op. cit., pp. 171-172.

[36]"O povyshenii roli agronomov, zootekhnikov i drugikh spetsialistov sel'skogo khoziaistva i razvitii kolkhoznogo i sovkhoznogo proizvodstva," *Sbornik*, pp. 588-595.

[37]Ibid., p. 594.

[38]Ibid.

[39]"O ezhemesiachnom avansirovanii kolkhoznikov i dopolnitel' noi oplate truda v kolkhozakh," *Direktivy KPSS*, vol. 4, pp. 604-605.

that bonuses should be paid for the fulfillment and overfulfillment of output targets and the lowering of cost of production. The decree established that in the animal breeding sector, bonuses should be paid quarterly, while in the remaining sectors of the farm they should be paid once or twice per year.[40]

In spite of the generality of the decrees of 1956 and 1962, we have noted that during 1961-62 rather specific rules for the payment of bonuses to all leadership personnel were established. For example, by recommendation of the Ministry of Agriculture of the RSFSR, branch specialists (for example, in the field crop sector) were to receive 100 percent of the average supplementary payments made to the brigadier. The brigadier, in turn, was to receive a certain percentage (varying with the type of brigade) of the bonuses paid on the average to each member of the brigade. In addition, the branch specialist would receive a one percent supplement to his annual base pay for every one percent reduction of production expenditures, as against the plan for the branch.[41] The system was similar in other areas although the precise percentages varied. For those specialists seen as not being engaged in production (the accountant, planner-economist, etc.), bonuses have normally been set as a percentage of those bonuses received by the chairman.

As with other leadership positions in the kolkhoz, the post-1966 period of guaranteed wage payments has seen an effort to introduce sovkhoz patterns, although it is as yet too early to fully evaluate the impact of these changes.

Thus far we have examined in some detail the formal rules pertaining to the payment of leadership personnel in the kolkhoz. The remainder of this chapter will be devoted to an examination of the efficacy of this system in terms of the following characteristics: methodology and consistency; simplicity; form and frequency of payment; magnitude.

Methodology and Consistency

By consistency is meant, broadly speaking, a system of base and incentive payments, the utilization of which tends to promote goal oriented economic activity. Thus given an objective function as represented by equation (1), the system is broadly consistent if the total income of the chairman (and other leadership personnel) is defined by equation (2) where all partial first derivatives are positive.

$$q = f(X_1, X_2, X_3, \ldots, X_n) \tag{1}$$

where: q = quantity of output

X_1 = changes in the quantity and/or quality of land

[40] "O povyshenii roli agronomov, zooteknikov i drugikh spetsialistov sel'skogo khoziaistva i razvitii kolkhoznogo i sovkhoznogo prioizvodstva," *Sbornik*, p. 595.

[41] I.A. Ivin, op. cit., p. 40.

$$X_2 \qquad = \qquad \text{changes in the quantity and/or quality of capital stock}$$

$$X_3 \qquad = \qquad \text{changes in the quantity and/or quality of the labor force}$$

$$(X_4 \ldots, X_n) \qquad = \qquad \text{inputs } X_4, \ldots, X_n$$

and the function (f) includes initial stocks of land, labor and capital when the manager assumes the post.

$$Y_t \qquad = \qquad g(q) \tag{2}$$

and:

$g'>0$, and the function g includes initial stocks of land, labor and capital when the manager assumes the post.

where:

$$Y_t \qquad = \qquad \text{total income of leadership personnel}$$

$$q \qquad = \qquad \text{quantity of output}$$

The efficacy of the reward system will be considered in the light of the following four goals: increasing output, reduction of inputs, increasing capacity and increasing welfare of farm members.

Undoubtedly the goal of increasing farm capacity was important during the early years of extensive cultivation, although more recently this goal has declined in importance. In a formal sense, the incentive system of the early years may have been more rational than that of recent years simply because increasing production capacity is probably more readily identified (and hence rewarded) than increasing efficiency in the utilization of existing inputs. Thus, quite apart from the merits of extensive cultivation, it is evident that the target of expanded sown area, for example, was rather easily understood and measured, making the payment of bonuses rather simple.

However, as both the goals and the means of their achievement have become more complex, the introduction of monetary variables may have assisted in the harmonization of means and goals, at least if prices were rational.[42]

In the late 1940s and early 1950s for example, given a need to expand capacity, bonus payments for the enlargement of sown area are relatively simple and make sense, though it is possible that sown area increases resulted equally from specific campaigns and Party directives, more than from any incentive system.[43]

---

[42]On the matter of prices and an appropriate parametric framework for a rational incentive structure, see Alfred Zauberman, *Aspects of Planometrics* (New Haven and London: Yale University Press, 1967), Ch. 10.

[43]There were significant increases in sown area for both kolkhozy and sovkhozy during the period 1950-1956. For this period and for kolkhozy alone, roughly half of the increases in sown area can be attributed to increased sowings of forage crops. Further, a breakdown of forage sowings (see *Sel'khoz-1960*, pp. 140-141), suggests that the entire increase in sowings of forage crops during this period can be accounted for by the corn program.

To the extent that the size of the farm increases, it would also seem reasonable to increase the pay of the leadership personnel.

In terms of expanding output, the incentive system of the early years can be viewed as rational only on a short time horizon, though with the production of foodstuffs running very little ahead of consumption, this aspect of policy cannot be overlooked. On the other hand, this incentive policy seems to have assumed that, in large measure, land could be substituted for capital and that adequate supplies of labor would be available. For the long run, both assumptions must be viewed as unrealistic, although we cannot ignore potential managerial pursuit of labor-days by expansion of sown area within certain constraints.

The use of money income as a basis for managerial compensation makes much more sense now than in the past. To the extent that money income is a measure of farm size, its presence in the formula might be explained by the Soviet view that, in general, the larger the farm the more difficult is the administrative task and accordingly the pay should be higher. However, one must question the extent to which collective farm management has active control and influence over the growth of money income, and to the extent such control is not present, the incentive system makes little sense.[44] Finally, since cost accounting was not introduced into the collective farms until the mid and late 1950s, one wonders what meaning should be given to the concept of money income and payment tied to this variable.

It is interesting to observe that the bonus system for yields was to operate in a negative as well as a positive direction. While theoretically rational, this system must have been highly unpopular if it in fact was applied according to the rules. First, agricultural production can be inherently unstable, especially given the climatic peculiarities of the Soviet Union. Second, Soviet agricultural planning has tended to be a short run operation where, at the whim of officials, targets could be adjusted in the middle of the production operation. Finally, in the past, managerial personnel must have had a limited influence over the allocation of resources, which in fact constitutes a rather broad indictment of any sort of reward system.

The notion of a reward for length of service may be rational especially given a tolerably good system of managerial selection. In the Soviet case, however, past emphasis upon short-term planning and the rapid rate of turnover of managerial personnel (see Table 5-2) must have weakened such a bonus. Also, given the seemingly contradictory policy of judging the competence of managerial personnel over a relatively short period of time, this particular bonus may have been directed towards a reduction of the number wanting to leave the agricultural sector for better opportunities in the cities and to move to higher level positions in the administrative hierarchy.[45]

---

[44]The question of managerial influence will be discussed in Chapter 6. However, to the extent that a manager is unable to exert influence over those variables for which bonuses apply, it matters little how theoretically well structured the system may be.

[45]Apparently there has existed a policy of paying agricultural specialists different salaries based upon their *place* of work, even though the tasks performed may be similar or the same. Thus pay for these specialists within the agricultural administrative hierarchy will be systematically less than for those engaged directly in collective farm operations.

90

Table 5-2

Collective Farm Chairmen According to Length of Service (Percent)

Length of Service as Chairman	1953[a]	1956[b]	1957	1958	1959	1962
Up to 1 year	23.8	29.7	16.9	17.3	4.6	9.7
1-3 years	35.6	33.9	41.0	33.7	38.9	37.1
3 years and more	40.6	36.4	42.1	49.0	56.5	53.2

Sources: Compiled from *Narkhoz-1961*, p. 466; *Sel'khoz-1960*, p. 474.

[a]July 1st.

[b]April 1st.

Note: Though not specified, these data probably refer to length as the chairman of *any* collective farm.

During 1955, approximately 23 percent of collective-farm chairmen were replaced with new recruits, primarily from the industrial sector. In 1956 there were 29.7 percent of collective-farm chairmen who had been in their posts for one year or less. But, since 23 percent of all chairmen were replaced in 1955, the difference (29.7-23.0), or 6.7 percent must have been chairmen who had been in their posts less than one year as of 1956, but who had been placed by a route other than the "thirty-thousander" campaign. In 1953, 23.8 percent of chairmen were in their first year of service. But, if we assume that length of service means the holding of a position on a *single farm* (the most restrictive form of this assumption), then, as of 1956, only 6.7 percent of those in the first year of their jobs could have been from the 1953 group (i.e. those from outside the 1955 recruitment campaign), and *at least* 17.1 percent (the remainder or 23.8-6.7) must have "moved up" in the hierarchy, or, be accounted for by a reduction in the number of collective farms. Given a *decline* between 1953 and 1956 in the proportion of collective farm chairmen in the 1-3 year and 3 year plus groups, the decline in the number of collective farms must have been an important factor. Further, the evidence would seem to support the view that many of those farms amalgamated or dissolved must have been ones with a chairman having held the position for less than one year.

In recent years, there have been some important shifts. First, there has been a shift away from physical towards monetary indicators, thus reflecting the introduction of cost accounting and the monetization of the collective farm sector. Second, there has been a tendency to eliminate the targeting of, and rewarding for, the fulfillment of what are essentially input targets, most notably sown area.[46] These sorts of targets have been replaced by rewards tied more closely to the *results* of production, normally some measure of gross value of output.

---

[46]This position should not be overstated. It is difficult to assess the longevity of the 1948 pay system based upon, for example, increases in sown area. While the rigid targeting of inputs may have declined somewhat, it remains difficult to assess the extent to which the reward system has changed accordingly. The bulk of available evidence does seem to suggest that leadership personnel are more likely to be paid on the basis of value of output, money income or some similar indicator. On the other hand, it might be noted that in a Soviet textbook published in 1965, the base pay of a kolkhoz chairman is said to depend, in part, upon the sown area (for which the labor-day payment ranges from 27 to 54), and upon the number of cattle per farm (for which the labor-day payment range is 5 to 18). It will be recalled that these labor-day ranges are identical to those postulated in 1948. See D.F. Kozyrev and V.F. Nemtsov (eds.), *Organizatsiia i planirovanie proizvodstva v kolkhozakh i sovkhozakh* (Moskva: Kolos, 1965), p. 198; and *Spravochnik predsedatelia kolkhoza*, vol. 1 (Moskva: Sel'khozgiz, 1956), p. 156.

Theoretically it is possible to define a system of the sort where appropriate rewards achieve a harmony between the patterns of managerial choice and the fulfillment of stated goals. Under such conditions, one would expect to find factor and product prices which accurately reflect rates of transformation in production and consumption, respectively, and freedom of managerial choice as to the allocation of resources. Neither can be said to exist given Soviet arrangements for the pricing of agricultural inputs and outputs, although the conclusions to be drawn are not completely clear since the period under study has been characterized by relatively limited managerial freedom. Thus managers have probably given little attention to prices as indicators of desirable resource shifts.

The use of gross value targets has been widely criticized for the industrial sector, mainly on grounds that they distort the output mix and lead towards maximization of inputs rather than minimization for a given output. It may be that the peculiarities of agricultural production partly offset these disadvantages, especially when the sector is in the early and crude stages of monetization.

In agriculture, the production process is typically long and, once started, there is limited flexibility for adjustment of the product mix. Further, it might be fair to generalize that in agriculture, the product range is narrower than that of industry and hence relatively more simple to plan and, on the other hand, difficult to pervert. However, the problem of lack of spare parts and the resulting idle machinery and equipment has plagued the agricultural sector in the Soviet Union. Indeed, it might be possible to draw a parallel between the shortage of spare parts in industry, and the continuing lack of adequate forage supplies in the Soviet agricultural sector.[47]

Throughout the period under study, and especially in recent years, there has been a tendency to tie the rewards of higher level managerial personnel to the performance (and rewards) of those personnel at lower levels. To a degree, higher level management should take an interest in managerial performance at lower levels though it would seem to be a most difficult task to insure that such a

---

[47]The practice in kolkhoz planning has been to create "funds" of seed and forage to insure appropriate future reproduction in the plant and animal sectors. According to Fedor Belov, *The History of a Soviet Collective Farm* (New York: Frederick A. Praeger, 1955), p. 86, these funds are seldom more than 40 percent of the volume called for in the statutes. The Soviet press abounds with reports pertaining to the inadequate provision of seeds. These reports frequently cite inadequate amounts, poor quality, inadequate processing, high moisture content, etc. See, for example, "Assure Each State and Collective Farm Its Own Seed," *Sovetskaia Rossia* (September 22, 1957), p. 1, translated and reprinted in *CDSP*, vol. IX, no. 43 (December 4, 1957), p. 29; A. Podkhomutnikov, "Actions, Not Resolutions Needed," *Izvestia* (December 11, 1957), p. 2, translated and reprinted in *CDSP*, vol. IX, no. 50 (January 22, 1958), pp. 30-31; D. Popel, "Save the Grain," *Izvestia* (October 23, 1958), p. 2, translated and reprinted in *CDSP*, vol. X, no. 43 (December 3, 1958), pp. 23-24; "Toward New Successes in the Development of Agriculture," *Pravda* (February 13, 1958), p. 1, translated and reprinted in *CDSP*, vol. X, no. 7 (March 28, 1958), pp. 31-32. One writer suggests that "We and our agronomist—we could plant seeds of pure gold, but no bonus or pay increment whatever is provided for us." See P. Ternovsky, "What Kind of Seed do you Have?— Little Concern About Planting Select Hard Wheat in Chkalov Province," *Izvestia* (October 23, 1957), p. 2, translated and reprinted in *CDSP*, vol. IX, no. 43 (December 4, 1957), pp. 29-30.

system is thoroughly consistent. Thus sub goals should mesh with overall goals and there should be a rational chain of influence from higher to lower levels. Such a system might lessen the positive motivating force of a bonus system at higher levels given the extreme difficulty of rational prediction as to expected magnitude of future bonuses.

There are other negative aspects of a hierarchial bonus system in the Soviet context. First, such a system would seem to be in contradiction to the frequently expressed Soviet view that such indicators as sales and money income are of no use at the brigade level insofar as the brigade is concerned solely with production, and not with the marketing of the product.[48] Secondly, accounting procedures are markedly weaker at the brigade level than for the farm as a whole.[49]

It might be noted that the practice of inter-connected pay scales between higher and lower levels is not new, though the direction of influence may have shifted somewhat. Thus during the 1950s, there was a prevailing notion that of fundamental importance was the establishment of an appropriate base and bonus payment system for the manager of the collective, after which other managerial personnel would receive a certain percentage of the chairman's pay.[50] In this connection, debate tended to focus upon the specific amounts that a person should receive rather than a questioning of the basic system of determination. One might suspect that simplicity was a major argument for this type of system.

To the extent that both the manager and the peasant were being paid in labor-days, the former should have been interested in the welfare of the latter insofar as increases in the value of the labor-day would increase the welfare of both. While there have been important limitations upon the ability of management to increase the value of the labor-day in the short run (to be discussed in Chapter 6), nevertheless, the labor-day as a method for calculating labor distributions deserves attention in the present chapter.

Since the general nature of the labor-day has been adequately treated by others,[51] we can focus upon one primary question: to what extent, if any, has the labor-day system of payments influenced managerial behavior? In particular,

---

[48]This point of view is adopted by G. Ia. Kuznetsov, op. cit., p. 150. In this connection, there is discussion on the efficacy of various different economic indicators. Various viewpoints are outlined by K.A. Shaibekov, op. cit., p. 228. Shaibekov argues in favor of gross production saying that money income does not give a "full picture" of the farm.

[49]According to one author, at the beginning of 1960, approximately 2,000 kolkhozy in the USSR were utilizing khozraschet at the brigade level (vnutrenii khozraschet). See I.V. Pavlov, Pravovye formy vnutrennogo khozrascheta v kolkhozakh (Moskva: Gosiurizdat, 1961), p. 5. It should be noted, however, that khozraschet at the brigade level normally means much less than the traditional interpretation of this term. Thus it does not mean that the brigade is a self-financing unit holding external economic relationships. Rather, it seems to mean the installation of basic accounting procedures such that revenues and costs for each production unit will be known. This might appropriately be described as "non-full" or nepolnyi khozraschet.

[50]See for example, Henri Wronski, op. cit.

[51]See ibid., for example.

if we assume that managers are motivated to increase their earnings, it is necessary to know how the labor-day as a peculiar method of calculation might have altered managerial behavior patterns while in the pursuit of increased earnings, and what impact this alteration might have upon the performance of the farm.

In general, the manager has faced two options: first, increase the *number* of labor-days that he receives or, second, increase the *value* of the labor-day. If we make some simple assumptions about managerial behavior, and if we ignore the time problem (long delays between effort and reward), it is possible to suggest that the pursuit of increased earnings may have been broadly consistent with prevailing goals.[52] Thus if we assume that the manager does not expand his labor-days by illegal means or by extracting them from peasants, then the pursuit of more labor-days would, especially in the early 1950s, lead to goal-oriented behavior: increasing sown area, cattle herds, etc. At the same time, the manager would, presumably, attempt to increase the value of his labor-days, an attempt which must have led to efforts to increase output and/or decrease inputs; that is, to increase the "residual," part of which is available for labor-day distributions. Within plan and other restrictions, the general motivation must have been in these directions.

If the connection between capacity and output increases (not to mention efficiency increases) was tenuous in the early 1950s, it must have been increasingly so as the planning structure changed and monetization engulfed the collective farm sector. However, the methodology of managerial payment was changing at the same time, although precisely at what rate and with what degree of consistency is not clear. Increasingly, however, monetary payment scales in ruble amounts were used; bonus payments were increasingly tied to cost reductions and output increases. While all the usual criticisms apply in this case (pricing problems, measurement of output and temporal aspects), this shift does seem to have reflected the monetization of the kolkhoz sector and the adjustment of kolkhoz means to goal achievement and the managerial role in that achievement. In short, there is some evidence to suggest that, as a methodology of calculation (apart from problems of form and frequency), the labor-day system was not wholly inconsistent with the goals of collective agriculture in the early years (although one might question the rationality of those goals). Further, there seems to have been some attempt, albeit *ad hoc* in many instances, to by-pass the labor-day system for management as the structure and operation of the kolkhoz underwent change. The ultimate culmination of this trend was certainly the abandonment of the labor-day system in its entirety in July of 1966.

---

[52] In particular, we must assume that the manager does not in some manner (legal or illegal) attempt to shift labor days away from peasants and towards himself, or to "pad" his own account either with more labor days or in some manner, higher valued labor days. Although the general direction of motivation appears to be in favor of increasing peasant welfare, it must also be noted that 1) managers have typically been "outsiders" governing increasingly large farms; 2) peasants have little real say in the selection or removal of the chairman; and 3) the nature of distribution of kolkhoz gross income (to be discussed in Chapter 6) would not make distributions to labor days a priority in the eyes of the state.

Simplicity

One of the basic requirements of a good payment system, especially the bonus component, is simplicity and, hence, utilization. Given the severe shortage of personnel trained in economics and available to collective farms, simplicity is especially significant in the Soviet case.[53] Second, it is important that the person receiving the bonus understand its application so that he will be motivated by the realistic expectation of receiving a bonus and the motivation will be in an appropriate direction in accordance with the "instructions" of the bonus system.

In general, the Soviet pattern for rewarding managerial personnel has tended to be overly complex. While some simplicity (if not rationality) has been gained by the use of unified systems for large geographic areas, the use of multiple indicators, themselves difficult to define and operating on several levels, must have left the participants in a state of confusion much of the time. The incentive systems studied to date are those existing on paper. Some Soviet writers have suggested that, in fact, bonus systems are frequently not used simply due to their complexity.[54] One solution to this problem has been the utilization of simple, short run plans where a bonus can be paid for the short run completion of a specific task or work project.[55]

[53] See, for example, V.P. Rozhin, op. cit., pp. 51-58. Rozhin cites the case of Krsanodarskii krai which is one of the best agricultural regions in the Soviet Union. At the beginning of 1958, there were on the average (with higher and secondary education), 13.4 agronomists, zootechnicians, veterinarians and engineers; and 0.3 planner-economists per kolkhoz. Furthermore, these figures include those employed by the MTS, many of whom did not enter the collective farms at the time of dissolution of the MTS. In general, there is considerable discussion in the Soviet press about the need for more planner-economists, while at the same time there is considerable confusion as to the nature of the tasks that they perform. Criticism of accountants centers upon their low educational levels and the inadequacy of their short-term training courses. On these questions see, for example, A.M. Galanov, "Ustranit' nedostatki v podgotovke kadrov," *Uchet i finansy v kolkhozakh i sovkhozakh*, No. 5 (May 1961), p. 57; A. Grigor'iants, "Kolkhoznyi ekonomist," *Kolkhoznoe-sovkhoznoe proizvodstvo Moldavii*, No. 12 (December 1964), pp. 1-3; and "Ob ekonomiste kolkhoza," *Uchet i finansy v kolkhozakh i sovkhozakh*, No. 1 (January 1962), pp. 29-32.

[54] V.I. Voropaev and P.P. Velichenko, op. cit., p. 168 suggesting that prior to 1962, many kolkhozy did not use bonus systems for kolkhoz specialists simply because the kolkhozy and those responsible for their operation did not know what to do.

[55] There seems to be a notion that where the pay of the kolkhoz members is sufficiently high, where output targets are filled on time and where quality is adequate, there is justification for the emphasis upon base rather than bonus pay. Thus V.P. Rozhin, op. cit., p. 127, suggests that bonus systems are more important for the weak farms. More specifically, however, the Soviet experience of the post-1952 period indicates a willingness to use bonus schemes for the achievement of specific priority goals. Thus in connection with the Virgin Lands program, it was decreed that workers of tractor and field brigades should receive a bonus in the form of up to 30 percent of the above-plan harvests from newly sown lands, and that for 1954-55, all personnel of newly organized sovkhozy should receive a 15 percent supplement to their earnings. On these schemes, see "O dal'nesihem uvelichenii proizvodstva zerna v strane i ob osvoenii tsellinykh i zalezhnykh zemel'," *Sbornik*, p. 124. A different sort of incentive was established in 1958. Thus for the creation of new strains of certain crops, the authors and those on collective and state farms associated with the development would receive ruble payments. On this sort of bonus, see "Ob izmenenii poriadka premirovaniia rabotnikov sel'skogo khoziaistva za vyvdednie vonykh i uluchshenie sushchestvuiushchikh sortov i gibridov sel'skokhoziaistvennykh kul'tur," *Sbornik*, pp. 307-308. While Soviet writers on agricultural matters advocate strongly the use of bonus systems, there seems to be a remarkable degree of skepticism and distrust of those who do in fact experience personal

Form and Frequency of Payment

If the payment of rewards is to be based upon effort expended, it would seem necessary that the two be temporally linked such that positive behavior is appropriately reinforced. In addition, payments should be in a *form* desired by the recipients. The latter question assumes great significance in the Soviet case given the importance of non-monetary transactions, especially in the rural sector.

During the period under study, there have been three significant trends. First, although the labor-day remained in official usage until July of 1966, the managerial group has always received a monetary component and, apparently, a guaranteed monthly component. Second, the proportion of kolkhozy with a guaranteed money payment system has increased quite rapidly though with marked regional variability as Table 5-3 indicates. It is clear that for most regions, the

Table 5-3

Selected Characteristics of Labor Payment on Soviet Collective Farms

Region	Percentage of Kolkhozy with Guaranteed Money Pay:[a]		Money Advances as a Percentage of the Money Portion of the Fund for Labor Pay:
	1959	1963	1961
USSR	7.2	20.3	75.4
RSFSR	8.1	25.6	77.4
Uzbekistan	17.1	78.6	73.5
Tadzhikistan	14.3	68.9	77.0
Estonia	14.0	88.6	81.3
Latvia	8.4	20.2	69.9
Ukraine	8.1	10.5	78.7
Kazakhstan	6.6	21.5	74.7
Moldavia	6.0	16.8	75.5
Kirgizia	4.7	18.6	78.3
Azerbaidzhan	4.5	7.2	54.2
Lithuania	2.5	3.6	66.5
Belorussia	1.9	4.2	69.9
Armenia	1.3	1.7	73.7
Turkmenistan	0.6	45.1	57.4
Georgia	0.4	4.9	66.7

Sources: Compiled from V.P. Rozhin, *Nekotorye voprosy pod'ema ekonomiki slabykh kolkhozov* (Moskva: Ekonomizdat, 1961), p. 113, Akademiia Nauk SSSR, Institut Ekonomiki, *Material'noe stimulirovanie razvitiia kolkhoznogo proizvodstva* (Moskva: Akademiia Nauk SSSR, 1963), pp. 54-55.

[a]In part, the increase in percentage of kolkhozy with guaranteed money pay can be ascribed to amalgamation and conversion, especially to the extent that economically weak kolkhozy were more likely to be amalgamated or converted.

gain from the operation of such a system. *Ex ante* the system appears necessary and desirable, while *ex post* the price paid always appears to be too high. This attitude may reflect the difficulty of being sure that the results achieved were in fact a result of extra effort expended by the person or persons receiving bonuses, and fear of illegal manipulations that may have led to the granting of a bonus.

major proportion of the money component of total pay has been for the purpose of making advances. Third, it is apparent from Table 5-4 that the frequency with which money advances have been given has increased significantly. Throughout the period 1957-1963 only a small proportion of collective farms gave *no* money advances, although this proportion did not decline substantially over time.

It is important to note that this data represents payment characteristics for all, not simply managerial personnel, of collective farms. At the same time, one can safely assume that although managerial personnel were supposed to receive monthly money components of their earnings, to the extent that this did not exist in reality (it was not centrally decreed), the monetization of labor payments must have been beneficial to the managerial group. Since managers have probably enjoyed greater mobility and, at the same time, less active participation in the private sector than peasants, the increasing availability of money income must have made the managerial task more attractive.

Magnitude of Managerial Rewards

How well do managerial personnel fare, and in particular, how important are bonuses as a managerial incentive in Soviet collective agriculture? The establishment of a base pay scale for the farm chairman is fundamental and one from

Table 5-4

Grouping of Collective Farms According to Frequency of Money Advances, 1957-1963 (USSR)

Year	Percentage of Collective Farms Giving the Indicated Number of Money Advances: Yearly				Percentage with No Advances
	Up to 3 Times	4-6 Times	7-9 Times	10 Times or More	
1957[a]	39.0	21.6	11.8	22.4	5.2
1958	37.0	20.3	25.1	13.4	4.2
1959	32.1	18.2	15.6	29.7	4.4
1960	27.8	17.3	16.8	32.2	5.9
1961	24.1	15.4	16.1	39.3	5.1
1962	18.9	13.8	15.5	45.5	6.3
1963	16.8	12.2	14.0	52.5	4.5

Source: G. Ia. Kuznetsov, *Material'noe stimulirovanie truda v kolkhozakh* (Moskva: Mysl', 1966), p. 29.

[a]For the year 1957 only, the third category is 7-11 times, and the fourth category monthly.

which other scales will follow.[56] In addition, Soviet writers indicate that the pay scale of the kolkhoz manager should closely reflect that of a nearby sovkhoz director.[57] While there has been a tendency to increase managerial payment, as the size of the farm increases, Soviet authors have suggested that as a "rule," the pay of managerial personnel should not exceed 2-3 times that of the average kolkhoz member. This figure was probably exceeded in many cases.

In the absence of more appropriate data, we have constructed in Table 5-5 a maximum-minimum estimated range of monthly earnings of a collective farm chairman for 1952.[58] This projection is based upon the 1948 payment rules and Alec Nove's estimated value of the labor-day for the year 1952. While necessarily very tentative, the estimated range of earnings (139 to 1723 old rubles) is probably a workable approximation. But if these extremes are reasonable, what can be said about the distribution of actual earnings?

To examine the latter question, consider the distribution of collective farms according to the main earnings components:

1. labor days for sown area and cattle holdings;
2. labor days for seniority;
3. rubles based upon the magnitude of farm money income; and
4. labor days (positive or negative) from the bonus system.

Considering sown area, the first portion of managerial earnings, it is apparent from Table 5-6 that labor-day earnings in this category were minimal for the early part of this period, though they increased significantly in the mid and late 1950s. Thus in 1949, 69.9 percent of collective farm chairmen must have earned 33 labor-days per month or less from this source, while for 1956, the corresponding figure was 17.7 percent.

Turning to that component of labor-day income derived from stage of work (see Table 5-2), the picture is less clear though the small relative importance of this component makes the question of minimal significance. However, at least 40 percent of kolkhoz chairmen received *some* supplement for tenure in their positions, and, throughout the 1950s, the number of chairmen receiving this type of supplement increased, though not substantially.[59]

---

[56]"O povyshenii roli agronomov, zootekhnikov i drugikh spetsialistov sel'skogo khoziaistva v razvitii kolkhoznogo proizvodstva," *Sbornik*, pp. 588-595 (especially p. 594).

[57]G. Ia. Kuznetsov, op. cit., p. 147, suggests that the pay of a kolkhoz chairman can be set at a level similar to that of a nearby sovkhoz director, but only as a guide. However, Soviet policy seems to be directed towards raising managerial rewards on collective farms up to the level of those on state farms. Such a view is expressed in M.V. Mikhailov, *Planirovanie i rezhim ekonomiki v kolkhozakh* (Moskva: Ekonomika, 1965), p. 26.

[58]See Alec Nove, "Incentives for Peasants and Administration," in Roy D. Laird (ed.), *Soviet Agricultural and Peasant Affairs*, (Lawrence: University of Kansas Press, 1963), pp. 51-68. See especially Tables 1 and 2 (pp. 51-52) and the footnotes thereto.

[59]Assuming that the data presented and the bonus both apply to the same indicator, namely length of service on a given kolkhoz *or* length as chairman of any kolkhoz.

Table 5-5

Maximum-Minimum Projected Earnings of Collective Farm Chairmen: USSR, 1952 (Old Rubles)

Payment Basis	Minimum	Maximum
Sown area (labor-days)	27	54
Livestock (labor-days)[a]	5	18
Horses (labor-days)	2	15
Fowl (labor-days)[b]	3	10
Stage of work as chairman	nil	28[c]
Base Pay Range (labor-days)	37	125
Income derived from farm money income (rubles)	25	400
Ruble valuation of base labor-days (labor-day = 5.4 rubles)[d]	200	675
Value of Total Base Pay	225	1075
Ruble Value of Bonus Pay[e]	−86	648
Projected Total Earnings	139	1723

Source: Compiled from *Spravochnik predsedatelia kolkhoza* (Moskva: Sel'khozizdat, 1956), Vol. 1, pp. 156-158.

[a]It is assumed that labor-days are not paid for *each* type of animal, and that each kolkhoz has 2 fermy.

[b]Assumes labor-day payment is not made for each type of fowl.

[c]Based upon a 15 percent supplement to base pay in labor-days (not including stage of work supplement).

[d]Valuation of the labor-day for 1952 from Alec Nove, "Incentives for Peasants and Administrators," as cited in Roy D. Laird (ed.), *Soviet Agricultural and Peasant Affairs* (Lawrence: University of Kansas Press, 1963), p. 52. Both cash and in-kind payment are included. Since this figure is an average value, we presumably overstate the minimum and understate the maximum earnings, thus narrowing the range of projected total earnings.

[e]Maximum "negative" bonus is 25 percent of base labor-days without stage of work supplement. The range is therefore −16 to +120 labor-days, here valued identically with the base labor-days.

Table 5-6

Distribution of Kolkhozy by Size of Sown Area and Resultant Potential Earnings of Kolkhoz Chairmen in Labor-Days (Percent Kolkhozy)

Labor-Day Earnings	Percentage of Kolkhozy with Indicated Managerial Earnings					
	1949	1950	1953	1956	1958	1959
27	14.0	5.4	1.9		2.2	
30	39.0	15.5	6.8	17.7	7.4	
33	16.9	13.8	9.8		8.6	5.8
36-42	19.2	28.9	28.9	24.6	23.3	18.3
48-52	10.9	36.4	52.6	57.7	58.5	68.1

Sources: Computed from *Sel'khoz-1960*, p. 53; and *Spravochnik predsedatelia kolkhoza* (Moskva: Sel'khozizdat, 1956), Vol. I, p. 156.

Data pertaining to ruble earnings based upon farm money income is assembled in Table 5-7. Here we see that no farm chairman could have received *more* than 175 old rubles per month in 1953, while in 1959, no farm chairman would have received *under* 175 old rubles. This represents a significant gain from an initially *very low* position.

Turning to the matter of bonuses, the lack of comprehensive plan fulfillment data (upon which bonuses are based) limits our analysis. Nevertheless, there is evidence that bonus payments were not of major importance. First, we have seen that *ex ante*, bonus payments to managerial personnel in collective agriculture were designed to be markedly smaller than those for similar types of positions in the industrial sector.[60] Second, the nature of the plan formulation and fulfillment process, especially in the early 1950s (and given the absence of any significant long term planning), must surely have dictated against persistence of significant overfulfillment of production and other plans.[61] Third, if one considers selected data, for example that offered by I.G. Suslov, it is apparent that bonuses must have been minimal. Suslov suggests that for the year 1964 (when one might have anticipated planning procedures to be somewhat improved vis-a-vis the early 1950s), percentage plan fulfillment (production-financial plans) for kolkhozy of the RSFSR ranged from a low of 65.5 percent (bee products) to a high of 90.0 percent (potatoes and vegetables) with an average fulfillment of 81.5 percent in the animal breeding sector and 79.5 percent in the crop growing sector.[62]

Table 5-7
Distribution of Kolkhozy by Money Income and Resultant Potential Ruble Earnings of Collective Farm Chairmen: Selected Years

Managerial Payment in Old Rubles	Percentage of Kolkhozy by Money Income		
	1953	1957	1959
25-125	58.4	18.9	0.7
125-175	41.6	54.9	4.3
175-225	...	17.7	6.7
225-350	...	...	18.0
400-	...	...	70.3

Sources: Computed from Nauchno-issledovatel'skii finansovyi institut, *Denezhnye dokhody kolkhozov i differentsial'naia renta* (Moskva: Gosfinizdat, 1963), p. 34, Sel'khoz-1960, pp. 53, 70; *Spravochnik predsedatelia kolkhoza,* Vol. 1 (Moskva: Sel'khozgiz, 1956), p. 157.

[60] Joseph S. Berliner, op. cit., pp. 29-32; David Granick, op. cit., pp. 130-134; Barry M. Richman, op. cit., pp. 134-135.

[61] During the period under study, there was no long-term planning of any significance in Soviet collective agriculture. In addition, the difficulties of defining capacity in combination with continual pressure from above created a "rachet" type of operation where initial plan targets bore little or no relation to final delivery demands. Under such uncertainty, bonuses for overfulfillment probably were of minimal significance as a managerial incentive.

[62] I.F. Suslov, *Ekonomicheskoe problemy razvitiia kolkhozov* (Moskva: Ekonomika, 1967), p. 203.

To the extent that bonus payments are based upon the fulfillment of state purchase plans, the picture is no brighter. Thus for kolkhozy in the RSFSR over the five year period 1959-1963, on the average, state purchase plans were fulfilled 90.3 percent for grain crops, 52.8 percent for potatoes, 68.1 percent for sugar beets, 88.8 percent for sunflower, 93.7 percent for milk and 95.7 percent for meat.[63]

In sum, our examination of Soviet collective farms from the point of view of earnings components of managerial personnel would indicate significant increases in potential *base* earnings of farm chairmen throughout the 1950s. The magnitude of potential bonus earnings seems to have been much more restricted, although very limited data necessarily limit the conclusions.

Turning to the question of managerial vis-a-vis peasant earnings, we accept labor-day earnings as a proxy for total earnings in both cases and examine the year 1954.[64] During 1954, each collective farm member earned on the average 423 labor-days, or 35 per month.[65] For the same year, the range of managerial labor-day earnings was from 21 to 245 per month (including seniority earnings). At first glance, it would appear that the level of managerial earnings could be significantly above (depending upon the nature of the distribution) the level of such earnings, on the average, for the peasants. There are, however, some necessary qualifications.

First, while ignoring the money component of total earnings may not be serious for the early 1950s, it must be recalled that roughly half of peasant earnings were derived from the private sector, hence labor-day earnings markedly understate total peasant earnings.[66] At the same time, it is doubtful that a significant component of managerial earnings could have been derived from the private sector of the kolkhoz given the time pressures of the managerial position and potential official displeasure as indicated by recurring campaigns against the private sector.[67]

Second, it is probably realistic to suggest that, at least for the early 1950s, the distribution of earnings for both groups was sharply skewed to the left, a result which would bring the earnings of the average kolkhoz chairman closely in line with those of the average peasant, given the nature of the minimal and maximal

[63] S.V. Rogachev, *Proizvodstvennyi kollektiv i khoziaistvennaia reforma* (Moskva: Mysl', 1969), p. 95.

[64] Is the labor-day figure a good proxy for total earnings? There are two questions involved. First, many farms began, in the 1950s, to switch from in-kind to monetary payment but using the labor-day as a measurement device. Second, some farms, when switching to monetary payment also abandoned the labor-day as a means of calculation. While we do not have data on the former and since the latter is a subset of the former, we can suggest that data for numbers of farms switching to guaranteed money payment would be an outside estimate of those abandoning the labor-day entirely. Thus in 1959 only 7.2 percent of collective farms in the USSR utilized guaranteed monetary pay. Thus for the early 1950s, the assumption is justified that labor-days represent total earnings. See V.P. Rozhin, op. cit., p. 113.

[65] Henry Wronsky, "Peasant Incomes," in Roy D. Laird and Edward L. Crowley (eds.), *Soviet Agriculture: The Permanent Crisis* (New York: Frederick A. Praeger, 1965), p. 124.

[66] V.P. Ostrovskii, *Kolkhoz'noe krest'ianstvo SSSR* (Saratov: Izd. Saratovskogo universiteta, 1967), p. 93.

[67] To the extent that the farm chairman has unofficial sources of fodder, and in addition his wife is in fact working on the private plot, this case is weakened.

earnings positions in both cases. In sum, it would seem that for the early years of our study, the average kolkhoz chairman typically earned more, though not substantially more, than the average kolkhoz peasant.·

Turning to the late 1950s and early 1960s, the data are somewhat better, though still inadequate. First, our examination of earnings components for the late 1950s would suggest a sharp upward trend in potential managerial earnings. Second, the data in Table 5-8 for the year 1961, indicate that average monthly earnings of a kolkhoz chairman for that year was 153 new rubles, including bonuses. In 1960, however, the average monthly earnings of rabochi and sluzhaschii in sovkhozy and subsidiary agricultural enterprises was 53.9 new rubles.[68] One would expect collective farm members to earn rather less, on balance, than their counterparts on state farms. Indeed, for the period 1953/54-1963/64, the *fund* for labor payments of kolkhozy as a percentage of the same fund in sovkhozy (calculated per able bodied worker) rose from only 35 percent to 50 percent, and, per work day (rabchii den'), from 53 percent to 79 percent.[69] Thus

Table 5-8

Basic and Supplemental Earnings of Kolkhoz Chairmen, 1961

	(1) Average Monthly Earnings: (New Rubles)	(2) Of Which Bonus (%)	(3) Chairmen Receiving Bonus (%)	(4) Bonus as % of Earnings for Those Receiving Bonus
RSFSR	143	7.6	23	33
Ukraine	162	11.8	71	17
Belorussia	152	29.2	64	46
Uzbekistan	147	3.3	22	15
Kazakhstan	107	17.8	38	47
Georgia	161	17.2	55	31
Azerbaidzhan	170	9.5	66	14
Lithuania	175	3.6	14	26
Latvia	150	...	20	...
Kirgizia	88	10.3	27	38
Tadzhikistan	186	0.7	3	23
Armenia	116	6.6	40	16
Turkmenistan	176	32.0	50	64
Estonia	203	0.7	17	2
Simple average	153	11.5 (excl. Latvia)	36.4	28.6 (excl. Latvia)

Source: Compiled from I.A. Ivin, *Oplata truda rukovoditelei i spetsialistov v kolkhozakh* (Moskva: Ekonomizdat, 1963), pp. 38, 39, 53.

[68]TsSU pri Sovete Ministrov SSSR, *Strana Sovetov za 50 let* (Moskva: Statistika, 1967), p. 227.
[69]T.I. Zaslavskaia, *Raspredelenie po truda v kolkhozakh* (Moskva: Ekonomika, 1966), p. 43.

the average collective farm chairman must have earned significantly more than the average peasant in the latter years of the period under study, and, in many cases, the "rule" of a 2-3 times differential must have been exceeded. This would be a significant improvement from an apparently limited differential between peasant and managerial earnings in the early 1950s.

How well do managerial personnel fare with regard to bonuses and, especially, vis-a-vis collective farm members as a group? One Soviet writer has suggested that they should be in the range of 6-15 percent of base pay.[70] For kolkhoz members as a group, they have apparently been of rather less importance, and certainly of minimal significance, when compared to Soviet industrial managers. Data assembled in Table 5-9 indicate that bonuses as a portion of money income of the farm going to labor have been small, increasing from only 8.3 to 11.5 percent for the period 1956-1959, and declining thereafter to 7.7 percent by 1963. At the same time, our data for the year 1961 indicate that 7.6 percent of the average monthly earnings of kolkhoz chairmen was in bonus form, while for the same year, 9.5 percent of money income going to labor was in the form of bonus payments (Table 5-9).[71] It is important to note that throughout the period 1955-1964, the in-kind portion of bonus payments declined significantly.[72]

Returning to Table 5-8 we can see that there has been marked regional vari-

Table 5-9

Selected Characteristics of Bonus Payments of Collective Farm Members of the USSR and RSFSR

	1955	1956	1957	1958	1959	1960	1961	1962	1963	1964
Bonus as a % of all money income going to labor: RSFSR	. . .	8.3	. . .	. . .	11.5	10.1	9.5	9.2	7.7	. . .
Portion of bonus pay in-kind: USSR	58.4	39.7	33.3	23.3	21.9	. . .	20.6	22.4	. . .	15.1

Sources: Compiled from G. Ia. Kuznetsov, *Material'noe stimulirovanie truda v kolkhozakh* (Moskva: Mysl', 1966), p. 163, and T.I. Zaslavskaia, *Raspredelenie po trudu v kolkhozakh* Moskva: Ekonomika, 1966), p. 307. Note that bonus payments are presented as a portion of money income rather than total income. Between 1959/60 and 1963/64, the share of money in payments to kolkhoz labor increased from 58.4 percent to 67.8 percent for those kolkhozy using labor-days, and from 77.0 percent to 75.3 percent (decline) for those kolkhozy not using labor-days. See Zaslavskaia, p. 151.

---

[70] K.A. Shaibekov, op. cit., p. 245.

[71] Note that since approximately 20 percent of bonus payments to peasants were in-kind in 1961 (Table 5-8), we understate total peasant bonus earnings. On the other hand, it is unlikely that managers received significant in-kind bonuses, hence their money bonuses roughly equal their total bonuses.

[72] The in-kind bonuses as a portion of all bonuses declined from 58.4 percent in 1955 to 15.1 percent in 1964 (USSR—all kolkhoz members). In-kind bonuses declined from 100 (index) in 1955 to 41 in 1964. See T.I. Zaslavskaia, op. cit., p. 307.

ability in the importance of bonus payments for managers. By importance we mean not only the proportion of personnel in a given class who actually receive a bonus, but also the relation of bonus to base pay for this group.

Supplementary Benefits

In addition to the monetary and non-monetary benefits associated with the formal reward system, managerial personnel in Soviet collective agriculture do reap certain benefits which, on balance, must add considerably to the satisfaction gained from the managerial position. Quite apart from the personal satisfaction associated with the operation of a "good" farm, a chairman is likely to receive a considerable measure of official recognition, medals and prizes, not to mention adulation in the local press.[73]

In addition to comfortable office facilities, the chairman may well be provided with a chauffer-driven automobile. Managerial personnel at lower levels will also be provided with transportation, possibly a motorcycle. These benefits cannot be viewed lightly in rural Russia where roads are typically bad, public transport is inadequate and distances are great. These means of transportation are a mark of distinction separating the managerial personnel from the average kolkhoz member who, at best, owns a bicycle.

Finally, the collective farm chairman has a significantly increased likelihood of travel, both to larger cities and to other farms and agricultural centers in the region. Travel may arise in connection with inter-kolkhoz competition, seminars, displays or service in the local organs of the state and Party.

Summary

This assessment of the managerial reward system of Soviet collective agriculture has focused upon selected aspects of income formation and related benefits. As such, treatment of the general incentive problem is limited. However, discussion of managerial rewards is deemed important on the assumption that both monetary and non-monetary benefits do mold managerial behavior patterns and, hence, farm performance.

[73]Throughout the period under study, there has been a continuing usage of various sorts of medals and prizes. In 1947, for example, 1,931 kolkhoz members and other agricultural workers received the "hero of socialist labor," 4,348 persons were awarded the "Order of Lenin," more than 12,500 received the "Banner of Red Labor," and 40,000 were awarded various medals. See T. Sokolov, *Organizatsionno-khoziaistvennoe ukreplenie kolkhozov* (Moskva: Gospolitizdat, 1948), p. 22. The practice has changed little in recent years. For example, in the Ukraine in 1958, 10 provinces received the "Order of Lenin," while more than 44,000 workers of various agricultural organizations received orders and medals of the Soviet Union. See N.V. Podgorny, "Toward a New Advance of Ukraine Agriculture," *Pravda*, February 27, 1958, pp. 3-4, translated and reprinted in *CDSP*, vol. X, no. 9 (April 9, 1958), p. 28.

In conjunction with monetization of the collective farm sector, the managerial payment system has undergone considerable change. The rules as to determination of base and bonus earnings were decentralized to some degree during the 1950s, though with some re-centralization evident in the 1960s. Most important, there has been a shift away from payment for fulfillment of what are essentially input targets (sown area, cattle, etc.), towards performance indicators (output, yields, and cost reductions). To the extent that these performance goals are expressed in value terms, the inadequacies of Soviet agricultural pricing will bear upon the success of the incentive system.

The managerial reward system of Soviet collective agriculture has been appraised on the basis of four interrelated guidelines: methodology and consistency; simplicity; form and frequency; and magnitude.

Are incentives formulated to motivate managerial personnel towards the achievement of collective farm goals? In general, the system must have provided reasonable motivation in generally appropriate directions—and increasingly so since the early 1950s. In addition to problems of price formation, however, the hierarchial structure is of questionable validity; that is, a system where rewards of higher level managerial personnel depend directly upon performance of lower level managers. This type of system in combination with multiple success indicators, changing over time, has made the system unduly complex. Many farms do not use bonus systems simply because the arrangements are not sufficiently simplified for all to comprehend. Indeed, complexity must be an important factor accounting for the relatively small magnitude of bonus payments in collective agriculture as opposed to bonuses in industrial management.

In terms of the form and frequency of payment, there has been significant improvement in recent years. Quite apart from the formal elimination of the labor-day system of payment as of 1966, throughout the period since the early 1950s, monetary income has replaced non-monetary income, and the frequency of payment has risen sharply for most personnel.

In recent years, the magnitude of managerial rewards has risen significantly. Thus while the average collective farm chairman of the early 1950s appears to have earned little more than the average peasant, this differential seems to have widened to the point that the typical manager will now earn 2-3 times the average peasant, and in many cases, 4-5 times. This represents an important improvement from an initially very low position. In part, however, this increased level of managerial rewards must be seen as compensation for the stewardship of a much larger and more complex organization. A more relevant comparison for the present day might be the earnings of brigadiers vis-a-vis the peasants.

Although regional differentials are important, bonus payments as a portion of managerial earnings have been small, especially when compared to those in industrial management. Although inadequate managerial performance and ignorance about complex bonus arrangements have been contributing factors, *prescribed* bonuses have been small vis-a-vis the industrial sector.

6

Planning and the Decision Making Process

In the preceding chapters the kolkhoz has been examined as a production unit with particular emphasis upon the changing internal organization and those political and administrative organs external to, but vitally connected with, kolkhoz operations. The present chapter will focus upon related, though substantially, different questions.

The purpose here is that of examining the internal decision making of the kolkhoz: who makes the important decisions and on what basis are they made. The focus is the post-1950 period and the most crucial decisions made by any production organization, namely, the determination of output on the one hand, and the determination of the volume and appropriate mix of inputs (land, labor and capital) on the other hand.

This analysis of the decision making procedures and practices of the kolkhoz rests upon the hypothesis that for the period under study there has been a noticeable shift, albeit limited, of the decision making system away from a net of physical targets operating within a rigid hierarchial command system (early 1950s), towards a semi-decentralized command system (late 1950s and the 1960s). While the former system was characterized by economic calculation largely in-kind: minimal attention to monetary incentives, absence of appropriate decision making tools within the kolkhoz (notably cost accounting) and a high degree of external control over kolkhoz decisions; the latter system has been characterized by increasing attention to: value parameters, monetary incentives, economic accounting with the introduction of appropriate decision tools at the local level and, finally, a measure of relaxation in terms of the decision making freedom enjoyed by managerial personnel within the kolkhoz.[1]

Changes in the decision making system of the Soviet kolkhoz have not always been positive. In this sense, the time classification suggested above is somewhat arbitrary. Further, the movement has been one of *degree*, and, above all, it is not suggested that a pure model (of either centralized or decentralized) decision making existed at any given time. Rather there has been a continuum of important changes, many serving to mold the kolkhoz in a new manner more suitable to the present and future role of agriculture in the Soviet economy.

---

[1] For a recent attempt to formalize these sorts of changes within the framework of organization theory, see Jerzy F. Karcz, "An Organizational Model of Command Farming," in Morris Bornstein (ed.), *Comparative Economic Systems*, rev. ed. (Homewood: Richard D. Irwin, Inc., 1969), pp. 278-299.

The Objective Function

Examination of a production enterprise must necessarily begin with consideration of its objective function, for, if one is to appraise and evaluate enterprise performance, the goals of the enterprise must be known. Thus in non-Marxian economic theory the firm is considered to be seeking maximum profits or some variant thereof. In the case of the socialist industrial enterprise, the profit mechanism has not been useful as a model of enterprise behavior. Thus western observers have turned to descriptive and organizational analysis, based in large part upon the incentive structure and the managerial motivation towards success within the planning system, to provide a mechanism around which a theory of the socialist firm can be constructed and managerial performance examined and appraised.[2] In the case of a producer cooperative, though the subject of relatively little attention by non-Marxian economists, the distribution of dividends per member of the cooperative is usually accepted as an appropriate maximand.

Though formally described as a cooperative, treatment of the Soviet kolkhoz within such a framework is rejected on two grounds: first, in practice as opposed to theoretical and propagandistic prescription, the kolkhoz lacks the significant structural and operational characteristics of a true cooperative, as we have seen in the early chapters of this study; second, and of greater importance, it will be argued in the remaining chapters that the kolkhoz does not operate as if it were a cooperative, and, although treatment of the kolkhoz as a formal cooperative is theoretically interesting, this type of analysis is not suited to the purposes of the present study.[3]

For the early years of this study, the kolkhoz manager was little more than an administrator of plan execution, operating on a short run time horizon, with only limited information inputs and within a myriad of constraints imposed by the planning apparatus. Thus the typical manager of the early years was motivated by multiple objectives (undoubtedly with major emphasis upon the physical volume of output) shifting over time and regionally but with no single objective forming the essence of managerial motivation. This pattern of behavior is in sharp contrast to that of the Soviet industrial manager, who, faced with conflicting and often irrational indicators, was, nevertheless, challenged by significant rewards for "success". The industrial manager in fact exhibited patterns of be-

[2] See, for example, Joseph S. Berliner, *Factory and Manager in the USSR* (Cambridge: Harvard University Press, 1957); David Granick, *Management of The Industrial Firm in The USSR* (New York: Columbia University Press, 1954). For a treatment of the Soviet firm in terms of organization theory, see David Granick, *Soviet Metal-Fabricating and Economic Development* (Madison: University of Wisconsin Press, 1967), Ch. 7. The Soviet firm is treated in terms of maximization theory in Edward Ames, *Soviet Economic Processes* (Homewood: Richard D. Irwin, Inc., 1965).

[3] For an interesting discussion of the formal properties of the cooperative, see Evsey D. Domar, "The Soviet Collective Farm as a Producer Cooperative," *American Economic Review*, Vol. LVI, No. 4, Part I (September 1966), pp. 734-757; and Walter Y. Oi and Elizabeth M. Clayton, "A Peasant's View of a Soviet Collective Farm," *American Economic Review*, Vol. LVIII, No. 1 (March 1968), pp. 37-59.

havior appropriate for the resolution of these conflicts within the system, though not always in terms of the priorities of the planning system. Collective farm chairmen, therefore, were simply not an important part of the system, for they were not integrated into the important information flows of the planning system, did not participate broadly in the important decisions of production and distribution of the product and were not sufficiently well trained to perform a significant managerial role. In a sense, managerial motivations and behavior patterns vis-a-vis the typical kolkhoz and its plan-directed production and growth goals may not have been of immediate importance.

The collective farm manager of the early years was, in large measure, an individual of limited ability and power operating from the center of a relatively primitive though highly planned and controlled organization. To a significant degree, the kolkhoz has been an "in-kind" operation directed by organs external to the farm itself. Within such a framework and in the light of our examination of managerial rewards during the early years, concern for survival and improvement of income position must have been fairly strong, although the absence of a strong linkage between this managerial motivation and the development path of the kolkhoz tended to leave the latter independent of the former.

The Centralized System
of Output Determination

If the typical kolkhoz manager of the early 1950s was, in fact, as ineffectual as the preceding characterization suggests, did he play any role in the production decisions of the farm? The managerial role in plan formulation has been less a policy of active *ex ante* participation in planning and more a matter of *ex post* response to the operation of the planning system. Thus for the formulation of planned output targets for a future period $(t + 1)$, plan execution or the past achievement of a similar target during period (t) has been of crucial importance for two reasons. First, the construction of a meaningful plan target for future output must be based upon a realistic appraisal of production capacity. In the Soviet case, appraisal of capacity has been in large measure an examination of past performance levels. Second, kolkhoz managerial personnel have had a minimal role in plan formulation in the face of continuing interference by external organs, notably the MTS, and the setting of targets to meet state demands. In the light of these considerations, it is difficult to discuss plan formulation in isolation from plan execution.

In theory, the production plan of the kolkhoz for a given year is the end result of deliberations within the kolkhoz carried on towards the end of the previous year. However, the extent to which continuous external control is practiced, especially by the raion level of government and the MTS, made planning within the kolkhoz largely a fiction.[4]

While both short- and long-term planning were said to operate within the kolkhoz, it is clear that long-term planning played no role whatsoever.[5] Thus in the absence of meaningful long term production targets, collective farm managers were faced with targets imposed by external organs and subject to continual change at the whim of those external agencies. The problem of production targets being continually changed throughout the plan period has plagued agricultural planning. The following comment by a Soviet writer is instructive:

Planning for the coming year usually begins on the collective farms and MTS in July and August. But by February and March the collective farms' plans have been revised by higher organizations two or even three times. And even after that the annual production plans are subject to change; the district and province centers send out additional instructions.[6]

This type of problem is not new to those familiar with the operation of centrally planned economic systems, nor is it peculiar to the agricultural sectors of such systems. However, it may be that the problem of setting appropriate plan targets is relatively more difficult in the agricultural than in the industrial sector.

If plan targets are to be useful in guiding and measuring enterprise performance, they must be based upon a realistic appraisal of enterprise capacity. Thus if managers exert effort to increase output (or to achieve some other goal), it is necessary that they be appropriately rewarded. However, if output achievements are based upon initially erroneous specifications of the firm's ability to produce, then the performance may have little to do with the managerial role, and rewards (for example, through the price system) will tend to leave some units earning large rents while others suffer large losses, both quite unrelated to effort and the basic ability of the unit to generate output.

To the extent that managerial and other rewards are closely tied to performance, and especially if there is a discontinuity in the earnings pattern, this "need to know" capacity will be crucial. Thus where the reward system gives little for 99 percent achievement of the plan targets but offers significant rewards for 101 percent plan fulfillment, the matter of capacity measurement becomes fundamental to the relevance of the planning mechanism.

[4]The problem of external interference in the planning of kolkhoz affairs is a continual theme in the Soviet press. Although steps were taken in 1956 (to be examined later) to change this state of affairs, it is only very recently that and significant effort has been made to make planning within the kolkhoz a meaningful concept.

[5]During discussions with collective farm chairmen in 1966, the writer was told that the most significant planning development in recent years was the introduction of long-term (five-year) targets. The significance derived not simply from the length of the planning period, but also from the fact that the targets were to be firm for the five-year period. However, the widespread and serious adoption of firm long-term targets remains to be achieved.

[6]Y. Yefimov, "When Farming Standards are Ignored," *Izvestia*, (January 29, 1957), p. 2, translated and reprinted in *COSP*, Vol. IX, No. 4 (March 6, 1957), pp. 35-36.

Capacity, however, is difficult to define and to measure. In addition, it may be significantly more difficult to measure in the agricultural as opposed to the industrial sector. In agriculture, the typical production run is the growing season. Thus once the production process is started, adjustment may be difficult. In addition, the production process is typically subject to random influences (for example weather changes and insects) which can markedly alter performance, but over which management may have only minimal if any control. In the face of these difficulties, Soviet planners have appraised agricultural production capacity by the following methods:

     a. On site inspection
     b. Past performance
     c. Managerial assessment of potential

Unfortunately, no single indicator has been used on a consistent basis, either for the general planning process or, for that matter, within the plan period. Thus within the plan period, the shifting of targets discussed above arises in conjunction with a change in the basis for determining capacity. For example, initial targets may have been based upon past performance, but, if on site inspection during the growing season seems to reveal greater "capacity," then the delivery demands placed upon the farm will most likely be shifted upward.

In recent years, managerial assessment of potential has become increasingly important although past performance has always been a guiding factor and probably will always serve as a base below which future production should not fall. As indicated, on site inspection has operated as a mechanism whereby during the growing season, and in accordance with expected progress (that is, expected by planners rather than farm managers), increased exactions have been made and base targets shifted upwards. These upward adjustments are frequently subsumed under "pledges," "socialist competition" and so on.

In any given year, therefore, planners have a minimal idea of what a farm is "really" capable of producing, hence, production targets have had little meaning. Such a system must have been especially confusing to a "good" farm manager who might have sought rewards through appropriate fulfillment of the demands of the system.

In addition to the difficulties of plan formulation, execution was hampered by the nature of the managerial incentive system. Given the relatively small potential earnings of a collective farm chairman, as indicated in Chapter 5, it is reasonable to assume that improvement of income position must have been an important objective. Moreover, it is evident that while income could be derived from the achievement of state directives, there have also existed a number of illegal or, at best, quasi-legal behavior patterns which, when practiced by managers, tended to undermine the planning system but at the same time produced rewards.[7]

Illegal behavior on the part of collective farm managerial personnel has been directed towards distinct though related ends. First, direct manipulation of inputs and/or outputs can generate illegal income (in money and in-kind), and/or the possibility of reduced targets and thus better performance in subsequent plan periods. This type of manipulation is familiar to students of Soviet industrial planning and arises in both the industrial and agricultural sectors for similar reasons, namely the difficulty of constructing appropriate "success indicators" for managerial personnel within a Soviet-type planning system. In the case of the kolkhoz, the manager might extend the area under cultivation (which within limits would be relatively simple) but without formally declaring the extended sown area.[8] The output produced on this new sown area might be sold in the kolkhoz markets (at prices substantially higher than those paid by the state), or it might be delivered to the state thus presenting an impressive gross output picture for which bonuses would be paid.

There is, of course, risk associated with these sorts of practices. With a short managerial time horizon, however, the risks may frequently have been outweighed by the potential rewards. Indeed, even on the basis of a longer time horizon, the kolkhoz manager might well pursue a quasi-legal path since future targets can be held down and thus fulfillment made easier by the hiding of capacity.

The crucial relationship here is between the managerial reward system and the methodology of plan formulation. Thus, to the extent that above plan performance is adequately rewarded, the manager would like to overfulfill the plan and receive these rewards. On the other hand, since future plans will be based upon present performance, overachievement in the present will tend to mitigate against the achievement of significant rewards in the future.[9] Under this type of

---

[7]It is difficult to appraise the impact of "illegal behavior" either upon managerial earnings in particular or the farm operation in general. The goal here is limited. The existence of such behavior must be recognized, and in addition, to the extent that it is directed towards plan fulfillment, it must be viewed as an important comment upon the pressures for plan fulfillment and "success" as viewed by farm managers.

[8]To the extent that managers did this, the earnings must have exceeded those possible from declaring only the sown area. Non-declaration was the illegal act. See for example, Fedor Belov, *The History of a Soviet Collective Farm* (New York: Frederick A. Praeger, 1955), p. 91. There is evidence that these sorts of procedures might be quite easy in the Soviet case. For example, the district surveyor of the Khobi district of Georgia stated that "finally, it should be noted that no one is responsible for the correct utilization of land—neither the collective farm boards nor the land surveyors nor the agricultural inspection services nor the district executive committees." See G. Klevakin, "Are There Virgin Lands in Georgia?," *Izvestia*, (June 16, 1959), p. 2, translated and reprinted in *CDSP*, Vol. XI, No. 24 (July 15, 1959), p. 26.

[9]The importance of this type of behavior depends in large part upon the nature of the managerial time horizon and especially the formulation of managerial *expectations* about the future. Given the very high turnover of managerial personnel in the early 1950s, the managerial time horizon could not have been very long.

system, the manager would probably try to overfulfill the plan, but only within certain narrow limits.

A second goal of illegal activity may relate not to the pursuit of illegal income nor the depression of future targets but rather the achievement of present targets. For example, where the wrath of local officials is likely to be especially great, the kolkhoz may simply purchase output from another area or farm and deliver this output for fulfillment of state demands. The tendency to maintain inadequate seed and feed reserves might be interpreted along these lines since the reserve can be described and sold as output.[10] This sort of behavior is, in a sense, an indirect measure of the extent to which kolkhoz managers view the importance of plan fulfillment for both monetary and non-monetary rewards.

It is difficult to assess the relative importance of legal and illegal managerial incomes. However, in the face of planning practices of the period and for a managerial group who were, on balance, poorly trained and rewarded, the potential importance of illegal earnings should not be underestimated.

Much of the planning system as described thus far remained operative throughout the 1950s and into the 1960s. At the same time, however, there have been a number of important changes, many of which have served to relax the most inflexible aspects of this early system.

The Relaxation of Controls

The purpose here is not that of cataloging the minutiae of administrative changes throughout the 1950s and 1960s, but rather to focus upon the economic significance of the most important adjustments to the planning system and, in particular, those changes that have found expression in practice.

The first important change of the period was a decree of March 9, 1955, foreshadowing significant changes in the planning methodology.[11] Rather than the external specification of detailed plan targets for such variables as sown area, deliveries, and so on, henceforward collective farms were to receive a delivery plan, and the farms themselves would work out a plan specifying changes in sown area and cattle herds as necessary for the fulfillment of the delivery targets. This plan was to be worked out within the kolkhoz, submitted to its general meeting for ratification and finally to the Raiispolkom for approval. If the Raiispolkom felt that the plan as constructed would not meet the delivery targets, it would have the final word in adjustments.[12] At the same time (and indeed frequently thereafter), the oft stated goal of kolkhoz activity was maximum value of output per unit of land with minimal expenditure of labor and means of production (cost) per unit of product.[13]

---

[10]Fedor Belov, op. cit., p. 86, has pointed out that "in practice the funds in kind were rarely more than 40 percent of the amount called for by statute, while the monetary reserves were usually about 75 percent of what they should have been under the plan."

[11]"Ob izmenenii praktiki planirovaniia sel'skogo khoziaistva," as cited in *Sbornik*, pp. 219-224.

[12]Ibid., p. 222.

[13]Ibid., p. 223.

The decree of 1955 represented a very important shift in planning strategy, for it emphasized for the first time the importance of targeting output, as opposed to input, variables as a fundamental directive to the farm. Unfortunately, this decree had little or no immediate impact upon the reality of planning in the kolkhoz sector, a fact continuously recognized in the Soviet press.[14] In March of 1964, Khrushchev suggested that, in many cases, sown area was still being specified from above.[15] Indeed, in April of 1965, V.V. Matskevich, the minister of agriculture went further, suggesting that planning remained a single year operation with frequent adjustments of targets not uncommon.[16]

In essence, the decree of 1955 had little or no impact upon the methodology of plan formulation in the collective farm sector. More recently, there has been a significant effort to introduce long-term (5 year) planning on a meaningful basis. To the extent that this sort of planning finds widespread acceptance, it will reduce the continual uncertainty as farm managers face frequently changing demands. However, to what degree managerial behavior will influence the setting of these targets is another question. In a system observed by the writer on several advanced farms of the Krasnodar region, output targets were projected into the future on a five year time horizon and were said to be "firm." These targets were based upon the average level of performance in several preceding years plus a growth rate (typically 5 percent, but apparently without theoretical foundation). All chairmen agreed that the implementation of such a system would remove the major curse of past planning methodology.

To the extent that the raion itself continued to receive and be responsible for the fulfillment of delivery targets, the distribution of these targets among farms

[14] Although the decree of 1955 may have initiated general tendencies towards less external interference in the affairs of the kolkhoz by upper-level planning agencies and gradual substitution of target variables, such as gross output instead of major emphasis upon sown area, Western observers have been in general agreement about the very slow pace with which these changes were actually implemented. For a discussion of these issues, see Douglas B. Diamond, "Trends in Output, Inputs, and Factor Productivity in Soviet Agriculture," *New Directions in the Soviet Economy*, (Washington: U.S. Government Printing Office, 1966), pp. 363-364; Jerzy F. Karcz, "Commentary," in Roy D. Laird (ed.), *Soviet Agricultural and Peasant Affairs*, (Lawrence: University of Kansas Press, 1963), pp. 44-47; Jerzy F. Karcz and V.P. Timoshenko, op. cit., pp. 138-140; Alec Nove, "Some Thoughts on Soviet Agricultural Administration," op. cit., p. 7; Howard R. Swearer, op. cit., pp. 17-18.

[15] N.S. Khrushchev, "Successfully implement Decisions of February Plenary Session of C.P.S.U. Central Committee on the Intensification of Agricultural Production," *Pravda*, March 7, 1964, pp. 1-6, translated and reprinted in *CDSP*, Vol. XVI, No. 10 (April 1, 1964), pp. 17-18.

[16] V.V. Matskevich, "Tasks Posed by Life," *Trud*, April 14, 1965, p. 2, translated and reprinted in *CDSP*, Vol. XVII, No. 17 (May 19, 1965), p. 10. While the original decree of 1955 was not specifically concerned with the *time period* for which plans were formulated, it was concerned with changing *what* was being planned. Each individual farm was to receive fewer directives from external sources. The time period is, however, of great importance. With long-term planning "on the books," but absent in reality, interference from above has been easily executed in the guise of insuring plan fulfillment. Unfortunately, into the 1960s collective farms continued to receive large numbers of directives (including those such as sown area). In addition, managers continued to complain about constant interference in the operations of their farms.

of the raion and pressure upon these farms for plan fulfillment, would remain of great importance. This type of planning has always facilitated a degree of bargaining between the raion authorities and the kolkhozy, for if the latter received targets not readily achieved either due to their magnitude or type of product requested, changes could be made. The burden of evidence seen by the writer seemed to indicate that such bargaining was, in fact, of marginal importance, and while it may be of assistance to the chairman in meeting plan demands, it appears to have had little or no impact upon the basic crop patterns and the level of specialization.

It should be noted that the problems of defining agricultural capacity remain as noted. Indeed, even on the best farms, annual output fluctuations must severely complicate the planning process, especially where long-term targets are to be meaningful.[17]

The abolition of the MTS in 1958 must have shifted a significant part of the planning apparatus into the collectives themselves, although the vastly increased size of the latter (as indicated in Chapter 4) would argue against considering such a trend as decentralization. However, control over both plan formulation and execution by the MTS had been especially close. In addition, to the extent that agricultural specialists came to be employed directly by the farms as opposed to the MTS, one might assume that information flows for managerial decision making must have improved. Whether these information flows penetrated to the brigade level is less clear. Certainly the placement of machinery and equipment at the brigade level and the re-organization of the brigade as a permanent production unit must have substantially increased the potential importance of the brigade as a decision making unit. And yet the very inferior quality of brigade management (see Chapter 8) will, in the immediate future, mitigate against any substantial improvement of decision making procedures at the brigade level.

In spite of these important changes, however, we have seen that agricultural capacity has been, and remains, very difficult to define—and this is the crux of the setting of "realistic" output targets upon which so much of the planning and operation of the kolkhoz rests. Output levels can and do fluctuate, both nationally and for individual farms, and on a wide scale. The extent to which the delivery demands are varied *within* the plan year may be reduced. However, there is

[17]The extreme difficulty of insuring a degree of stability in agricultural plan targets and results is evident in the following indicators of sales to the state (centners) by the kolkhoz "Michurin" in Slaviansk Raion of Krasnodar Krai:

Product	1964	1965	Average, 1964-65	1966 Plan
Grain	105,194	66,799	85,996	100,000
Sunflower	5,963	4,140	5,100	8,000
Rice	60,710	49,904	55,307	48,000
Vegetables	11,120	7,728	9,424	26,000
Milk	15,148	20,957	18,052	18,400
Meat	4,013	5,436	4,724	6,300
Eggs	663	1,347	1,005	1,500

little question that the raion level of administration faces pressure from above and much of this pressure will be transmitted to the farm. In this sense, state demands are bound to be primary determinants of farm plans and, in the formulation of the latter, the farm manager has only minimal room for maneuverability. Thus, at the present juncture, we would not anticipate major adjustments of crop patterns and specialization based upon cost-price variables or other decentralized information available to managerial personnel.

Thus far the focus has been solely upon the methodology and practice of output determination in the kolkhoz. However, in the absence of a viable managerial system within the kolkhoz, the planning system has tended to focus as much or possibly more upon the appropriate level and mix of inputs—decisions not to be left to local managers.[18] It is thus crucial to our examination of the kolkhoz to understand the procedures for input planning.

Land Utilization

From the vantage point of the farm manager, the upper constraint upon land utilization is the borders of the individual farm.[19] Further, given the Soviet practice of shifting targets upward over time, the sown area for any given period will likely form a minimal constraint upon sown area for any succeeding period. Thus the general limits of flexibility afforded the manager are defined.

In addition to a multitude of other targets received from the raion and channeled through the MTS, the kolkhoz receives a target for sown area, output and state deliveries.[20] At this point, the formulation of the annual tasks for the brigade and ferma and their short run (ten day) elaboration might proceed strictly according to the plan or with some modification. For example, suggested sown area might be changed; that is, within technological restrictions and where inspection was weak.[21] For the vast majority of kolkhozy in the past, crop

[18]Kolkhoz managers could better be described as plan administrators insofar as they have not been actively concerned with the making of input-output decisions on a decentralized basis as a response to economic variables.

[19]Expansion of sown area through amalgamation was an important exception. It is very doubtful, however, that the manager could play an important role in implementing such a program.

[20]The deliveries are not expressed in the original formulation of the production plan which includes sown area, yields and so on. Prior to harvest, MTS and kolkhoz officials estimated the potential field harvest which was then reported to raion officials from which compulsory delivery targets would be derived. For a discussion of this methodology, see Fedor Belov, op. cit., pp. 84, 97. Belov argues that the reports tended to be fairly accurate, since overstatement and subsequent underfulfillment would bring on the wrath of raion officials, as would the hiding of sown area. However, given considerable fluctuations from year to year there must have been some room for error. There is also the important question of the accuracy with which yields can be determined in advance, and in particular, the significant differentials between "field yield" and "barn yield." In addition, the determination of compulsory delivery levels at such a late stage in the production process must have been a severe brake upon managerial incentive to increase output.

[21]The vastly increased size of the typical kolkhoz must have led to a decrease in the frequency and quality of inspection in recent years.

specialization has been minimal and thus there were severe limitations upon adjustments to sown area by farm managers.

In the absence of a rental charge for land utilization, the major constraints upon land usage are: the physical limits; the fear of being "discovered" and, hence, receiving higher subsequent targets based upon the revelation of previously undeclared sown area; and, finally, the extent to which other inputs, especially labor, can be brought to bear upon illegally sown land. With the area of the private plot closely constrained, the private sector could not add to managerial flexibility.[22]

To the extent that the decree of 1955 becomes a reality in the future, central pressure over input targeting may be reduced. However, throughout the Khrushchev period, the very limited extent to which farm managers were able to resist the mass sowing campaigns (for example, those of the corn program) indicates only marginal flexibility in this respect.

Quite apart from plan targets and their formulation, however, the pressure for conformity in crop rotation patterns, along with the physical land limits and the necessity of registering changes in land utilization, have produced amazing stability; not only in terms of total sowings, but also the structure of sowings in terms of different crops.

Apart from those areas peculiarly suited to a specific crop, for example, cotton growing in Central Asia, there is a high degree of conformity and stability in land utilization patterns among the large and prosperous collective farms. Further, this stability has been altered more by conversion to sovkhozy than by structural changes outlined in the preceding chapters. The farms examined by the writer in the Krasnodar region conform to this type of pattern. These farms were very large, having been subjected to amalgamation in the early 1950s. Their sown area was, therefore, stable. In terms of crop structure, the amalgamation simply meant that rotation patterns are now carried out within a large, permanent brigade (formerly a small, single kolkhoz), whereas it would previously have been carried out among small, temporary brigades. To a small degree the fields may have increased in size, but this change has been handled within the context of amalgamation, while the numbers and types of crops being grown have remained basically the same. While some experimentation with new crops (notably rice) has been tried, this was not on the initiative of the farm manager. Indeed the permanence of land utilization within this type of farm would suggest that, for the large successful kolkhoz, managerial flexibility in the matter of land utilization is very limited.

Labor Allocation

During the early stages of economic development, agricultural production is typically labor intensive. Accordingly, even though the payments to labor may

---

[22]While official attitudes toward the private plots have varied over time, their size has always been relatively very small in terms of land area, and specified within the kolkhoz charter. The utilization of this plot is basically a function of the peasant family in pursuit of personal income.

be low relative to those in a more developed economy, labor productivity is also low and thus one would expect the labor share of total production costs to be relatively high vis-a-vis the more highly developed economy. In this sense, the labor input is an important element in the production process and an important consideration for the kolkhoz manager. Although one would expect regional, product and other sorts of differentials to be important, in the Soviet case, the labor input accounts for approximately 40 percent of the production costs *(izderzhiki proizvodstva)* of gross agricultural production.[23] Since labor is an important input to Soviet agricultural production, what role can the kolkhoz manager play in its utilization?

The labor supply curve facing the kolkhoz is partly a function of the mobility of labor into and within the kolkhoz sector, and, also, the behavior of peasants within a given kolkhoz as they attempt to strike an appropriate income-leisure balance faced with alternative employment possibilities in the public and private sectors of the kolkhoz.[24] This section will begin by considering a formal model of labor allocation within a kolkhoz, thereafter relaxing the restrictive assumptions to conform more closely to the reality of the typical kolkhoz. Finally, the formation of peasant incomes will be considered as a crucial determinant of the labor supply function.

With the assistance of Figure 6-1, a formal analysis of labor allocation within the kolkhoz can be constructed.[25] In addition, the following assumptions prevail:

1. The analysis is short run (fixed capital stock) and membership of the farm is closed.
2. Discrimination in hiring is not possible.
3. Perfect information and certainty prevail.
4. A minimum labor contribution ($0Q_1$ units) is required from every "able bodied" (Soviet definition) member. Those who don't qualify cannot "fill in" for those who do qualify.
5. The labor supply curve ($0Q_1 S_p^1 S_p$) is that which faces the farm manager when he wishes to induce members to participate. Thus it already incorporates the peasant evaluation of alternative incomes and represents peasant expectations for the present period based upon evaluation of past achievements.

[23]For the years 1964 through 1966 as measured in 1965 prices. For a detailed breakdown of production costs, see V.R. Boev, *Zakupochnye tseny i chistyi dokhod kolkhozov* (Moskva: Kolos, 1969), p. 35.

[24]It is unlikely that a peasant could maximize income without working in both sectors of the kolkhoz. Also, given the limited mobility of rural labor, the initial assumption of a closed farm is not wholly unrealistic. These matters will be treated in detail in subsequent sections of this chapter.

[25]Although differing in several important respects, the analysis presented here follows the pattern suggested by Evsey D. Domar, "The Soviet Collective Farm As A Producer Cooperative," *American Economic Review*, Vol. LVI, No. 4, Part I (September 1966), pp. 734-757; and Walter Y. Oi and Elizabeth M. Clayton, "A Peasant's View of a Soviet Collective Farm," *American Economic Review*, Vol. LVIII, No. 1 (March 1968), pp. 37-59.

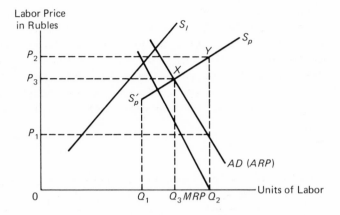

Note: S_p = labor supply; VMP = value of marginal product; $AD = ARP$ = average dividend. Average Dividend (AD) — defined as output price multiplied by output quantity and divided by labor input. ARP is net of state deliveries and managerial labor days. A single price is paid for all output.

Figure 6-1. Labor Allocation on a Collective Farm.

Under the conditions postulated, how will the manager behave? If he is operating on the upward sloping portion of the supply curve (a point to be discussed later) and if he wishes to maximize the gross value of output (under constraints), he will produce until the value of the marginal product (VMP) is zero. Thus he will try to utilize an amount of labor equal to $0Q_2$ in Figure 6-1. However, given that labor is not a free good and is not viewed as such by the manager, equilibrium will be reached when the farm manager utilizes an amount of labor equal to $0Q_3$ paying a dividend equal to $0P_3$.[26] To approach the reality of the kolkhoz, however, it is necessary to relax some of the assumptions.

If the peasant wishes to maximize his income, he can presumably allocate accordingly between the socialized and private sectors of the kolkhoz. However, as the labor supply curve is presented in Figure 6-1, it is apparent that, owing to the minimum labor contribution required from every able bodied peasant, the individual peasant has little choice, and the total labor supply will be, at a minimum, $0Q_1$ units. If this is, in fact, the case, and if the demand curve for labor (AD) intersects the supply curve within this range, management may well see the labor input as a "free good." Whether or not such a situation prevails will depend upon the nature of the minimum labor requirement and the slopes and positions of the VMP and AD curves.

[26]Notice that with any positive price of labor, Point X will always lie to the left of Point Y and hence the manager will be constrained to produce where $VMP > 0$.

The minimum labor contribution is probably not very significant vis-a-vis the total output of the socialized sector of the kolkhoz and the labor input required to produce that output. The evidence for this is presented in Table 6-1. Thus it is apparent that very few peasants (roughly 3-10 percent) in fact fail to meet the minimum labor requirement. Also, for the year 1954, kolkhoz members earned on the average 423 labor-days, or significantly more than the minimum range of 100-150 labor-days required annually from each peasant.[27] At the same time,

Table 6-1

Proportion of Adult Able-bodied Kolkhoz Members not Working the Established Minimum Labor- or Man-days, 1959

	Percentage of Kolkhoz Members not Working Min. Labor- or Man-days	In Addition, not Working at All
USSR	10.8	3.0
RSFSR	10.6	2.7
Belorussia	15.8	2.4
Armenia	15.5	6.9
Moldavia	14.0	4.7
Georgia	12.2	4.7
Lithuania	12.0	2.0
Estonia	11.6	2.7
Ukraine	11.3	3.2
Latvia	10.3	1.6
Tadzhikistan	9.8	5.2
Azerbaidzhan	7.5	4.3
Kazakhstan	7.2	2.7
Kirgizia	6.4	1.8
Turkmenistan	5.2	1.5
Uzbekistan	4.7	2.0

Source: V.P. Rozhin, *Nekotorye voprosy pod'ema ekonomiki slabykh kolkhozov* (Moskva: Ekonomizdat, 1961), p. 79. The material in this table has been derived from the annual accounts and accordingly cannot be checked against Soviet statistical publications. In particular, the table must be used with caution, for in spite of several checks for internal consistency, it is not possible to determine whether those kolkhoz members included in column 1 are inclusive or exclusive of those in column 2. Also, it is not clear to what extent this table includes those who may have been "legally" excused from full or partial participation. The number so included may have been set within the kolkhoz thus allowing for special cases—women with children, etc.

[27] On the number of labor-days earned in 1954, see Henry Wronski, "Peasant Incomes," in Roy D. Laird and Edward L. Crowley (eds.), *Soviet Agriculture: The Permanent Crisis* (New York: Frederick A. Praeger, 1965), p. 124. There are assumed to be 23.3 million kolkhoz members as cited in *Narkhoz-1961*, p. 461. On the labor day requirement, see Abram Bergson, *The Economics of Soviet Planning* (New Haven and London: Yale University Press, 1964), p. 223.

while there is a continuing campaign to induce greater and more productive participation in the socialized sector by the peasants, it is not clear that kolkhoz management has in fact utilized any special penalties for those who do not fulfill the minimum requirement.[28] It seems most likely, therefore, that the manager will be operating on the upward sloping portion of the labor supply curve.

The above line of reasoning might be strengthened. In the absence of discrimination,[29] and without a strong administrative mechanism to guarantee fulfillment of minimum requirements, one might seriously question the existence of a vertical portion of the labor supply curve. It may well be that, in the typical case, the labor supply curve is upward sloping throughout and will be seen in this light by the kolkhoz manager. Even if all peasants meet the minimum requirement at the same time (so that further "hiring" need not discriminate as between those who have fulfilled the minimum and those who have not), one does not find a situation where all receive a very low dividend prior to fulfillment (that is the "free good" portion of the labor supply curve), and a larger dividend thereafter.

To the extent that performance in the private sector was not a "success indicator" for kolkhoz management, there would be an interest in encouraging peasants to greater participation in the socialized sector of the kolkhoz. If managers are so motivated, their reaction is here presented as pertaining solely to variations in the magnitude of the dividend as derived from the socialized sector of the kolkhoz. It is apparent, however, that the peasant's utility function will be maximized through the pursuit of leisure and earnings, the latter derived from both the private and the socialized sectors of the kolkhoz. In fact, the nature of the supply curve faced by the kolkhoz manager will depend crucially upon the nature of the reward system and the peasant response to that system.

The Nature of Peasant Income

A full treatment of peasant income levels is beyond the scope of the present study, though consideration of the matter is essential on two grounds.[30] First,

---

[28] One major exception could be when collective farm managers utilize fodder supplies for cattle of the private sector as a weapon to enforce peasant participation in the socialized sector. However, non-participation is most likely a major problem among those technically qualified but for age, illness or other reasons. The new charter does spell out certain penalties (for example, deprivation of "supplementary benefits") for those who fail to participate without valid reason. See Appendix B.

[29] By absence of discrimination it is assumed that "old" employees cannot be paid less than "new" employees, and hence the wage for the final person hired will be the wage for all. Thus in the case of the kolkhoz, it is assumed that labor not having fulfilled its minimum, and labor having fulfilled its minimum, are identical as far as the manager is concerned. Thus it is not possible to pay less to labor *not* having fulfilled its minimum while at the same time paying more to those workers who *have* met the minimum.

[30] For a detailed study of rural incomes, see David W. Bronson and Constance B. Krueger, "The Revolution in Soviet Farm Household Income, 1953-1967," in James R. Millar (ed.), *The Soviet Rural Community* (Urbana: University of Illinois Press, 1971), pp. 214-258.

since Soviet policy has been directed towards increasing the performance level of the socialized as opposed to the private sector of the kolkhoz, it is necessary to know something about income formation in both sectors in order to appraise the results of prevailing policy. Second, since the question of labor supply is so crucial to managerial decision making within the kolkhoz (especially the slope of the labor supply curve), it is necessary to appraise the incentive system in terms of its ability to bring forth the desired participation and effort.

Peasant family income is derived from two main sources, namely, work in the socialized sector of the kolkhoz and on the private plot.[31] There is also the possibility of work outside the kolkhoz though this is likely a marginal source of income. Income from both the private and socialized sectors has typically been in both in-kind and money forms; in particular, part of the income from the socialized sector consists of forage, not readily grown on the plots but required for animals in the private sector. At the same time, income from the private plot has been in-kind (primarily food and animal products) plus a portion of money income derived from sale of these products in the collective farm markets.

To the degree that managers are attempting to induce greater peasant participation and effort in the production activity of the socialized sector of the kolkhoz, not only the magnitude, but also the form and frequency of income payments will be of great importance. For most of the period under study, the labor-day *(trudoden')* has been the basic manner of labor payments calculation.[32] Suffice it to say that as a method of rewarding effort and participation, the labor-day must have had a limited appeal vis-a-vis the ruble income that might have been earned from the private plot. As many authors have pointed out, the labor-day was a very arbitrary method of calculation and could vary widely both regionally and temporally without variations in labor effort. Furthermore, normal procedures for much of this period dictated labor-day distributions as a residual at the end of the year; partly "in-kind" and partly in money form.

It is generally assumed that frequent distributions of money income would be a much stronger motivating force for peasants than infrequent distributions on an in-kind basis. As we have seen in Chapter 5, the labor-day as a method of calculation was formally abandoned in 1968. However, in the preceding years, there was significant improvement in both the frequency with which income payments were made and also the portion of income in money form (see especially Tables 5-3 and 5-4). Although there have been important fluctuations from year to year, the long term trend towards money income is clear. It can be

---

[31] We ignore transfer payments from the social consumption funds of the kolkhoz. They are estimated by Bronson and Krueger for the early 1960s to be approximately 1 percent of peasant incomes. See David W. Bronson and Constance B. Krueger, op. cit., p. 224.

[32] The labor-day system has been treated at length by others and thus need not detain us here. The classic treatment is Henri Wronski, op. cit., or for an introductory discussion see Alec Nove, *The Soviet Economy*, 2d ed. rev. (New York: Frederick A. Praeger, 1969), pp. 56-57.

computed from the Bronson and Krueger study that in 1953, 41 percent of wages in the socialized sector of kolkhozy (paid to collective farm members and administrative-technical staff) were in money form, while in 1967, the comparable figure was 92 percent.[33]

In addition to changing the form and frequency of payments to kolkhoz members, the absolute level of these payments grew significantly from a very low base. In Table 6-2, the distributions of grain and money per labor-day for the Soviet Union in 1950 are presented. Recalling that this money income data is in old rubles, the incredibly low payments for labor-days in 1950 is abundantly clear, surely an important deterrent to work in the socialized sector of the kolkhoz in spite of the fact that this sector must have accounted for something less than 30 percent of the income of collective farmers at this time.[34]

Since the early 1950s, aggregate earnings of collective farm members have grown significantly, although much of this growth can be accounted for by growth in income derived from the socialized sector, this taking place primarily in the early 1950s and the mid 1960s. In 1953, wages from the socialized sector and private plot income accounted for 29 percent and 71 percent, respectively, of income of collective farm members and administrative-technical staff.[35] The comparable figures for the year 1967 were 53 percent and 47 percent for socialized and private income, respectively.[36]

Table 6-2
Distribution of Grain and Rubles per Labor-day on Collective Farms of the USSR as a Percentage of the Total, 1950

Grain in Kilograms[a]					
None	Up to 1	1.1-2.0	2.1-3.0	3.1-5.0	5 Plus
2.1	48.9	28.4	12.7	6.5	1.4
Money in Rubles					
None	Up to 0.6	0.6-1.0	1.01-2.50	2.51-4.0	4 Plus
22.4	39.3	12.7	16.5	4.2	4.8

Source: V.P. Ostrovskii, *Kolkhoznoe krest'ianstvo SSR* (Saratov: Izd. Saratovskogo universiteta, 1967), p. 59.

[a]For comparison in value terms, the average procurement price of grain in 1950 was 90 rubles per ton or approximately 10 kopecks per kilogram. See Nancy Nimitz, "Soviet Agricultural Prices and Costs," as cited in United States Congress, Joint Economic Committee, *Comparisons of United States and Soviet Economies* (Washington, D.C.: U.S. Government Printing Office, 1959), p. 251.

[33]Computed from David W. Bronson and Constance B. Krueger, op. cit., Table 1, p. 241.

[34]Ibid. In 1953 wages from the socialized sector accounted for 29 percent of the income of collective farm members. Thus it is safe to assume that for 1950, the comparable figure must have been somewhat lower.

[35]Ibid.

[36]Ibid.

The growth of income of kolkhoz members was especially rapid in the early 1950s. This growth can be traced in detail from the selected data pertaining to the Ukraine as presented in Tables 6-3 and 6-4.

Turning briefly to the matter of bonuses, our limited data would suggest that, as a portion of income derived from the socialized sector of the kolkhoz, bonuses have been very small. In the Ukraine, for example, bonuses formed 6.7 percent of the general pay of kolkhoz members in 1950, 8.2 percent in 1954 and by 1955, 18.3 percent.[37] For the RSFSR as a whole and, as a portion of the general sum of money for distribution to labor, 8.3 percent consisted of supplementary payments in 1956, 11.5 percent in 1959 and, thereafter, the proportion declined steadily to 7.7 percent in 1963.[38] At the same time, there has been a

Table 6-3

Groups of Collective Farms in the Ukraine According to Rubles Distributed per Labor-day, 1951-1955 (Percentages)

Distribution in Old Rubles:	1951	1952	1953	1954	1955
Up to 60 kopecks	30.5	34.1	21.4	11.4	3.2
From 61 k. to 1 ruble	16.3	13.9	16.1	17.9	10.3
1.01 to 2.50	39.8	37.7	44.6	47.4	37.8
2.51 to 4.00	10.6	11.1	12.8	14.9	31.5
4.01 to 6.00	2.2	2.4	3.8	5.7	13.2
More than 6.00	0.6	0.8	1.3	2.7	4.0

Source: N.I. Nizhnii, A.M. Onishchenko, N.I. Romanenko, A.A. Storozhuk, *Denezhnaia oplata truda v kolkhozakh* (Moskva: Sel'khozgiz, 1961), p. 46.

Table 6-4

Groups of Collective Farms in the Ukraine According to Quantity of Grain Distributions per Labor-day, 1951-1955 (Percentages)

Grain Distributed:	1951	1952	1953	1954	1955
Up to 0.5 kilograms	18.5	1.7	4.3	18.7	4.3
0.5 to 1.0	35.0	15.1	22.1	46.3	15.4
1.0 to 2.0	38.0	44.9	55.5	31.6	30.0
2.0 to 3.0	7.7	21.9	15.6	3.3	23.4
More than 3 kilo.	0.8	16.4	2.5	0.1	26.9

Source: N.I. Nizhnii, A.M. Onishchenko, N.I. Romanenko, A.A. Storozhuk, *Denezhnaia oplata truda v kolkhozakh* (Moskva: Sel'khozgiz, 1961), p. 47.

[37] N.I. Nizhnii et al., *Denezhnaia oplata truda v kolkhozakh* (Moskva: Sel'khozgiz, 1961), p. 55.

[38] G. Ia. Kuznetsov, *Material'noe stimulirovanie truda v kolkhozakh* (Moskva: Mysl', 1966), p. 163. Bonus payments as reported for the Ukraine are as a portion of aggregate earnings of kolkhoz members, whereas those reported for the RSFSR are as a portion of total money income distributed to labor. The two series presumably differ though they are treated as broadly comparable.

tendency to substitute money for in-kind bonus payments. Although regional variations have been significant, 58.4 percent of bonus payments were in-kind in 1955, while the corresponding figure for 1964 was only 15.1 percent.[39]

Thus far the payment system of the Soviet collective farm has been examined as representing an inducement to greater participation by the members in the socialized sector of the farm. Apart from the continuing problem of the labor-day as a residual payment throughout much of the period under study, changes in the form, frequency and magnitude of payment since the early 1950s should have assisted the manager in his task of inducing greater peasant participation and effort. Was this in fact the case?

It is apparent (Table 6-5) that collective farm peasants have not favored great-er participation in the socialized sector of the kolkhoz. Although our data does not measure effort, if increased rewards to peasants is to induce greater partici-pation, such a pattern should be apparent for the period 1953-1963 when the growth of peasant incomes was significant, especially during the early years of this period.[40]

Table 6-5

The Structure of Work Time for Kolkhoz Members of the RSFSR, 1953 and 1963

	All Family Members				Of Which							
		Of Which			Men: 16-59 Years				Women: 16-54 Years			
			Of Which			Of Which				Of Which		
	Total Worked Hours = 100	in Kolkhoz	External	Work on the Private Plot	Total = 100	In Kolkhoz	External	Private Plot	Total = 100	In Kolkhoz	External	Private Plot
1953	100	62	12	26	100	75	16	9	100	59	10	31
1963	100	60	10	30	100	78	13	9	100	55	10	35

Source: I.F. Suslov, *Ekonomichsekie problemy razvitiia kolkhozov* (Moskva: Ekonomika, 1967), p. 193.

---

[39]T.I. Zaslavskaia, *Raspredelenie po truda v kolkhozakh* (Moskva: Ekonomika, 1966), p. 307.

[40]Although peasant incomes stagnated in the late 1950s, the study by Bronson and Krueger suggests that the differential in average pay per day worked in the private and socialized sectors has always been great and has remained so over time in spite of efforts to make it otherwise. See David W. Bronson and Constance B. Krueger, op. cit., p. 234.

Table 6-6

The Structure of Aggregate Family Income of Kolkhoz Members of the RSFSR (Percent of Total)

	1953	1958	1963
Income from the kolkhoz	33.4	41.3	42.7
Income from the private subsidiary economy	45.7	42.0	42.9
Income from the state and cooperative orgs.	18.5	14.7	12.2
Other income	2.4	2.0	2.2

Source: V.P. Ostrovskii, *Kolkhoz'noe krest'ianstvo SSSR* (Saratov: Izd. Saratovskogo universiteta, 1967), p. 93.

Although many factors may account for the pattern observed in Table 6-5,[41] the continuing importance of income derived from the private sector probably remains paramount. The data in Table 6-6 indicate that the portion of aggregate family income of kolkhoz members derived from the socialized sector grew from 33.4 percent in 1953 to 42.7 percent in 1963. At the same time, however, earnings from the private sector declined relatively little, from 45.7 percent of family earnings in 1953 to 42.9 percent in 1963. The difference has been accounted for by a decline in that portion of aggregate family income originating from state and cooperative organizations. In essence, the private plot continues to be a crucial source of income for the typical kolkhoz member. It is also worth noting that for the decade 1953-1963, the structure of income derived from the private sector has undergone very little change (Table 6-7). For the selected case of Vitebskii Oblast, where disaggregated data is available for the period 1958-1967 (Table 6-8), a similar picture emerges. Thus we find the structure of earnings quite stable within the private sector but, within the socialized sector, money income has come to replace income in-kind.

The sorts of data presented here would suggest that the labor supply curve in the typical kolkhoz is very steeply sloped indeed, thus greatly complicating the managerial task in the recruitment of labor inputs. Although regional differentials are important, the global data on this matter is of interest. Thus, as a portion of total hours of labor time expended in agriculture, the private sector accounted for 32.4 percent in 1950 and 39.8 percent in 1965 (Table 6-9).[42] At

[41]Changes in the age and sex composition of the rural labor force are undoubtedly important. See, for example, Norton T. Dodge, "Recruitment and The Quality of The Soviet Agricultural Labor Force," in James R. Millar (ed.), *The Soviet Rural Community* (Urbana: University of Illinois Press, 1971), pp. 180-213; and Karl-Eugen Wädekin, "Manpower in Soviet Agriculture—Some Post-Khrushchev Developments and Problems," *Soviet Studies*, Vol. XX, No. 3 (January 1969), pp. 281-305.

[42]This result could be partially accounted for on the basis of changing factor proportions in the socialized and private sectors. Thus as development proceeds, one would anticipate the socialized sector to become relatively less labor intensive, as production of mechanized crops on a large scale tends to be concentrated in this sector.

Table 6-7

The Structure of Family Income Derived from the Private Sector in the RSFSR: Selected Years

		As a Percent of Income Received from Private Sector	
	Value of Crops	Value of Cattle Bred and Products of Animal Sector	Other
1953	32.5	58.7	8.8
1958	36.6	57.8	5.6
1963	35.1	61.3	3.6

Source: V.P. Ostrovskii, *Kolkhoznoe krest'ianstvo SSSR* (Saratov: Izd. Saratovskogo universiteta, 1967), p. 85.

Table 6-8

The Structure of Family Income of Kolkhoz Members, Vitebskii Oblast, 1958-1967 (In Prices of the Corresponding Years)

Type of Income	1958	1961	1963	1965	1967
From the Socialized Sector as a Portion of Total Income from that Sector (%)					
Money receipts	56.3	64.5	69.1	74.9	94.3
Value of crops	42.4	35.4	30.6	24.9	5.6
Value of meat and animal products	.7	.08	.2	.2	.05
Other receipts	.6	.02	.07	.04	.05
From the Private Sector as a Portion of Total Income from that Sector (%)					
Value of crops	42.7	39.9	45.3	37.8	42.7
(of which)					
Grain	2.1	1.9	1.9	1.4	1.3
Potatoes	25.9	28.4	33.2	28.5	29.2
Veg. & Fruits	13.2	7.2	7.3	4.9	9.5
Value of meat and animal products	52.3	56.0	50.7	58.9	53.7
(of which)					
Milk	24.9	25.5	26.6	26.8	25.2
Cattle	23.6	25.7	20.3	28.4	24.1
Eggs	2.8	3.9	3.2	3.0	3.7
Other receipts	5.0	4.1	4.0	3.3	3.6

Source: A. Ia. Pesin, *Garantirovaniia oplata i raspredelenie po trudu v kolkhozakh* (Minsk: "Urozhai," 1969), p. 111.

Table 6-9

The Structure of Labor Inputs to Agriculture in Hours, by Category of Farm, 1940-1965 (USSR: in Percentages)

Year	Kolkhozy (Inc. MTS)	Sovkhozy	Private Sector	Total
1940	61.8	3.7	35.5	100.0
1950	62.4	5.2	32.4	100.0
1960	49.2	13.1	37.7	100.0
1965	41.4	18.8	39.8	100.0

Source: Ia. B. Lapkes, *Tekhnicheskii progress i proizvoditel'nost' truda v sel'skom khoziaistve* (Moskva: Ekonomika, 1968), p. 161.

the same time, the structure of labor time expenditures in collective and state farms shifted, reflecting primarily the changing roles of these institutions in Soviet agriculture. It is interesting to note that between 1952 and 1965 the number of kolkhoz households in the Soviet Union declined from 19.9 million to 15.4 million, while the volume of labor expenditure in the private sector (in millions of hours) fluctuated but declined very little: from 20,039 to 19,265.[43]

Returning for a moment to the analysis presented in Figure 6-1, it is apparent that managerial flexibility vis-a-vis the labor input can be visualized through relaxation of certain assumptions. Ignoring the matter of skill differentials and the question of membership requirements it is clear that there is a significant degree of flexibility in the magnitude of the labor force available to the agricultural sector in general.[44] Thus Douglas Diamond in his study notes that for the year 1958, "... between 82 and 83 million persons probably participated at some time during the year in farming activity as compared to only 41.5 million persons engaged principally or exclusively in agricultural pursuits."[45]

Flexibility also arises from the seasonal nature of agricultural production.[46] Several approaches have been adopted to handle the seasonality of production. First, labor can be, and is, directed from industry to rural areas for meeting peak demands, notably harvest. Normally, the worker who is directed to assist in the rural sector will be partially paid by his enterprise and, also, the collective on

[43]Ia. B. Lapkes, *Tekhnicheskii progress i proizvoditel'nost' truda v sel'skom khoziaistve* (Moskva: Ekonomika, 1968), p. 158.

[44]Membership requirements are probably a minimal brake upon labor mobility. More important will be the absence of any decentralized mechanism of labor recruitment, especially one that is available to the individual farm manager.

[45] Douglas B. Diamond, op. cit., p. 349.

[46]This is especially true for those engaged in the raising of field crops. See for example the discussion in G.I. Shmelev, *Raspredelenie i ispol'zovanie truda v kolkhozakh* (Moskva: Mysl', 1964), pp. 79-103 and especially Table 20, p. 86. At the same time, it should be noted that data presented by Bronson and Krueger suggests that participation in the socialized sector of the kolkhoz is no greater even when the pressure of campaigns is brought to bear. See David W. Bronson and Constance B. Krueger, op. cit., pp. 234-235.

which he will temporarily serve. Second, youths, especially in agricultural institutions, normally spend part of their summer vacations in some sort of "practical training," at which time they will provide labor services in the rural sector as needed. This pattern can extend to late return to classes in the fall.[47] Third, it is possible to hire local individuals (for example, women with children who might not otherwise participate) to complete specific tasks at a given time and for a specific daily wage rate.[48] Fourth, it is possible for the kolkhoz to attract new members, although given the pattern of out migration from the agricultural sector, this option must have been of minimal importance.[49] Finally, although full treatment of this question is well beyond the present study, it must be apparent that Soviet agricultural policy has, in several respects, been directed towards the resolution of the seasonal labor problem. The development of interkolkhoz organizations, utilization of processing and related industrial establishments in the rural areas and the restructuring of the production brigade have all been factors working in this direction.

In spite of these techniques through which increased flexibility in labor force participation may be gained, the picture is not bright. First, it is not clear that there exists any significant mechanism through which the manager can, himself, actively control labor supply on a decentralized basis. The collective farm system lacks any decentralized basis of labor allocation, a factor which could be of great importance to any potential expansion of decision making powers at the kolkhoz level. Second, the policy pursued by Soviet leaders has been predicated upon the assumption that collective farm members can achieve a better standard of living through expansion of *money income*.

We do not know enough about the preference function of a typical collective farm peasant to be sure that improvement of a standard of living is, in any sense, a strong motive to participation in the labor force. Indeed, those in the rural sector who possess this sort of motivation would most likely be the first to seek greater opportunities in the industrial sector, thus reinforcing a self-selection process whereby the remaining members of the rural sector may have only very limited aspirations. Quite apart from motivations, however, the structure of rural incomes must be an important factor restricting peasant participation in the socialized sector. Peasant income from this source has been in the past primarily in-kind and typically fodder.[50] One would expect that having achieved the

---

[47] Observed by the author at Timiriazev Agricultural Academy.

[48] The author observed such a case in the Krasnodar region where women, otherwise external to the kolkhoz labor force, were being hired on a five ruble daily wage rate to complete the harvest tasks.

[49] For a discussion of the legal implications of membership in a collective as opposed to employment by an enterprise, see Peter B. Maggs, "The Law of Farm-Farmer Relations," in James R. Millar (ed.), *The Soviet Rural Community* (Urbana: University of Illinois Press, 1971), pp. 142 ff.

[50] Grain has frequently represented 80 percent or more of the in-kind distributions of the labor-day. The private plot is not suited to the production of this type of crop, and yet the peasant demand for such a product is likely very inelastic with respect to peasant labor inputs to the socialized sector.

necessary fodder supplies for animals in the private sector, the typical peasant would be reluctant to contribute further labor time, especially given the substantially better rewards from the private sector.

Finally, the utility of money income in the Soviet rural sector may be minimal. For the period 1950 through 1967, the average size of rural savings deposits in the Soviet Union grew from 52 to 413 rubles.[51] For the same period, the relative importance of rural savings deposits as a portion of all savings deposits in the country grew from 11 percent to 26 percent.[52] Such a pattern could suggest a lack of desired goods and services and/or a desire to wait until quality improves. Certainly the distribution of goods and services in the rural sector, where roads and transportation are bad, must be a barrier to consumption.

The ability of management to recruit labor for the socialized sector is also hindered by the basic nature of Soviet agricultural production. Given, for example, the inadequate supplies of meat and fresh vegetables, any contribution to output within these spheres certainly cannot be overlooked even though it may come from the private sector. The improvement of both meat and vegetable production has been a continuing problem.[53]

The very nature of the collective farm labor force has produced a pattern of non-participation which in many cases is beyond the immediate control of farm management. The non-participation of women is much higher in the socialized sector than that of their male counterparts. At the same time, it might be noted that in 1962, for example, of the entire number of workers in the economy, 48 percent were women while the comparable figure for kolkhozy was 56 percent.[54] For the same year and, on the average for the entire country, able-bodied kolkhoz males worked 232 man days while able-bodied females worked 173 man days.[55]

In essence, it is the male contribution (per kolkhoz member) which is of greatest importance, yet at the same time it is the young and energetic males who leave for more attractive pursuits in the cities. Child rearing for those women who remain with the collectives is also a problem. For 1959, it has been reported that more than 75 percent of those not fulfilling the minimum number of labor-days were women caring for several children.[56] Another Soviet author has indicated that, in 1960, in the collective farms of 22 oblasts of the RSFSR there were no kindergartens whatsoever.[57]

[51]V.R. Boev, op. cit., p. 63. For the period 1950 through 1967, the average size of a savings deposit in city areas grew from 151 rubles to 421 rubles. Part of the rapid expansion of rural savings deposits may arise from those rural dwellers who work in the cities, but in the main it must represent the significant monetization of incomes in the rural sector and hesitance to consume out of those incomes.

[52]Ibid.

[53]See, for example, Naum Jasny, "The Failure of The Soviet Animal Industry," Parts I and II, *Soviet Studies*, Vol. XV (October 1963), pp. 187-218, and (January 1964), pp. 285-307.

[54]G.I. Shmelev, op. cit., p. 113.

[55]Ibid.

[56]V.P. Rozhin, *Nekotorye voprosy pod'ema ekonomiki slabykh kolkhozov* (Moskva: Ekonomizdat, 1960), p. 79.

[57]G.I. Shmelev, op. cit., p. 117.

It must also be noted that female members of the kolkhoz labor force have tended to be placed in the least desirable jobs. As we shall see in Chapter 8, the proportion of women serving in managerial positions declines sharply as one moves up in the managerial hierarchy, and, indeed, their role is negligible at the highest levels. Even in the case of the war years, when increasing numbers of women were moved into responsible positions due to the absence of men, there was a sharp post-war reversal. In 1944, 11.8 percent of kolkhoz managers were female, whereas by 1956, the comparable figure was less than 2 percent.[58] The same pattern seems to have prevailed for those jobs requiring technical skills. Women represented 7 percent of those servicing machinery in the MTS in 1948, a figure which declined to 5.2 percent in 1950 and 3.7 percent in 1954.[59] In 1959, 0.8 percent of tractor drivers and combine operators were women.[60]

Although organizational adjustments to the kolkhoz (changing size and nature of the brigade for example) may enhance managerial flexibility vis-a-vis the labor force, it is apparent that, at least up to the mid 1960s, the monetization of rural incomes and sharp increases in magnitude have not been successful in inducing greater participation. The continued implementation of this policy would suggest only limited gains in the future, especially since non-participation also arises from several very basic characteristics of the Soviet rural labor force.

Capital Investment and Utilization

The general question of financial management in the collective farm sector is beyond the present study and indeed has been treated adequately elsewhere.[61] Attention will be focused upon two questions: first, who determined the magnitude of capital investment within a collective farm and on what basis is this determination made?; second, how is the distribution of investment funds among alternative uses evaluated?

While the production-financial plan does in theory originate from deliberations within the kolkhoz, we have seen that such discussions have had a minimal impact upon the nature of the plan. For the early years of our study, the rate of capital investment was established, along with other norms, by higher level planning authorities and remained essentially unchanged from year to year. Specifically, the kolkhoz was directed to deduct a certain percentage of gross income

[58] For data on the war years see Iu. V. Arutiunian, *Sovetskoe krest'ianstvo v gody velikoi otechestvennoi Voiny*, 2d ed. (Moskva: Nauka, 1970), pp. 408-411. For the post-war years see Table 8-2.

[59] G.I. Shmelev, op. cit., pp. 120-127.

[60] G.I. Shmelev, op. cit., p. 121.

[61] In particular, see James R. Millar, "Financing the Modernization of Kolkhozy," in James R. Millar (ed.), *The Soviet Rural Community* (Urbana: University of Illinois Press, 1971), pp. 276-303. For an extended treatment, see James R. Millar, "Price and Income Formation in The Soviet Collective-Farm Sector Since 1953," unpublished Ph.D. dissertation, Cornell University, 1965.

which would then enter the indivisible funds *(nedelemye fondy)*[62] This percentage would be spelled out in the kolkhoz charter, and thus, while absolute amounts would vary from farm to farm, relatively speaking in inverse proportion $I/Y = -t(Y)$ to ability to invest as measured by the size of money income, the percentage amount will be relatively stable.

Prior to 1952, these deductions were decreed at 12-15 percent of money income in the grain regions and 15-20 percent in the regions where technical crops and animal breeding predominated.[63] While there may have been a degree of regional variability, it is interesting to note, as evidence of lack of managerial flexibility, the marked stability of deductions for the country as a whole. Thus between 1950 and 1957, the portion of money income deducted for use in the indivisible funds remained at approximately 16-17 percent.[64] This pattern did not hold true in subsequent years as the rules were changed.

The methodology for allocating investment funds among alternate uses is less clear although one can observe significant constraints upon managerial behavior. In general, utilization of funds is spelled out in the production-financial plan.[65] However, to the extent that plan formulation is centralized, so will the disbursement of capital funds be centralized. A general pattern for the utilization of funds consists of roughly 15 categories (such as land reclamation, electrification, construction, preparation of roads and so on) all of which tend to introduce a measure of conformity into the plan.

Within the production-financial plan there are a number of regulations curbing managerial freedom. First, during the plan year the management board cannot spend more than 70 percent of the income earmarked for expenditure on capital projects. The remainder is a residual to be utilized after harvest results are known. Second, since the general meeting has approved the income-expenditure estimates in total, the manager does not have the right to alter usage of funds throughout the year without permission of the kolkhoz membership. In practice, however, there seems to be some flexibility on this point, especially when the sums involved are not large.[66] Unfortunately, investment data is highly aggregated and does not tell us much about the direction in which investment funds have been allocated. The data in Table 6-10 does suggest a degree of conformity over time although with notable exceptions, such as the purchase by kolkhozy of machinery and equipment from the MTS in 1958.

[62]The indivisible funds *(nedelemye fondy)* are the capital funds of the kolkhoz. They consist of the capital assets plus cash held and are formed by deductions from gross income. For a detailed discussion of sources and uses of funds, see James R. Millar, "Financing the Modernization of Kolkhozy," op. cit.

[63]A. Mishchenko, *Novyi poriadok planirovaniia kolkhoznogo proizvodstva* (Moskva: Moskovskii rabochii, 1957), p. 100.

[64]P.V. Alekseev and A.P. Voronin, *Nakoplenie i razvitie kolkhoznoi sobstvennosti* (Moskva: Ekonomizdat, 1963), p. 57.

[65]The production-financial plan contains a section devoted to an estimate of sources and uses of funds for capital investment and capital repair. For each category, annual totals are subdivided on a quarterly basis.

[66]Based upon personal interviews with kolkhoz chairmen in the Krasnodar region.

Table 6-10

The Structure of Capital Investments of Collective Farms, USSR (Percent)

Direction of Investment	1950	1957	1958	1960	1961
Buildings and installa- tions	22.1	42.5	21.8	32.7[a]	34.6[b]
Purchase of machinery, inventory and equipment [c]	22.1	17.2	53.2	18.1	19.0
Long term crops (forests,[d] etc.)	3.1	2.0	1.2	1.9	1.6
Irrigation and reclamation	2.1	2.7	1.6	2.0	2.4
Capital repair of buildings installations and equipment	12.6	11.0	7.8	16.8	15.0
Purchase of productive cattle, fowl and bees	26.3	17.4	10.0	...	...
Purchase of work cattle	7.4	0.8	0.4	...	...
Other expenditures	4.3	6.4	4.0	3.9	3.9

Source: P.V. Alekseeva, A.P. Voronin, *Nakoplenie i razvitie kolkhoznoi sobstvennosti* (Moskva: Ekonomizdat, 1963), p. 106.

[a]Including investment in roads, bridges, means of communication and also objects of a cul-tural-personal nature.

[b]The authors point out that the relative weight of investment in animal breeding remained at the 1958 level of 10 percent in 1960, and by 1961 had fallen to 4 percent, the remaining means compensating only for the value of young animals transferred into the basic herd.

[c]The absence of significant change in the share of investment funds devoted to machinery and equipment (as between 1950-1957 and 1960-1961) in spite of dissolution of the MTS can be explained in large measure by the decline of state production (and shipments) of machinery and equipment. On this matter, see for example, Jerzy F. Karcz, "Seven Years on the Farm: Retrospect and Prospects," as cited in United States Congress, Joint Economic Committee, *New Directions in the Soviet Economy* (Washington, D.C.: U.S. Government Printing Office, 1966), pp. 402-410.

[d]Classified as capital in Soviet accounting practice.

It should be noted that prior to 1958, the MTS role as a budget financed organ of state control was significant. This relationship was not limited to tech-nical assistance but also involved "organizational" assistance by which was meant both plan formulation and execution, for which both the director of the MTS and the kolkhoz manager were held responsible. Although the MTS would be responsible for the utilization of major machinery and equipment, this did not relieve the kolkhoz of major problems. In particular, the close interaction of the MTS and the kolkhoz under typically contradictory goals must have been a source of constant irritation for kolkhoz management.[67]

[67]Alec Nove has observed: "The collective farm was interested in maximizing the harvest and its net revenues in cash and kind. The MTS was rewarded by the authorities for carrying out its work plan (expressed in standard work units) and for earning produce in payment for its services; this encouraged it to carry out such work as was 'profitable' in respect of the above criteria, even if it was wasteful from all other points of view." See Alec Nove, *The Soviet Economy*, op. cit., p. 53.

With the abolition of the MTS in 1958, the procedure for determination of the share of income to be devoted to capital investment purposes was changed. The decision was decentralized and the norm of 15-20 percent abandoned. With the growth of kolkhoz money income in the 1950s, it was hoped that decentralization of this decision would lead to an expansion in the share of income devoted to investment purposes and, in particular, assist in the purchase of the MTS machinery and equipment. The data in Table 6-11 would seem to suggest that, on balance, deductions did increase, and, in addition, that collective farms really did have a new measure of freedom in making this decision. Nevertheless, regional differentials remain important. The average level of deductions for the country as a whole was 16.8 percent, in Latvia 17.5 percent, in Lithuania 17.8 percent, in Tadzhikistan 18.8 percent and in Uzbekistan 19.4 percent.[68] As money income of collective farms grew in the 1950s, both the share of income going to labor and to capital investment would be established within the farm. An important test of managerial decision making freedom was developing.

The initial result was, on the average, a reduction in the size of deductions to capital investment. Alekseev and Voronin point out that after the collectives were given the right to decide the deductions themselves, "... many of them lessened the percentage deduction from money income into the indivisible funds."[69] Initially the state and Party responded with a campaign to encourage greater deductions for capital investment, along with the suggestion that, for labor payments, nearby sovkhoz wage payments should be a major guide.

According to formal procedures, the utilization of capital funds is a decision of the management board, spelled out in the annual production-financial plan and approved by the general meeting. In reality, the latter body approves only limits and, as we have seen, there is an element of managerial flexibility in shifting funds.

Table 6-11

Groups of Collective Farms According to Percent Deduction from Money Income for the Indivisible Funds: USSR

	Percentage of Collective Farms Deducting from Money Income into Indivisible Funds		
	Less than 20 Percent	20-25 Percent	25 Percent and More
1958	40.4	36.1	22.7
1959	27.5	39.7	32.8
1961	27.1	40.5	32.4

Source: P.V. Alekseeva, A.P. Voronin, *Nakoplenie i razvitie kolkhoznoi sobstvennosti* (Moskva: Ekonomizdat, 1963), p. 57.

[68] P.V. Alekseev and A.P. Voronin, op. cit., p. 57.

[69] Ibid., pp. 56-57.

Although changing rules appear to have introduced new managerial flexibility in the utilization of funds within the kolkhoz, it appears as if kolkhoz managers as a group are quite unwilling or possibly unable to seize the opportunity to utilize this power for the good of the farm. Millar in his study of the financial development of the kolkhoz sector has noted that financial policy is, on balance, very conservative.[70] He notes that while this sector has had access to credit, it has for the most part utilized funds obtained from increased prices and has tended to pursue a policy where income must precede outlays.[71] Although one would expect state control over utilization to be greater in those cases where funds are granted through credit channels, kolkhozy have been reticent to utilize these means. At the same time, where financing has been realized by increased prices, here, too, policy has been conservative suggesting that, on balance, financial mechanisms for the stimulation of kolkhoz performance by kolkhozy are somewhat alien to kolkhoz managers.

Finally, the case of machinery and equipment is instructive. It gives us insight into an area where kolkhoz management has new decision making freedom, and yet, in the face of continuing problems shifted from the MTS to the kolkhozy, decisions made in this sphere by kolkhoz management may be little better than those under the MTS regime. In this sense, and considering the greatly expanded size and changing structure of the typical kolkhoz, new freedom for kolkhoz managers may have little meaning in terms of decentralization.

We have noted that the complex brigade or, in many cases the department *(otdelenie)*, has been used with increasing frequency in recent years. In these cases, machinery and equipment is most likely held at this level and this is where its purchase and utilization will be planned. The utilization of equipment will be a function of the targets facing the brigade and the technical norms translating these targets into specific fulfillment tasks. This translation is typically planned with the use of a technological map *(tekhnologicheskaia karta)*. If additional equipment is needed, the brigadier forwards a request to kolkhoz management which in turn is forwarded to the raiispolkom. If the request is for a deficit commodity, the decision as to who will in fact receive the equipment is apparently made at the raion level.

This equipment is recorded at the brigade level as an asset and depreciated according to standard norms (usually over a ten year period). Capital repairs are planned in advance and based upon anticipated usage. The costs of these repairs are recorded at the brigade level although the brigade does not make payment. This procedure establishes a measure of freedom within the kolkhoz certainly not held under the MTS system. However, old problems remain.

---

[70] James R. Millar, "Financing The Modernization of Kolkhozy," op. cit., p. 289.

[71] Millar comments as follows on the period 1952-1962: "Disregarding the MTS transaction, the pecuniarization and improvement in money and total earnings and the increased money expenditures on capital account were financed almost exclusively by increased average realized procurement prices." See ibid.

Under the MTS system, a frequent complaint centered upon the extent to which the distribution of equipment was decided centrally and not in accordance with the needs of each MTS. Thus a bank official of the Stavropol territory made the following comment in 1957:

A checkup of 48 M.T.S. conducted in March 1957, showed that they have 2580 unneeded farm machines, which have been idle for a long time. . . . It is significant that some of these farm machines have not been used since 1950, and yet some of them were received in 1956.[72]

The conversion of approximately 80 percent of the MTS to RTS (repair tractor stations) did not seem to improve the situation. The RTS served as the supply system until the formation of the all-union supply organization *(soiuzsel' khoztekhnika)* in 1961.[73] In Stavropol territory in 1959, a senior engineer of one RTS could say:

The RTS warehouses now have 500,000 rubles' worth of machines on hand for which they have no market, and such machines continue to come in.[74]

Further, the writer suggested that the problem would continue as long as delivery of machinery was planned from "above." The complexity of this problem may well increase to the extent that operations most readily mechanized have already been serviced while those operations that remain to be mechanized will require more complex equipment.

A second problem facing management is the poor quality of machinery and equipment and the constant shortage of spare parts. One writer has suggested that in spite of equipment shortages, 15 percent of tractors stand idle every year due to technical inoperability.[75] In addition, repair facilities established by the RTS frequently proved to be inadequate. Thus the chairman of a collective farm in Rostov province pointed out in December of 1959 that the RTS under khozraschet had no interest in the quality of the repairs or, for that matter, the provision of repairs in harmony with peak demand for machines at harvest time. The solution suggested was the purchase of the RTS by the kolkhoz and the advocacy of a share system for weaker farms.[76]

The shortage of spare parts remains unresolved as a perennial problem in the Soviet system. There are continual complaints focusing upon idle equipment and/or repairs not completed on time thus hampering the harvest effort and

[72]V. Loginav, "Without Taking the MTS' Needs Into Account," *Pravda*, May 25, 1957, p. 2, translated and reprinted in *CDSP*, Vol. IX, No. 21 (July 3, 1957), p. 37.

[73]Formed by a decree of February 20, 1961.

[74]V. Kozlitin, "In The Old Way," *Pravda*, March 3, 1959, p. 3, translated and reprinted in *CDSP*, Vol. XI, No. 9 (April 1959), p. 68.

[75]I.A. Gladkova (ed.), *Razvitie sotsialisticheskoi ekonomiki SSSR v poslevoennyi period* (Moskva: Nauka, 1965), p. 274.

[76]V. Matskevich, "Are RTS Needed Everywhere?," *Pravda*, November 11, 1959, p. 3, translated and reprinted in *CDSP*, Vol. XI, No. 45 (December 9, 1959), pp. 28-29.

other tasks for which time pressure is important. In February, 1960, the new chairman of the Caucasus collective farm in the Kurgan district asked another farm chairman how spare parts could be obtained, to which the response was: "We buy stolen goods."[77]

While the physical possession of machinery and equipment passed to the farms, and the system of dual management (for which the MTS were so frequently criticized) was ended, collective farm managers began to face those sorts of problems previously faced by the MTS. In fact, during the initial years of this new freedom, there was a reduction in the size of the machine tractor park. Between 1959 and 1961, the number of tractors on collective farms fell by 55,000 while the number of grain combines fell by 61,000 and the number of heavy duty trucks by 17,000.[78]

Summary

In this chapter the focus has been decision making patterns pertaining to the determination of both inputs and outputs. Although plan rules have been relaxed somewhat over time, the kolkhoz manager has typically had very little effective control over production decisions. With farm production capacity difficult to measure and continuing central pressure for increased product contribution, farm production plans have tended to be of short term duration and subject to continual upward ratcheting minimizing any positive role for the managerial incentive system.

At the same time, however, there has been an effort to change the nature of plan targets enhancing the importance of *output* and related performance indicators. Also, there has been an effort to introduce serious long term planning.

Managerial control over input utilization though increasing over time due to changing decision rules has, nevertheless, been very limited.

In the case of labor allocation, for example, the farm manager lacks any significant mechanism to afford flexibility of labor supply, and markedly increased rewards have failed to elicit the desired response from labor.

Where farm managers have been granted a new measure of freedom to determine the *share* of kolkhoz income devoted to capital investment, it seems that the distribution of these funds among alternate uses remains circumscribed.

[77]V. Darmodekhin, "How Are The Collective Farm Billions to Be Realized?," *Izvestia*, February 19, 1960, p. 3, translated and reprinted in *CDSP*, Vol. XII, No. 7 (March 16, 1960), p. 30.

[78]I.A. Gladkova (ed.), op. cit., p. 227.

7

Pricing and the Managerial Framework

Thus far, decision making in the kolkhoz has been treated within the context of the planning system—the nature and extent of plan rules as they bear upon managerial decision making flexibility. The present chapter focuses upon the transition away from a system of plan rules based mainly on physical targeting and towards a system of plan rules based mainly upon value indicators. This transition represents the introduction of money into the collective farm system in a significant way and increasing reliance upon the price system, both as mechanisms for the appropriate expression and achievement of plan goals.

Although pricing arrangements in Soviet agriculture have been treated in detail by others, the importance of the subject to an understanding of kolkhoz management necessitates further consideration at this point.[1]

Pricing in the collective sector of Soviet agriculture is of great importance in both macroeconomic and microeconomic terms. First, in a macroeconomic sense, since kolkhozy both purchase inputs for the production process and sell the resulting output according to prices fixed by the state, clearly the level of prices will be a crucial factor determining the terms of trade between kolkhozy and the non-kolkhoz sector of the Soviet economy.[2] In this respect, the kolkhoz has been a unique organizational mechanism.

From the early 1930s through the late 1950s, the Soviet government utilized a two-level pricing system for the procurement of collective farm output. The basic compulsory deliveries of output (frequently determined on the basis of

[1] For a general treatment of initial problems relating to monetization, see Frank A. Durgin, Jr., "Monetization and Policy in Soviet Agriculture Since 1952," *Soviet Studies*, vol. XV, no. 4 (April 1964), pp. 375-407. For a detailed treatment of pricing and marketing arrangements during the Stalin era, see Jerzy F. Karcz, *Soviet Agricultural Marketings and Prices, 1928-1954* (Santa Monica: The Rand Corporation, 1957). For the 1950s, see Nancy Nimitz, "Soviet Agricultural Prices and Costs," in *Comparisons of United States and Soviet Economies* (Washington: U.S. Government Printing Office, 1959), pp. 239-284. For a general discussion, see Lazar Volin, *A Century of Russian Agriculture* (Cambridge: Harvard University Press, 1970), Ch. 16. For a recent discussion of reform proposals, see Morris Bornstein, "The Soviet Debate on Agricultural Price and Procurement Reforms," *Soviet Studies*, vol. XXI, no. 1 (July 1969), pp. 1-20.

[2] For much of the period under study, it is only partially true that the kolkhozy purchased their inputs. Thus in the absence of land charges (with the exception of differential MTS charges based upon varying land quality), scarcity charges for capital, payments to labor as a residual and the absence of cost accounting until the mid-1950s, economic calculation could have very little meaning in the collective farm sector. This pattern is, however, changing as monetization creates an economic organization out of what was formerly an administrative mechanism. Also, any terms of trade discussion would of necessity consider the important role of the private sector.

inputs, for example, sown area), were to be sold to the state at low, fixed prices, while above plan deliveries would be paid for in higher, fixed prices. Given the nature of targeting arrangements discussed earlier, the very low level of compulsory delivery fixed prices and the importance of the compulsory deliveries as a portion of farm output, production costs were simply not covered and hence much of the time peasants bore a heavy tax, in part as a mechanism for financing the industrialization effort.[3] As we shall see, however, state purchase prices were increased significantly throughout the 1950s and 1960s. Also, the two-level pricing arrangement was abandoned in 1958 although it was partially re-introduced (for grain crops) in 1965. These price adjustments, along with the introduction of cost accounting in the mid 1950s, gave meaning to the concept of profitability.

A second and most important aspect of pricing is its microeconomic implications. To the extent that any important decision is made within the collective farm, the price system may serve as a framework for decision making—in a sense, providing appropriate rules for decision makers as they respond to various incentives and pursue the goals of the organization. The cost-profit calculus may be designed to pursue various organizational goals, not necessarily profit maximization. In any such system, however, the nature of prices for inputs and outputs becomes crucial to the success of the organization for it is these prices to which managers will respond when making decisions. Hence it is essential that the "instructions" of the price system be accurate in their reflection of enterprise goals.

Since the price system has been playing an increasingly important role in the operations of the typical kolkhoz during the past twenty years, we must ask to what extent this system has encouraged appropriate managerial response.[4] In particular, has the pricing system encouraged managers to expand the output and improve the quality of agricultural products, while at the same time lowering production costs? To answer this question, we must re-examine working arrangements for the determination of kolkhoz output and input patterns.

On the input side, we have already examined in some detail the planning arrangements for the allocation of land, labor and capital, although the role of prices was not discussed. The pricing of inputs has two related facets. First, to the extent that inputs are scarce, prices should reflect relative scarcities thus allowing management, within given technological constraints, to produce a desired output level with minimum expenditure of resources. Second, with appropriate product pricing, managerial decisions could then be evaluated on the basis of profitability or the difference between revenues and costs.[5]

---

[3] Although there have been important variations regionally and over time, state procurements have for most products represented an important portion of gross kolkhoz output, and have generated a major portion of gross kolkhoz income. For details, see Nancy Nimitz, op. cit., pp. 242-248; Lazar Volin, op. cit., Ch. 16.

[4] For a discussion of resource allocation procedures in Soviet collective farms, see Abram Bergson, The Economics of Soviet Planning (New Haven and London: Yale University Press, 1964), Chapters 9 and 10.

[5] This sort of argument does some violence to the nature of the collective since there is an inherent assumption about the nature of goals. However, although an assumption such as profit maximization would be pretty unreasonable, lower costs, greater output and similar sorts of goals seem fairly reasonable, at least as a general starting point.

To the extent that monetization of the kolkhoz has meant the introduction of a cost-profit type of calculus, much will depend upon the nature of prices which are, after all, the basis of the whole framework. It is for this reason that much attention has been focused upon the nature of agricultural prices and especially the role that they should play in the operation of the kolkhoz.

In the case of land utilization, there has not been a charge for use and hence probably only a minimal possibility that land might be viewed by management as a scarce resource. To the extent that land use has been constrained, however, management might generally attempt to improve utilization to the extent that such behavior might improve the managerial success position. On the other hand, the absence of a charge for land has left the cost-profit calculus largely meaningless since any residual between revenues and costs may stem largely from the quality of the land on which the farm is fortunate enough to be located and may have nothing whatsoever to do with the manner in which the land is cultivated.

Although differential charges for MTS services may have partly alleviated the land rent problem, the solution was short run and haphazard. The entire question of land charges has been the subject of much debate over an extended period of time in the Soviet Union.[6]

In the absence of charges for capital, our conclusions as to the allocation pattern for capital must be broadly similar to those for the allocation of land. Indeed, since much of the financing of the kolkhozy has been an internal matter, even those cases where minimal capital charges have been made have not been of importance. Once again, for most of the period under study, the tendency to relax plan controls has been very slow, and thus centralized dictates as to the volume and distribution of investment funds has largely taken precedence over any decentralized mechanism for allocation. Also, from a cost-profit point of view, the absence of a capital charge makes such a calculus rather meaningless.

The question of labor allocation has already been treated at great length in Chapter 6. Suffice it to say that for the period under study, the wage (dividend) has apparently been below the equilibrium level and even in the face of considerable effort to induce greater participation the results have not been encouraging. For most peasants, their marginal product is higher in the private sector and in that sector they are paid their marginal product, hence in the absence of powerful sanctions to force participation in the socialized sector, it is limited. The equilibrating mechanism is only partly operational given the administrative controls and the inability of the individual farm manager to hire labor from other farms or, for that matter, the inability of that labor to move from farm to farm according to regional wage (dividend) differentials. The difficulty of predicting *ex ante* the value of the dividend must have restricted any potential movement of farm labor, although in some areas, undoubtedly, amalgamation and conversion have been attractive to weaker farms whose members would forsee increased earnings with a given or lower level of participation and effort.

[6]For a detailed treatment of the land rent question in the Soviet case, see James R. Millar, "Price and Income Formation in the Soviet Collective-Farm Sector Since 1953," op. cit.

Turning to the question of output determination, what sort of managerial response might we expect given the nature of pricing arrangements in the collective farm sector? If we assume even a limited degree of flexibility within the guidelines of the plan, would the price system induce managers to produce more, and in particular, to adjust the product mix according to price differentials? Could cost reduction and some form of profitability, however crude, be considered an operative part of the managerial system?

In spite of significant upward price adjustments in 1953, 1956 and 1958, only in a few cases did average procurement price cover average costs of production.[7] At the same time, it must be remembered that for these years, farm managers were not, for the most part, calculating costs of production, so neither they nor central planners could have made input or output decisions on a cost basis.[8] Price differentials must have been utilized, if at all, on much cruder grounds.

If average procurement prices did not, in most cases, cover average costs of production by 1956, the same cannot be said for above quota delivery prices. From the data assembled in Tables 7-1 and 7-2 it is clear that for many non-animal products as of 1956, the above quota prices covered the average costs of production. The crucial question here is the extent to which kolkhoz managers would in fact be motivated by the higher above quota prices.

Quite apart from production costs and the absence of any costing procedures prior to 1956, it is theoretically correct that under a two-level pricing system, managers should form their expectations and be motivated in doing so by the higher prices. On this basis, one would expect the above quota prices to be a strong stimulus towards expansion of output, and with the introduction of cost accounting and a concern for earnings, presumably a stimulus to improve farm performance in general. Can we conclude, then, that the relevant comparison in the Soviet case is the average cost of production and the above quota price? The answer is apparently in the negative, due in large part to the nature of planning arrangements, especially the formation of output targets. In particular, with a two-level pricing system, the extent to which above quota prices are relevant will depend upon the formation of managerial expectations for which three possible cases can be postulated:

1. For any one (or all) of several possible reasons, the manager may well anticipate significant overfulfillment of plan targets of output. For example, the

[7]Procurement prices were also raised in 1962, 1963 and 1965. For a discussion of debates on price levels, see Morris Bornstein, op. cit., pp. 3-4. The usual procedure when comparing prices and costs has been to utilize an average of base and above quota prices weighted by state procurements.

[8]Cost accounting, to be discussed later in this chapter, was non-existent prior to 1956. Most data utilized here is from Nancy Nimitz's study of prices and costs during the 1950s, a period when the methodological problems of cost calculation, especially the costing of labor and MTS services, made cost data most difficult to derive. Necessary assumptions have been elaborated in footnotes to the various tables.

Table 7-1

Average Costs of Production and Procurement Prices of Selected Products of Collective Farms, USSR

	Average Cost of Production, 1953-1956[a]	Average Procurement Price	
		1950	1956
Grain	690	91	530
Potatoes	350	40	410
Vegetables	480	150	540
Milk	1,570	300	970
Meat	12,010[b]	700	3,640
Sugar beets	160	110	240
Raw cotton	2,000	3,600	3,680
Flax fiber	6,800	4,423	14,488

Source: Compiled from Nancy Nimitz, "Soviet Agricultural Prices and Costs," *Comparisons of United States and Soviet Economies* (Washington, D.C.: U.S. Government Printing Office, 1959), pp. 269, 271.

[a]Nimitz accepts as broadly comparable those cost calculations utilizing different methodological bases, and accordingly, does not specify for the above data the bases used. However, they probably include labor value at state farm norms, materials and supplies at prices actually paid by the kolkhoz, and MTS services based on state outlays (not including depreciation) for the provision of those services.

[b]Pork only.

Note: Costs expressed in rubles per ton, and for eggs, per 1000.

Table 7-2

Procurement Prices Received by Collective Farms for Selected Products, 1956

	Average	Compulsory Delivery	Above-Quota Delivery
Grain	530	235	800
Potatoes	410	330	530
Vegetables	540	425	615
Meat	3,640	2,000	5,100
Pork, meat grade	...	3,200	7,000
Milk	970	550	1,200
Eggs	250	200	500

Source: Nancy Nimitz, "Soviet Agricultural Prices and Costs," *Comparisons of the United States and Soviet Economies* (Washington, D.C.: U.S. Government Printing Office, 1959), p. 266.

manager may "know" that the targets are "easy" vis-a-vis his perception of available production capacity; he may have "hidden" capacity available and so on. In this sort of case, the manager would be motivated by above quota prices.

2. At the other extreme, there may be reasons why the manager knows (or be-

lieves) that output targets cannot be achieved. The targets may be very high relative to past performance, the manager may anticipate upward adjustment throughout the plan year or he may simply expect unfavorable natural conditions. In this case, above quota prices would not be relevant for managerial decision making.

3. In this case, which would seem to be the most applicable to the realities of Soviet collective agriculture, let us assume that we are not talking about large overfulfillment or large underfulfillment, but rather are operating within the immediate range of the plan targets, possibly slightly under or over. How will the manager be motivated in this case? The answer will depend upon the nature of managerial expectations as to plan fulfillment. Thus if the manager expects to overfulfill, even by a small amount, the above quota price would be relevant.

Although there are bound to be variations from farm to farm, if the planning system roughly approximates our picture presented in the previous chapter (upward ratcheting of targets, significant underfulfillment, small managerial rewards from the bonus system), it would seem very unlikely that above quota prices would be of any relevance. To the extent, therefore, that above quota price did in fact cover cost, this would still not provide a meaningful mechanism for motivating management towards expansion of output.[9] This sort of argument would seem to apply whether we are speaking about expansion of output of a single product or the shifting of effort to expand output as among a variety of products. The latter shifts may, of course, take place depending upon the degree of differentiation as among products of the degree of plan tautness and the magnitude of differentials as between base and above quota prices for all products under consideration. In this latter case where multiple products are involved, the degree of specialization resulting from managerial behavior would seem to be largely a function of the plan targets vis-a-vis managerial expectations and rather less a function of price levels.

If we cannot say that prices have been a positive motivating force for kolkhoz management, what can be said about cost reductions? In particular, to the extent that cost-price comparisons utilize cost data generated on the basis of sovkhoz rates for wages, do we not overstate costs to the farm (at least where sovkhoz wage rates are higher than kolkhoz distributions) and, accordingly, understate the extent to which management will be motivated to produce more? While it is true that cost were not being calculated until the mid and late 1950s and management was not being evaluated on the basis of cost performance per se, nevertheless it would seem reasonable to suggest that management must have

[9] Bonuses may motivate managers to overfulfill targets. However, since overfulfillment will likely induce higher targets in the following period, significant overfulfillment would be avoided. Whether above quota prices are important here would depend upon the specific nature of the bonus arrangements.

had some motivation to conserve inputs given the fact income (even though gross) was a success indicator. Also, management must have understood to some degree the possibility of increasing distributions by reduction of inputs to the extent that targets for the latter did not appear explicitly among plan goals.

The basic difficulty with this sort of theorizing is the fact that a significant portion of kolkhoz costs (and indeed the entire operation of the kolkhoz) was "in-kind." Much of the labor and MTS payments, for example, were not in monetary form, yet in the absence of valuation of some sort, the tools of economic theory are simply of no use. The question remains, how do we value the in-kind portion of labor payments, for example?

Given the labor intensive nature of agricultural production during the early stages of industrialization, the question of labor payments is significant. From the point of view of the individual farm, though probably not from the point of view of the economy as a whole, it would seem that the relevant "cost" for the in-kind portion of labor payments would depend upon whether the farm is operating according to case #1, #2 or #3 as outlined above. One can argue that from the managerial point of view (which is relevant since the center was not involved in cost calculation), the manager was rewarded for above quota output, and since it was this product that must have been utilized to induce labor to participate in its production, the "cost" of labor is the opportunity cost of the products with which labor is paid. If the manager is in fact motivated by above quota prices, one could argue that this price is in fact the opportunity cost, and accordingly, the in-kind payment to labor should be valued at the above quota (or possibly the kolkhoz market) prices. In this case, kolkhoz production costs would surely be above those calculated on the basis of sovkhoz norms. On the other hand, to the extent that base prices are said to be the relevant "motivators" then these should be utilized to value the labor payment.

A similar argument could be made for the in-kind portion of the payment for MTS services. These, together with labor payments, must have accounted for a significant portion of kolkhoz costs of production.

Returning to our cost-price comparisons, it would seem that where above quota prices are thought to be relevant and accordingly are utilized to value the labor input, kolkhoz production costs will most likely be significantly higher than those calculated on the basis of sovkhoz wage rates (even for the early years when presumably the difference between sovkhoz wages and kolkhoz distributions must have been greater), given the significant difference between base and above quota prices. In contrast to what is frequently argued, therefore, we may not be significantly wide of the mark if managerial motivation is characterized in terms of a comparison between cost as calculated at sovkhoz wage rates and average procurement price. To the extent that such a comparison is justified, managerial motivation to increase output by increasing the magnitude of labor inputs beyond that called for under the compulsory minimum levels must not have been great in light of the cost-price data assembled in Table 7-4. However, if management is maximizing gross output under constraints, pursuit of labor-day earnings will remain relevant though managerial expectations re the "price" of labor will be revised upward and, other things equal, less will be utilized.

In light of what has been said thus far, can we consider the long run development and general health of the farm, and indeed, the personal development and promotion of management as success indicators of any significance? To answer in the affirmative, it would be necessary to demonstrate that there were managerial rewards greater than those available for the peasants, and that the manager was in fact able to move towards the achievement of these rewards.

The results of our investigation of managerial rewards would suggest that these rewards, at least for the early years, must have played a minimal role in motivating management. Although both absolutely and vis-a-vis peasant earnings managerial earnings have risen significantly, the bonus portion, or that portion of earnings tied directly to priority goals, has risen very little. Also, these gains in managerial earnings must have been partially illusory insofar as a mechanism for managerial motivation was concerned. Managerial control over the utilization of the farm resources remains limited, and improved incomes were in large part generated from forces outside the kolkhoz. Finally, there has been a significant expansion of the responsibilities placed upon the farm chairman, especially in the light of a greatly expanded farm over which management must have control. Quite apart from the source of increased managerial rewards, these increases were surely well beyond the time horizons of many chairmen. In a real sense, therefore, there were no long-term managerial rewards for chairmen, a picture not improved by high mobility and the relative absence of promotion into better positions.

Under these circumstances, the degree to which a manager could feel either immediate or long run pride in farm operations must have been limited and certainly would not have been enhanced by low income, short tenure, "outside" status vis-a-vis the kolkhoz members and the sharply increasing size of the typical kolkhoz which greatly complicated communication with the membership.

At least for the early years of the period covered by this study, kolkhoz managers must have had very limited freedom of decision making. Quite apart from the absence of a concern with and quest for economic efficiency and rationality during these years, centralized targets and external control remained the essence of the system. The latter was significant and tended to increase through mechanisms such as the MTS and the Communist Party structure within the kolkhoz. A high degree of external control must have been especially confusing to the competent manager, and even more so in light of multiple and not always clearly delineated goals.

If the system itself did not always provide a consistent and complete set of goals and "rules of the game," the management team was itself no better prepared to meet the challenge. In the absence of cost accounting techniques and with the generation and utilization of technological information largely a function of specialists external to the farm, management simply lacked the tools and the framework for decision making.

While it is true that price increases (apart from their questionable role in directly motivating management) did serve to improve farm income and, thus, rewards to labor, these gains were limited in the early years of our study. In addition, we have noted that some gains were achieved through means largely beyond the control of the individual manager, for example, amalgamation.[10]

The system of multiple prices in combination with administratively determined production (and other) targets raises complex questions pertaining to managerial behavior. For the post-1958 period, however, we find a substantially new system with the introduction of cost accounting and the abolition of multiple pricing (until the mid 1960s).

The price reform of 1958 was important in two major respects. First, multiple pricing was abolished and in its place was to stand a set of prices which would be basically stable though subject to change according to the production conditions of the particular year.[11] Second, with the introduction of cost analysis, a new policy would encourage regional specialization by the state purchase of agricultural produce where production costs were lowest. In theory, these changes could be of great importance, for with price adjustments in combination with cost analysis and a procurement policy based upon this analysis, the rudiments of a fundamental economic mechanism to direct agricultural activity was in the making.

From the point of view of managerial behavior, single level pricing and the introduction of costing procedures should allow us to depart from the sort of analysis previously considered. In particular, cost reductions and the motivational role of price policy need no longer be viewed as *independent* of each other. Further, a new procurement policy should allow a degree of managerial freedom in the determination of output patterns rather than the full determination of these within the plan.

Quite apart from the utilization of relative procurement price levels as a mechanism to manipulate production patterns, we have noted that during the early and mid 1950s, for many products, average state procurement prices did not cover kolkhoz costs of production, and hence farms were forced to bear significant losses. This undesirable state of affairs, especially from the point of view of incentives, was one of the major revelations when cost accounting was first introduced in the mid 1950s.

Throughout the 1950s and into the 1960s, however, substantial price increases for the products purchased from kolkhozy reduced or eliminated the

[10]Increased payment for the stewardship of a larger farm is quite proper, although this sort of increase is within the control of the manager himself only to the degree that those "promoted" to the chairmanship of a bigger farm were in fact selected for their prior performance, and that this procedure would in fact be known to managers.

[11] A.N. Malafeev, *Istoriia tsenoobrazovaniia v SSSR (1917-1963 gg.)* (Moskva: Mysl', 1964), p. 302.

undesirable cost-price relationships of earlier years. By the late 1950s, the production of most field crops was profitable (see Table 7-3), although through 1960, the production of most animal products remained unprofitable (see Table 7-4).[12]

Table 7-3

Profitability of Selected Field Crops on Collective Farms of the USSR, 1958 (Rubles Per Centner)

	Kolkhoz Cost of Production	Actual Purchase Price	Profit (%)
Grain	4.0	6.1	53.0
Sunflower	3.2	14.8	363.0
Potatoes	3.4	4.2	24.0
Vegetables	5.5	7.8	42.0
Sugar beets	1.2	2.3	92.0
Cotton	16.5	33.7	104.0
Flax	63.7	16.6	161.0
Tobacco	84.6	116.8	38.0

Source: A.N. Malafeev, *Istoriia tsenoobrazovaniia v SSSR* (1917-1963 gg.) (Moskva: Mysl', 1964), p. 294. See Table 7-4 for a comment on methodology employed in the calculation of production costs.

Table 7-4

Profitability of Selected Meat Products on Collective Farms, USSR (Rubles per Centner)

	Cost	1958 Purchase Price	Profit (%)	Cost	1960 Purchase Price	Profit (%)
Increase in weight of young and fattened animals:						
Cattle	93.2	54.6	(−41)	91.6	59.1	(−46)
Sheep	41.3	49.3	19	52.6	51.6	(−2)
Swine	130.2	79.3	(−39)	122.6	82.3	(−33)
Chicken						
(live weight)	125.4	81.5	(−35)	140.5	82.2	(−41)
Milk	12.6	11.3	(−10)	13.3	11.4	(−14)
Wool	267.8	376.1	40	260.7	373.4	43
Eggs ('000)	92.2	61.7	(−33)	93.0	60.0	(−35)

Source: A.N. Malafeev, *Istoriia tsenoobrazovaniia v SSSR* (1917-1963 gg.) (Moskva: Mysl', 1964), p. 297. Malafeev cites the statistical handbook *Narodnoe khoziaistvo* as the source for cost data. The official practice for cost calculation has been: (1) seed, forage, etc. at internal kolkhoz cost; (2) purchased materials at purchase prices plus transport charges; (3) labor at sovkhoz norms; (4) amortization at state farm norms.

[12]In 1962, an effort was made to improve the very unfavorable cost-price ratios in the animal breeding sector. See "O povyshenii zakupochnykh (sdatochnykh) tsen na krupnyi rogati skot, svinei, ovets, ptitsu, maslo, zhivotnoe i slivki i roznichnykh tsen na miaso, miasnye produkty i maslow zhivotnoe," as cited in *Sbornik*, pp. 595-597.

During the 1960s, kolkhoz production costs for most products increased, most likely accounted for by increases in payments to labor (see Table 7-5). However, state procurement prices also continued to increase during the 1960s (see Table 7-6), and indeed for some products, these increases were very significant. For most agricultural products, production became profitable by the second half of the 1960s (see Table 7-7).[13] Considering the magnitude of price increases for some products (in the animal sector for example), it is little wonder that Khrushchev achieved minimal success in attempting to increase meat output under the very unfavorable cost-price ratios prevailing in the 1950s. It must be noted, of course, that regional differentials remain important, and, in the absence of significant differentiation in regional purchase prices (and with existing costing procedures), some kolkhozy will necessarily earn large "profits" while others will suffer large "losses."

With the abolition of compulsory deliveries and the establishment of a single level pricing system in 1958, the state instituted a policy of purchasing grain in

Table 7-5
Index of Average Production Cost of Selected Agricultural Products on Kolkhozy of the USSR (1960 = 100)

	1964	1968
Grain (without corn)	120	122
Cotton	136	172
Sugar beets	129	150
Sunflower	84	135
Potatoes	125	159
Vegetables	116	143
Cattle[a]	108	123
Swine	108	97
Sheep	121	141
Milk	122	126
Eggs	91	76
Wool	117	137

Sources: Computed from *Narkhoz-1961*, p. 426; *Narkhoz-1964*, pp. 394-395; *Narkhoz-1968*, pp. 428-429.

Note: Data for the years 1960 and 1964 are based upon kolkhoz labor costed at sovkhoz norms; for the year 1968, kolkhoz labor is costed by actual distributions in money and product. This procedure may introduce a downward bias in the index since in most instances for the early years sovkhoz norms would be higher than actual kolkhoz payments, while for the latter years, actual distributions would remain below, though probably only marginally, the sovkhoz norms.

[a]Includes newborn cattle and increases in weight through fattening.

[13]In 1965, a modified form of the two-level pricing system was restored in the form of a 50 percent bonus for above quota delivery of grain to the state. The criticisms made of the earlier system could also apply here. For a discussion of these changes, see Alec Nove, "Soviet Agriculture Under Brezhnev," *Slavic Review*, vol. 29, no. 3 (September 1970), pp. 379-410.

Table 7-6

Index of Average State Purchase Price of Agricultural Products Purchased from Kolkhozy, Kolkhoz Members and Workers(1952 = 100)

	1953	1954	1955	1956	1957	1958	1959	1965
All agr. products:	154	207	209	251	266	296	302	413
Field crops	132	171	169	207	209	203	206	253
Grain crops	236	739	553	634	617	695	743	1,081
Wheat	245	752	524	647	603	621	656	918
Rye	169	730	668	625	622	1,047	1,114	1,610
Oats	119	617	561	550	642	783	862	1,440
Barley	152	601	592	458	598	888	926	1,485
Millet	718	1,426	1,029	1,014	1,033	1,260	1,342	2,342
Corn	207	564	685	572	738	819	1,008	1,667
Buckwheat	221	460	496	441	535	886	1,386	2,129
Rice-silk	146	243	748	887	846	957	967	1,520
(Technical crops)	122	125	137	163	166	155	154	158
Cotton-silk	105	102	96	114	115	106	107	122
Flax	139	166	215	213	216	239	218	176
Sugar beets	144	111	130	229	243	219	217	276
Sunflower	528	626	987	928	947	774	881	854
Grapes and fruits	119	135	138	192	188	179	169	160
Potatoes	316	369	368	814	859	789	834	1,470
Animal products	214	307	319	371	420	546	561	845
Cattle	338	476	464	508	604	1,147	1,226	2,430
Pigs	453	786	806	976	1,151	1,156	1,181	1,990
Milk and milk products	202	289	303	334	362	404	404	535

Sources: *Sel'khoz-1960*, p. 117; P.A. Ignatovskii, *Sotsial'no-Ekonomicheskie izmeneniia v Sovetskoi derevne* (Moskva: Nauka, 1966), p. 242.

Note: The data in this table should be utilized with an element of caution. Although the methodology of calculation is not explicit in *Sel'khoz-1960*, presumably we have a weighted index. However, to consider field crops as an example, the overall increase for all field crops is troublingly small in the light of increases for each of the sub-categories.

low cost regions where, it was asserted, zonal prices should allow all kolkhozy and sovkhozy to be profitable.[14] These zonal prices were established on the basis of sovkhoz costs of production in the immediate region (sovkhoz costs were normally lower than kolkhoz costs).[15] Prices were to be differentiated by union republics and, within the republics, by zones. For the entire area of the RSFSR, however, there were only eight purchase zones for grain, seven for sun-

[14]Nancy Nimitz, "Soviet Agricultural Prices and Costs," op. cit., p. 268.

[15]Ibid., p. 260.

Table 7-7
Production Costs and Actual Receipts from Sales to the State by Kolkhozy, 1960-1967 (Rubles Per Ton)

Product	1960		1962		1964		1966		1967	
	Cost	Receipts	Cost	Receipts	Cost	Receipts	Cost	Receipts	Cost	Receipts
Grain	40	62	37	80	44	85	45	101	48	103
Sunflower	37	139	30	139	30	173	45	224	45	214
Sugar beets	14	23	16	23	17	29	22	29	21	27
Cotton	207	341	224	341	281	390	332	438	352	452
Milk	133	114	129	122	151	123	160	156	163	149
Meat (from cattle)	916	591	834	764	927	805	1,048	1,151	1,089	1,201
Swine	1,226	823	1,146	953	1,250	1,061	1,173	1,401	1,183	1,451
Mutton	526	516	512	541	609	537	692	760	718	849

Sources: Cost data for 1960 from *Narkhoz-1961*, p. 426; all remaining cost data and all receipts data from V.R. Boev, *Zakupochnye tseny i chistyi dokhod kolkhozov* (Moskva: Kolos, 1969), pp. 51, 57.

Note: All kolkhoz cost data is based upon actual distributions of money and product for the costing of labor inputs. The cost and receipts data in this table can be considered as broadly comparable, although a measure of caution is suggested. An examination of the above cited monograph by V.R. Boev indicates that the product categories are not fully consistent as between cost and receipts data.

flower, seven for cattle and so on.[16] Furthermore, the largest zonal price difference (in 1961) for the purchase of grain was 35 percent, for sunflower 41 percent, and for cattle 36 percent.[17] At the same time, the maximal zonal cost of grain production in kolkhozy exceeded the minimal zonal cost by six times, the comparable figure for sunflower was three times and for cattle roughly two times.[18] In effect, regional price differentiation was wholly inadequate to meet the very wide regional cost variations, a criticism which has remained relevant throughout the 1960s.

Regional production specialization and the utilization of appropriate pricing arrangements to achieve such an end may be a very worthwhile pursuit, and yet it would probably be a mistake to view the late 1950s and early 1960s as even a preliminary attempt to generate specialization through local managerial response to profit indicators. Throughout this period, as we have noted, plan targets brought down from above remained the essential determinant of farm activity. The notion of profitability is seen as desirable, and yet to jump from this position to one where profit becomes a determinant of future managerial action is a significant step, since profitability has always been an element of the khozraschet system and has meant little more than the general notion that revenues should cover costs.

On those collective farms visited by the writer, specialization, either by farm or by brigade within farms, simply did not exist. For the most part, each farm grew the main crops and each farm also raised animals and produced various animal products. In addition, each brigade was organized on the basis of producing some of most of the crops grown by the farm as a whole. While cost analysis was introduced at the brigade level, where one brigade might be operating at high cost vis-a-vis other brigades, the strategy was one of treating the high cost brigade as a sick member of the group. Either the accounting department or, in some cases, a team from the local agricultural institute would be called in to seek out the causal factors. In short, plan targets determined output patterns, and while it was desirable that the kolkhoz should be profitable, the costs of production in each brigade would be roughly similar and all should resemble those on neighboring kolkhozy—and this would be a normal and desirable state of affairs.

Production specialization need not, of course, arise as a local managerial response to cost-price differentials. The desire for profitability at the kolkhoz level might be viewed as the development of an improved *incentive* system to insure appropriate managerial response to plan goals, specialization and other patterns of change being expressed within the plan goals. The case of grain production, clearly a high priority crop in the Soviet case, is instructive.

Under the policy instigated by Khrushchev, the state was to purchase grain from low cost regions and hence encourage regional specialization. The cost-

[16] A.N. Malafeev, op. cit., p. 302.
[17] Ibid.
[18] Ibid.

price data assembled in Table 7-7 indicate that in some regions, average purchase price did not cover production costs. To the extent that managers could significantly manipulate their crop patterns, one would expect to see output decline in the high cost regions, and at the same time the proportion of state purchases obtained from the high cost areas should decline.

Turning to Table 7-8, it is apparent that, in general, the proportion of grain

Table 7-8

Cost and Average Purchase Price in Rubles Per Ton of Grain (Without Corn) on Collective Farms, 1962

Region	Cost of Production (Labor Valued at Actual Outlays)	Average Purchase Price
USSR	37.00	80.00
RSFSR	35.10	76.00
North-West	119.40	59.00
Central	62.40	73.00
Volga-Viatka	56.20	77.00
Central Chernozem	28.40	75.00
Volga	31.60	84.00
North Caucasus	22.00	73.00
Urals	33.10	75.00
West Siberia	41.20	73.00
East Siberia	43.30	71.00
Far East	70.90	75.00
Ukrainian S.S.R.	33.00	92.00
Belorussian S.S.R.	79.00	88.00
Uzbek S.S.R.	75.00	109.00
Kazakh S.S.R.	40.00	79.00
Georgian S.S.R.	79.00	76.00
Azerbaidzhan S.S.R.	68.00	79.00
Lithuanian S.S.R.	106.00	82.00
Moldavian S.S.R.	40.00	71.00
Latvian S.S.R.	126.00	79.00
Kirgiz S.S.R.	48.00	78.00
Tadzhik S.S.R.	84.00	87.00
Armenian S.S.R.	82.00	63.00
Turkmen S.S.R.	83.00	76.00
Estonian S.S.R.	84.00	77.00

Source: N.M. Studenkova, *Metodika ischisleniia sebestoimosti produktsii v kolkhozakh i sovkhozakh* (Moskva: Ekonomika, 1965), p. 31.

procured has been higher in the low than in the high cost areas.[19] However, it must be noted (Table 7-9) that while the proportion of grain procured in high cost regions declined (1958-1960) there was no proportionate increase in exactions from the low cost areas. In fact, after 1960, such exactions increased in

Table 7-9

Share of Grain Procurements in Total Grain Output: U.S.S.R., 1954-58, 1958-64 (Percentages)

	1954-1958	1958	1959	1960	1961	1962	1963	1964
USSR	39.5	42.0	39.0	37.2	39.8	40.4	41.7	44.9
RSFSR	41.2	41.3	39.4	38.1	40.0	41.9	42.6	44.8
Northwest	9.4	3.8	2.6	.9	10.0	6.7	16.0	11.7
Center	22.3	18.1	14.0	8.5	19.5	18.7	24.6	20.4
Volga-Viatka	25.2	20.2	22.7	16.2	15.2	22.3	26.1	20.8
Central Chernozem	37.4	37.0	37.9	29.6	39.3	36.4	37.0	38.6
Volga	42.7	48.5	42.9	43.5	50.0	51.3	48.8	53.1
North Caucasus	43.6	42.6	40.8	40.6	47.0	48.3	57.0	47.5
Urals	38.4	32.9	44.1	42.4	41.8	46.5	42.1	45.9
West Siberia	52.5	55.0	47.8	48.8	43.8	32.4	13.9	52.3
East Siberia	41.0	37.2	39.8	36.2	36.2	39.2	42.6	38.1
Far East	26.7	16.2	21.0	28.2	24.6	32.8	34.3	31.3
Ukrainian SSR	31.0	32.9	31.6	27.0	37.9	37.1	44.1	37.8
Belorussian SSR	13.5	9.3	10.2	8.5	11.6	14.3	16.1	15.2
Uzbek SSR	31.8	29.3	20.0	17.1	19.8	24.8	34.2	47.8
Kazakh SSR	60.4	67.4	60.5	56.2	51.5	51.7	45.2	64.7
Georgian SSR	10.9	5.1	3.3	.3	10.4	5.8	28.8	15.2
Azerbaidzhan SSR	24.1	21.3	16.2	14.9	12.2	20.1	31.2	25.9
Moldavian SSR	18.2	14.6	16.2	17.4	20.9	24.4	40.3	25.7
Latvian SSR	8.8	3.6	4.3	2.8	12.2	5.2	25.6	15.7
Kirgiz SSR	22.1	16.8	12.0	19.3	7.0	22.6	26.6	23.5
Tadzhik SSR	13.1	10.7	6.5	2.3	11.6	12.6	22.0	21.4
Armenian SSR	14.7	11.0	1.2	.6	2.3	14.0	23.2	18.8
Turkmen SSR	7.0	5.5	.2	2.5	20.0	12.1	29.0	27.7
Estonian SSR	5.5	.2	4.5	.3	8.2	3.6	16.8	11.3

Source: Jerzy K. Karcz, "Seven Years on the Farm: Retrospect and Prospects," *New Directions in the Soviet Economy* (Washington, D.C.: U.S. Government Printing Office, 1966), p. 411.

Note: Output in physical weight; procurements in accounting weight.

[19]Ideally, one should consider the proportion of total state grain procurements exacted from each region. As a proxy, we utilize the proportion of grain output of each region procured by the state on the assumption that this proportion would decline in high cost regions were Khrushchev's policy actively implemented.

all areas. In the light of this evidence, what can be said about state purchase policy? Given the importance of grain in the Soviet planners preference function, and also given the fact that Soviet grain stocks declined steadily from 23 million tons in 1956 to 2.1 million tons in 1963, it is not clear why the proportion of grain purchases from low cost areas (as a proportion of their output) did not increase during the period 1958-1960.[20] It may be that attempts were made, but, in the absence of higher relative prices for grain crops, managers or local officials may have been unwilling to shift further into grain production. In the period after 1960, it would appear that faced with declining domestic grain stocks and the continuing importation of grain from abroad, Soviet leaders opted to return to increased grain exactions from all regions. Thus the possibility of greater specialization through greater price differentials was, at least implicitly, rejected.

It should be noted that in those areas indicated by Karcz to be marginal grain production regions, there were some important shifts in the period 1959-1965.[21] The relevant data are assembled in Table 7-10. After 1960, the share of grain procured tended to increase in all areas, while the area sown to grain tended to decline in the marginal areas, although rather slowly. In part, therefore, increased grain exactions from the high cost areas may have come about after kolkhoz managers had begun to shift to the production of more profitable crops. If this was in fact the case, subsequent pressure by the state for

Table 7-10

Area Sown to all Grain Crops on Collective Farms: Selected Regions ('000 Hectares)

Region	1959	1962	1965
RSFSR			
Northwest	1,190	. . .	541
Center	3,933	. . .	3,884
Volga-Viatka	4,329	. . .	3,173
Georgian SSR	465	352	347
Azerbaidzhan SSR	752	672	470
Lithuanian SSR	783	644	692
Latvian SSR	432	407	425
Armenian SSR	218	184	148
Estonian SSR	209	191	193

Source: *Narkhoz-1959*, p. 431; *Narkhoz-1962*, p. 345; *Narkhoz-1965*, p. 290.

[20] Nancy Nimitz, *Soviet Government Grain Procurements, Dispositions and Stocks, 1940, 1945-1963* (Santa Monica: The Rand Corporation, 1964), p. 58.

[21] The data is presented and the case discussed in Jerzy F. Karcz, "Seven Years on the Farm: Retrospect and Prospects," op. cit.

continued grain deliveries might tend to make kolkhoz managers increasingly conservative when future specialization programs are at stake.

It is apparent that throughout the period under study, price-cost relationships must have been of very limited value in promoting appropriate managerial responses, even responses to the achievement of plan targets. While it is true that significant price increases have improved this situation, it remains to consider the extent to which the other side of the coin—costing techniques—are in any sense rational.

Cost Accounting

The pre-1956 period was characterized by a high degree of centralization of decision making, planning largely in physical terms and the direct plan specification of input-output mixes. Cost accounting was not discussed, and accordingly the extent to which kolkhozy were being asked to suffer "losses" was unknown. In the mid 1950s, however, it was generally assumed that production costs on kolkhozy were higher than those on sovkhozy, and Khrushchev intended to change this undesirable state of affairs.

When the introduction of cost accounting was first discussed in the early and mid 1950s, there were two broad sorts of difficulties.[22] First, there were necessarily questions pertaining to the inadequacy of basic data available for costing purposes. Second, and more important for the present discussion, there were difficulties of measurement, especially pertaining to the labor input (partly due to the labor-day per se, but also due to its large in-kind component) and, in addition, the payment for MTS services largely carried out on an in-kind basis.

The labor input in kolkhozy was valued in two ways. In some instances, state farm wage rates as utilized on nearby sovkhozy were utilized, while in other instances actual distributions to kolkhoz members were utilized, the in-kind portion of payment being valued at state purchase prices. The techniques for handling the MTS payments were similar. In some cases, MTS costs were calculated as costs to the state, that is, outlays on fuel, wages and so on. In other instances, the definition was based upon outlays actually made by the farm, in-kind payments being valued according to kolkhoz costs of production. The differences were probably not of major importance, and hence the debate need not be pursued at this point.[23] The question of valuing MTS services was resolved in 1958 with the abolition of the MTS, and the matter of labor costing was resolved in 1966 when state farm norms were used to introduce a wage system into kolkhozy thus ending the famous labor-day system. In fact, during the years im-

---

[22]This discussion is based upon Nancy Nimitz, "Soviet Agricultural Prices and Costs," op. cit., pp. 239-284. See especially p. 256 ff.

[23]Ignoring the differences arising from methodological differences, Nancy Nimitz observes that ". . . their results may have been broadly comparable." See ibid., p. 258.

mediately preceding the abandonment of the labor-day as a measurement device, distributions to kolkhoz members by kolkhozy increased substantially, gradually bringing them closer to the level of wages being paid on state farms.

Apart from the mechanics of cost accounting, the introduction of this management tool raises broader issues. For those economists trained in the competitive cost-profit calculus of the introductory economics textbook, the entire range of issues associated with cost accounting procedures, pricing and so on raises the issue of a managerial system or, in essence, the extent to which there is a parametric framework in which managers operate. Is there such a framework in which there is operative a cost-profit calculus, however crude, such that when appropriate motivation prevails (presumably managerial rewards for profit achievement, or at a minimum, incentive towards cost reduction and output expansion), the decentralized responses of the managerial personnel to the "signals" of the system will in any significant measure produce appropriate (goal oriented) behavior? That is, will there be a long run tendency for output expansion, cost reduction and a general pattern of innovative behavior to enhance the health of the organization?

To some degree, our examination of the Soviet kolkhoz has been couched within this sort of framework, and when we examine the "rationality" of monetization, it is normally along the lines of examining the nature of managerial behavior within the context outlined above. To proceed on this basis probably overstates, possibly in signficant degree, the functions to be performed by the khozraschet system. In a significant sense, monetization has been subservient to the planning system, and while the introduction of cost accounting is certainly a significant improvement in the nature of the managerial system in kolkhozy, the fine tuning of managerial decisions will not be one of the functions of this new tool. Rather, cost accounting will point out broad changes which will be made through the conventional arrangements of the planning system.

These considerations are important for two reasons. First, cost accounting is not, in and of itself, of any value to an organization. The purpose of cost accounting is to provide *information* such that managerial decisions can, in some sense, be more rational. Second, in the case of the kolkhoz, the costing arrangements have to a large extent produced a system of "messages" which differed depending upon whether they were read centrally or locally. It matters, therefore, who uses the cost data and for what purposes.

In general, costs are calculated for individual crops, being the aggregate of direct and indirect expenditures. By-products are properly excluded and cost is defined as expenses incurred, thus recognizing the traditional concept that cost need not involve outlay. For the compilation of an aggregate cost figure, two concepts are distinguished: production cost *(proizvodstvennyi sebestoimost')* defined to include all actual expenses up to and including the storage of the final product; full cost *(polnyi sebestoimost')* defined to include all actual expenses associated with "realized" production or sale of the product. Thus full cost would be greater than production costs to the extent that there are transportation and other costs associated with the sale of the product. Profit is the difference between full costs and the monetary proceeds realized from the sale of the product.

In addition to methodological problems already discussed, the introduction of costing procedures in Soviet kolkhozy raises a fundamental problem—that of utilizing an economic calculus based largely upon physical "norms" rather than value parameters. In the case of labor costs, for example, various means have been utilized to move away from an in-kind, and hence non-additive, cost to a value, and hence additive, cost. The ultimate resolution of the problem through the introduction of state farm wage rates is itself only a partial solution. Thus in the absence of a labor market (with due recognition of the likelihood of greater market influence in the allocation of labor than other factors of production), we do not know whether wage rates represent rates of transformation in production in sovkhozy, let alone in kolkhozy.

But what about material inputs, where prices are centrally determined? Consider the utilization of a tractor. In a competitive system, the costing problem is one of allocating a certain portion of the capital cost of the tractor (that utilized on the given job), plus those current inputs also for the specific job. The usual procedure would be on a time or area basis, where outlays on current expenditures are added to a portion of the expended life of the tractor, and accordingly, a cost per unit of land or per time unit for cultivation is achieved.

In the Soviet case, the determination of cost is typically a two stage procedure based not upon outlays, but rather upon the subjective evaluation of "norms" which are usually generated for regions and interpreted within each farm. For example, the volume of tractor services allocated to the plowing of a particular piece of land is spelled out within the plan documents, and, in particular, the technological map *(tekhnologicheskaia karta)*. Land will be ranked according to degrees of plowing difficulty (for example in terms of the terrain, presence of rocks and so on). This scale, according to Soviet comment is typically different in different regions and in each is given local interpretation. Thus where a particular piece of land falls on the scale (for purposes of allocating tractor services within the plan) will be a subjective determination of management within the collective farm. In a sense, one can criticize depreciation norms in a market system insofar as they may not, for a given job, accurately represent that portion of the asset (the tractor) actually "used up," and yet, in the Soviet case, the subjective interpretation of regional scales may well make intra-regional and indeed inter-regional comparisons meaningless.

For accounting purposes, the value expression of the above physically allocated tractor services will be based upon a state scale setting forth the appropriate ruble "cost" of a given tractor operating on a given type of land for a specified period of time. Again, at this stage, the value translation of the previously physically expressed tractor services will be based upon a regionally developed value scale interpreted subjectively within each kolkhoz.

To the extent that these technological norms and their value interpretation differ from "reality" but are similarly interpreted for each farm *within* a region, intra-regional norms differ by significant amounts, inter-regional comparisons may be less meaningful, and it is these that are of primary interest to central planners.

The question of norm setting is the subject of continual discussion in the Soviet press. In addition to the setting of norms on a regional basis, thus presenting the possibility of non-comparability as among regions, there is also the problem of infrequent revision of norms in spite of constantly changing conditions, for example: the introduction of new equipment, new levels of mechanization and so on. In theory, each collective farm is to have a commission which, on an annual basis, is to revise norms in accordance with higher directives, with research carried out by local agricultural institutes and with the perception of changing local conditions. The setting of these norms is the subject of continual complaint, focusing upon their technical inaccuracy and/or the exaggeration of their transformation into value terms. The following comment was made by a Soviet author in 1959:

To this day many collective farms are using obsolete model output norms that were established about ten years ago. They are considerably lower than the state farm norms. The piece rate payments, on the other hand, are too high.[24]

Another author, commenting upon the ranges normally specified by "local agricultural agencies" comments:

In fact what happens is that the collective farm established the lowest norm and sets the highest valuation on it.[25]

In some cases, for example, vegetable growing, norms are frequently not worked out at all.[26] When these norms are utilized, they are seldom changed even when procedures are mechanized. In short, the problem of establishing proper norms, whether they be for deciding appropriate input or output levels, remains a problem for kolkhozy. In a recent work, one Soviet economist has pointed out how fundamentally the problem of norm setting can complicate the operations of the kolkhoz:

Thus in practice kolkhoz plan indicators of yield and productivity on the average significantly outstrip their factual level, and if in the economy the plans are fre-

[24]"Double Labor Productivity on Collective Farms," *Izvestia*, March 29, 1959, p. 1, translated and reprinted in *CDSP*, vol. XI, no. 13 (April 29, 1959).

[25]A. Larionov, "On Establishing Norms for Collective Farm Labor," *Izvestia*, November 21, 1958, p. 3, translated and reprinted in *CDSP*, vol. X, no. 47 (December 31, 1958), p. 14.

[26]A. Mischenko, *Novyi poriadok planirovaniia kolkhoznogo proizvodstva* (Moskva: Moskovskii rabochii, 1957), p. 16.

quently not fulfilled, then the system of payment for production is not activated and earnings are carried out only for the fulfillment of work.[27]

The writer suggests that these sorts of norms be established on the basis of an examination of actual performance of the previous 4-5 years with a 5-10 percent annual increase, a system similar to that being used for output determination in the Krasnodar Region.[28]

Apart from methodological problems of establishing a useful and rational cost accounting system, there are a number of practical complications.

First, there is the range of issues associated with accounting at brigade and ferma levels as opposed to a system which operates at the kolkhoz level only. This is an important issue to the extent that the brigade structure of the 1970s will be similar to the overall kolkhoz structure of the 1950s. While khozraschet and accompanying cost accounting procedures have been discussed for both the kolkhoz and brigade levels, there has been a continuing emphasis in Soviet writings suggesting that the brigade is fundamentally different from the kolkhoz in the sense that the latter is concerned with both production and distribution of the product, while the former should be concerned solely with production matters. On this basis, there has been a tendency to define cost differently at the kolkhoz and brigade levels, and, in particular, to assign costs associated with distribution, and more important, overhead costs, to the kolkhoz level.

Second, as we shall see in Chapter 8, there has been a critical shortage of adequately trained accountants in the Soviet rural sector, and in general, only very limited training of other personnel in financial and economic matters. This lack of personnel has been especially severe at the brigade level, and yet it is precisely at this level that the application of costing procedures is most important.

The initial moves towards the development of an adequate accounting system will undoubtedly benefit both local managers and central planners. For the period under study, however, the system has basically been in an introductory stage. To some degree, planners have begun to consider the messages from the costing system, although within the individual farm, the system seems to have operated mainly in terms of setting constraints or upper cost limits, thus allowing a comparison of performance as among brigades and farms.

Summary

In this chapter we have examined selected aspects of the pricing system, which in conjunction with the introduction of cost accounting into Soviet collective

---

[27]M.V. Mikhailov, *Planirovanie i rezhim ekonomiki v kolkhozakh* (Moskva: Ekonomika, 1965), p. 36.
[28]Ibid.

farms bear significantly upon the nature of the framework within which managers make decisions.

For the 1950s, average state procurement prices were typically below, and in some cases substantially below, kolkhoz costs of production, although the latter were unknown until the introduction of cost accounting into kolkhozy in the mid and late 1950s. This state of affairs must have had a strong negative impact upon any potential managerial motivation to expand output and/or lower production costs. At the same time, the two-level pricing system (abandoned in 1958), in addition to suffering from the undesirable features emphasized by Alec Nove and others (i.e. higher average prices in good years), may have lacked any redeeming features in terms of above-quota prices motivating output expansion. In the light of the prevailing planning arrangements (short-term targets, frequent adjustment and so on), it would seem that managers could expect only marginal and at best short run gains to be achieved from the attempted expansion of output in pursuit of the higher above quota prices. These sorts of criticisms remain relevant to the system prevailing in the mid and late 1960s when partial two-level pricing was re-introduced, although the introduction in practice of meaningful long-term planning could remove a major defect of the system.

Throughout the 1950s and 1960s price increases (state purchase prices) have been significant, and indeed for some products dramatic. Thus while kolkhoz production costs are on the average generally covered by the new higher purchase prices, the precise meaning of a "profitable" kolkhoz remains to be elaborated. In particular, if a cost-profit calculus is intended to serve as an operative framework for managerial decisions, even to a limited degree, certain problems must be resolved. In fact, even if the messages of a cost-profit system are to bear upon a limited number of decisions made within the traditional planning system and at the center, costing methodology, land rent charges, capital charges and related issues must be resolved.

It is significant that the kolkhoz has shifted away from a physical planning system towards the utilization of value-targeted variables, and yet the utilization of this system to make regional and temporal cost comparisons and related input-output adjustments is at a very early stage.

8 Characteristics of Managerial Personnel

Thus far the focus of this study has been the decision making patterns of the kolkhoz and certain organs closely related to the kolkhoz. The present chapter focuses upon the characteristic features of managerial personnel—examining age structure; the role of the Communist Party and Party membership; and finally, nature, source and amount of education.

The theoretical underpinnings of the present chapter are at best ill-defined. If this is true for the study of industrial management in the west, it is all the more true for the study of agricultural management in the east. Furthermore, the nature of the data limits our analysis and in particular necessitates heavy reliance upon a cross-section view utilizing the 1959 census of the Soviet population.

In spite of the above complication, characteristics of managerial personnel are of interest to the extent such characteristics are thought to measurably influence, in roughly definable directions, the outcomes of the decision making process. To the extent possible, these directions will be spelled out in relation to each characteristic. We shall examine managerial characteristics and their impact upon decisions, but with an interest, also, in the Soviet attitude towards agricultural managers, and in particular, how Soviet leaders perceive "appropriate" training and development of managerial personnel. To the extent that light can be shed on these matters, it will be possible to comment more sensibly on the possible future patterns of local decision making in conjunction with a changing economic environment, for example, changing managerial patterns at the brigade level.

Age and Sex Structure

Examination of age and sex variables can tell us something about the nature of the managerial group and especially Soviet attitudes on the question of who should perform managerial functions. Soviet writers have themselves suggested that there is discrimination against women which increases proportionately with the importance of the position.[1] To what extent does this hold true for agricultural management? Also, is the stewardship of the collective farm to be given to

---

[1] See, for example, G.I. Shmelev, *Raspredelenie i ispol'zovanie truda v kolkhozakh* (Moskva: Mysl', 1964), pp. 119-127. There are, of course, many potential reasons other than discrimination solely on the basis of sex that might explain the very low participation of women in managerial positions. These, however, will not be pursued in this study.

the young and ambitious, or is it to be entrusted only to older and possibly more reliable managers?

With regard to age and sex, one would think that as the Second World War and its aftermath draw farther back into history, planners would be able, in greater degree, to specify appropriate types of managerial personnel as a policy variable. On the other hand, given the female-male imbalance and the relatively attractive demands of industrial employment, planners cannot, in the absence of force, wholly dictate patterns of employment.[2]

In Table 8-1 we compare, for the year 1959 and by republics, the age distribution of collective farm chairmen and their assistants with the age distribution of the collective farm population as a whole. With some regional variability, the vast majority of chairmen and their assistants fall within the 30-50 year age range, a not surprising result. Compared with the kolkhoz population at large, there appears to be a bias against both young and old persons in these top posts. The most notable deviation from this pattern is demonstrated by the Baltic republics, where, compared to the general kolkhoz population, there is a marked tendency to utilize younger managerial personnel, and at the same time to avoid those in older age brackets (an exception to the latter being Estonia).

The nature of the data in Table 8-1 may somewhat overstate the emphasis upon middle age, since women are an important part of the general kolkhoz population but play a miniscule role in top management. First, the age distribution of male and female kolkhoz members tends to vary somewhat. Second, the apparent pattern may in part result from high turnover rates in the early 1950s and the mass recruitment campaign of 1955, neither of which necessarily reflect a long-term negative judgment of older managerial personnel by Soviet leaders.

It should be apparent from Table 8-2 that women play a negligible role. Where this has not been the case, it has been for decidedly abnormal conditions such as the Second World War, and even then, on a short-run basis.[3] There is, therefore, an apparently strong bias against women as heads of collective farms. To what extent does this bias arise from age and/or educational barriers?

Turning to the census data assembled in Table 8-3, it is apparent that the age distribution of female farm heads and their assistants is markedly similar to their male counterparts—there is a bias against the young and the old. It would appear that insofar as age is concerned, regardless of sex, those in the 30-50 year range are the best managerial group. It is worth noting, however, that while the distribution of female kolkhoz population does not differ markedly from that of the

---

[2]For a more comprehensive treatment of these questions see Norton T. Dodge, op. cit.; and Karl-Eugen Wädekin, op. cit.

[3]In almost all regions of the Soviet Union, the proportion of women among collective farm managers rose significantly during the war, but declined again thereafter. Thus for the RSFSR as a whole in 1940, 3.1 percent of farm chairmen were women while the corresponding figure for 1944 was 14.7 percent, and for 1945, 10.4 percent. The same can be said for other positions such as accountant, brigadier, ferma leader, etc. On this question, see Iu. V. Arutiunian, *Sovetskoe krest'ianstvo v gody velikoi otechestvennoi voiny*, 2nd ed. (Moskva: Izd. Akademii Nauk SSSR, 1963), pp. 408-417.

Table 8-1

Age Distribution of Collective Farm Chairmen and Assistants (Both Sexes) by Republic, 1959 (Age Distribution of Total Kolkhoz Population Given in Brackets Below)

	-20	20-29	30-39	40-49	50-54	55-59	60 Plus
USSR	. . .	6.1	41.9	34.9	10.6	4.7	1.8
	(11.9)	(26.0)	(20.7)	(18.1)	(8.7)	(6.2)	(8.4)
RSFSR	.022	6.0	41.5	35.0	11.0	4.9	1.8
	(12.4)	(26.3)	(19.7)	(19.6)	(9.0)	(5.7)	(7.3)
Ukraine	.015	4.5	42.6	37.2	10.0	4.3	1.2
	(11.5)	(23.5)	(22.2)	(19.7)	(9.5)	(6.3)	(7.3)
Belorussia	. . .	6.3	44.0	34.2	9.6	4.0	1.9
	(11.0)	(24.0)	(18.9)	(16.0)	(9.1)	(8.1)	(12.9)
Uzbekistan	.11	4.0	36.8	36.6	13.9	6.1	2.4
	(13.2)	(33.2)	(23.0)	(11.6)	(5.7)	(6.0)	(7.3)
Kazakhstan	.12	4.7	37.6	38.0	12.8	4.5	.2.1
	(12.9)	(29.3)	(21.3)	(16.0)	(6.9)	(5.6)	(8.0)
Georgia	. . .	4.5	42.7	36.3	9.5	4.6	2.4
	(10.0)	(26.1)	(19.2)	(13.7)	(6.8)	(7.7)	(15.9)
Azerbaidzhan	. . .	4.1	38.4	35.6	12.2	6.3	3.3
	(11.1)	(36.7)	(19.1)	(11.3)	(5.3)	(5.3)	(11.2)
Lithuania	. . .	19.0	46.4	17.9	10.4	3.8	2.3
	(10.4)	(19.5)	(18.5)	(16.0)	(1.8)	(8.9)	(14.9)
Moldavia	. . .	7.3	54.4	29.9	5.7	2.2	.5
	(13.9)	(26.5)	(22.7)	(16.5)·	(6.6)	(5.9)	(7.9)
Latvia	. . .	16.4	43.3	23.5	9.0	4.3	3.4
	(9.2)	(16.1)	(15.5)	(19.2)	(12.3)	(10.4)	(17.3)
Kirgizia	. . .	3.8	42.6	33.6	10.5	6.0	3.4
	(10.3)	(16.1)	(15.5)	(19.2)	(12.3)	(10.4)	(17.3)
Tadzhikistan	. . .	3.3	33.4	42.3	13.9	5.3	1.8
	(13.1)	(34.0)	(23.7)	(11.9)	(5.4)	(5.1)	(6.8)
Armenia	. . .	3.2	42.2	34.6	13.0	5.0	1.8
	(11.4)	(37.4)	(20.1)	(11.5)	(6.4)	(5.1)	(8.1)
Turkmenistan	. . .	4.2	39.7	43.2	8.3	2.9	1.6
	(11.8)	(32.6)	(23.5)	(14.1)	(5.6)	(5.4)	(7.0)
Estonia	. . .	6.6	42.2	29.5	26.1	4.4	2.7
	(4.9)	(12.2)	(13.9)	(20.0)	(13.0)	(13.0)	(23.0)

Source: TsSU, *Itogi vsesoiuznoi perepisi naseleniia 1959 goda* (Moskva: Gosstatizdat, 1962), all volumes.

Table 8-2
Proportion of Kolkhoz Chairmen Women: Selected Regions

	July 1 1953	March 1 1954	1955	1956	(April 1) 1957	1958	1959	1960	1961
USSR	...	...	...	1.5[b]	1.3[a]	...	...	...	...
RSFSR	2.8	...	...	...	...	...	1.7	1.7	2.1
Irkutsk Oblast	.3[c]	...	...	...	...	...	.2	.2	...
Kirov Oblast	...	...	...	1.6	...	...	...	...	...
Saratov Oblast	...	...	...	...	...	...	1.1	1.2	...
Bashtir ASSR	.4	...	...	...	...	...	.3	.3	.3
Moldavia	2.8	2.0	1.6	1.3	1.3	1.3	.9	.9	1.1
Kirgizia	1.4	1.2	.9	1.0	...	1.3	.9	.9	1.1
Lithuania	1.8	...	1.6	1.6	1.7	1.7	1.7	...	...
Azerbaidzhan	...	...	...	...	...	...	2.1	...	...

Sources: *Narkhoz RSFSR v 1958 godu*, p. 326; *Narkhoz RSFSR v 1959 godu*, p. 366; *Narkhoz RSFSR v 1960 godu*, p. 345; *SSSR v tsifrakh* (1958), p. 232; *Dostizheniia Sovetskogo Azerbaidzhana za 40 let v tsifrakh*, p. 134; *Narodnoe khoziaistvo i kul'turnoe stroitel' stvo Bashkirskoi SSR*, p. 213; *Narodnoe khoziaistvo Irkutskoi oblasti*, p. 141; *Narodnoe khoziaistvo Kirovskoi oblasti*, p. 94; *Narodnoe khoziaistvo Kirgizskoi SSR*, p. 109; *20 let Sovetskoi Litvy*, p. 215; *Narodnoe khoziaistvo Moldavskoi SSR v 1962 godu*, p. 198; *Narodnoe khoziaistvo Saratovskoi oblasti v 1960 godu*, p. 175.

[a]End of the year.
[b]As of December 1, 1956.
[c]End of the year.

total kolkhoz population (there are some regional differentials), the proportion of female chairmen in the 20-29 year age bracket is typically higher than the proportion of male chairmen in the same age bracket. Given a tendency towards increasing tenure in office, this pattern could suggest a slightly expanded role for women as kolkhoz managers in the future.

Education will be examined in detail later in this chapter. However, it can be seen from Table 8-4 that the educational level of kolkhoz women is rather lower than that for men. But the size of this differential could not by itself account for the very large differential between the proportion of male as opposed to female kolkhoz managers. Finally, it is only a very partial indicator of the educational potential of these women.[4]

It might be noted that Norton Dodge, while examining the role of women in the Soviet economy, considers the number of female kolkhoz managers as op-

---

[4]Thus we cannot assume that because female kolkhoz members are on balance less educated than their male counterparts, they would necessarily be less effective in managerial posts. Further, this fact of lower education does not necessarily indicate that given appropriate opportunities, they would not be able to raise their education to a level necessary for participation in managerial ranks.

Table 8-3
Age Distribution of Collective Farm Chairmen and Assistants (Female) by
Republic, 1959 (Age Distribution of Female Kolkhoz Population Given in
Brackets Below)

	-20	20-29	30-39	40-49	50-54	55-59	60 Plus
USSR	.1	9.5	44.8	34.8	6.5	3.3	1.0
	(10.4)	(24.4)	(22.1)	(21.8)	(9.5)	(6.3)	(5.5)
RSFSR	...	7.5	42.5	37.9	7.2	3.6	1.0
	(10.0)	(23.0)	(21.0)	(24.2)	(10.5)	(6.2)	(5.1)
Ukraine	...	7.2	41.8	43.1	5.9	1.3	...
	(9.8)	(22.5)	(20.2)	(18.7)	(9.6)	(8.8)	(11.0)
Uzbekistan	...	11.8	58.8	25.5	3.9	...	...
	(14.3)	(37.6)	(23.9)	(12.3)	(4.4)	(4.5)	(3.0)
Kazakhstan	2.6	17.9	33.3	40.8	10.2	5.1	...
	(12.7)	(28.2)	(24.0)	(19.4)	(6.9)	(5.7)	(3.1)
Georgia	...	5.1	30.8	43.6	5.1	7.7	7.7
	(10.4)	(26.2)	(18.9)	(15.5)	(7.0)	(9.6)	(13.0)
Azerbaidzhan	...	...	57.1	31.4	8.6	2.8	...
	(12.5)	(37.8)	(18.7)	(12.1)	(5.3)	(5.8)	(7.8)
Lithuania	...	32.7	52.7	7.3	1.8	3.6	1.8
	(9.1)	(20.6)	(20.8)	(19.1)	(10.3)	(8.5)	(11.6)
Moldavia	...	22.2	61.1	16.6	...	...	...
	(14.0)	(27.0)	(23.1)	(16.9)	(6.3)	(6.0)	(6.7)
Latvia	...	20.0	58.5	15.4	3.0	3.0	...
	(7.5)	(15.8)	(17.8)	(22.8)	(12.8)	(10.3)	(13.0)
Kirgizia	...	12.5	56.2	18.7	0.6	0.6	...
	(9.8)	(34.3)	(25.4)	(15.0)	(5.5)	(6.1)	(3.9)
Belorussia	...	11.3	52.8	26.4	7.5	...	...
	(9.2)	(22.5)	(20.2)	(18.7)	(9.6)	(8.8)	(11.0)
Tadzhikistan	...	6.6	60.0	33.3	...	...	...
	(13.5)	(40.1)	(24.2)	(12.0)	(4.2)	(3.5)	(3.5)
Armenia	...	...	50.0	25.0	25.0	...	...
	(12.8)	(39.8)	(19.9)	(13.0)	(5.8)	(4.6)	(4.1)
Turkmenistan	...	6.9	48.3	41.4	...	3.4	...
	(12.3)	(35.2)	(25.2)	(14.8)	(4.9)	(4.6)	(3.0)
Estonia	...	9.0	39.4	36.4	12.1	3.0	...
	(3.7)	(10.2)	(14.9)	(23.3)	(14.4)	(13.3)	(20.2)

Source: TsSU, *Itogi vsesoiuznoi perepisi naseleniia 1959 goda* (Moskva: Gosstatizdat, 1962), all volumes.

Table 8-4

Educational Attainment of Male and Female Kolkhoz Members: USSR, 1959 (Percentage)

	Completed Higher Education	Spec. Secondary and Incomplete Higher Education	Secondary General Including Incomplete Spec. Sec.	Primary and Incomplete Seven-Year	Less Than Four-Year
Men	0.2	1.4	24.9	41.1	32.4
Women	0.1	0.6	19.2	30.8	49.3

Source: *TsSU, Itogi vsesoiuznoi perepipsi naseleniia 1959 goda, SSSR* (Moskva: Gosstatizdat, 1962), pp. 125, 127.

posed to the number of female able bodied kolkhoz members.[5] Although this practice has been followed here, in doing so, the participation of women in managerial positions may be understated. Thus female participation in the social sector of the kolkhoz is significantly lower than that of the male kolkhoz member.[6] It might be more relevant to compare the portion of female kolkhoz chairmen to participating able bodied female kolkhoz members, their contribution in man-hours or some such variable.

Unfortunately, the data pertaining to middle level managerial personnel are for kolkhozy and sovkhozy combined. These combined indicators will be accepted as an appropriate proxy for kolkhozy only.

With regard to ferma leaders and brigadiers of all types, there tends to be a concentration of these positions among "middle age" kolkhoz members. As with the farm chairmen, this concentration is typically greater than that for the kolkhoz population as a whole, though markedly less than that for higher level management. Note for example, that in 1959, only 6.1 percent of kolkhoz managers in the Soviet Union were from the 20-29 year age group, while 18.9 percent of the brigadiers of the field brigades (kolkhozy and sovkhozy) fall within this age group. For both the upper and the middle level managerial personnel, however, there is discrimination against those in the age group above 50 years, and at approximately the same rate. It would appear from the data presented in Table 8-5 that for middle level management, there is an emphasis upon youth not found at higher levels. Furthermore, there is a significant degree of consistency of this pattern as among different *types* of brigades. To the extent that top level man-

[5]Norton T. Dodge, *Women in the Soviet Economy* (Baltimore: The Johns Hopkins Press, 1966), pp. 202-204.

[6]See, for example, V.F. Mashenkov, *Ispol'zovanie trudovykh resursov sel'skoi mestnosti* (Moskva: Ekonomika, 1965), pp. 53-54. Mashenkov points out that for the year 1959, only 41.2 percent of the total expended time of able-bodied female kolkhoz members was spent in the social sector of the kolkhoz and in state-cooperative enterprises, while the corresponding figure for the male members was 77.3 percent.

Table 8-5

Age Distribution of Middle Level Managerial Personnel (Both Sexes) on Collective and State Farms, 1959

	-20	20-29	30-39	40-49	50-54	55-59	60 Plus
			Brigadier Field Brigade				
USSR	1.1	18.9	38.0	25.2	9.4	4.8	2.6
	(10.9)	(26.0)	(20.7)	(18.1)	(8.7)	(6.8)	(8.4)
RSFSR	1.4	21.6	36.8	24.8	8.9	4.1	2.3
	(12.4)	(26.3)	(19.7)	(19.6)	(9.0)	(5.7)	(7.3)
			Brigadier Tractor Brigade				
USSR	1.0	12.8	34.0	29.1	11.6	6.8	4.7
	(10.9)	(26.0)	(20.7)	(18.1)	(8.7)	(6.8)	(8.4)
RSFSR	.3	19.6	41.6	31.8	5.5	1.0	.1
	(12.4)	(26.3)	(19.7)	(19.6)	(9.0)	(5.7)	(7.3)
			Brigadier Complex Brigade				
USSR	.5	15.8	40.9	30.4	7.9	3.2	1.3
	(10.9)	(26.0)	(20.7)	(18.1)	(8.7)	(6.8)	(8.4)
RSFSR	.5	16.3	41.2	30.0	7.7	3.0	1.2
	(12.4)	(26.3)	(19.7)	(19.6)	(9.0)	(5.7)	(7.3)
			Brigadier Animal Brigade				
USSR	1.8	19.8	32.7	23.5	9.8	6.4	6.0
	(10.9)	(26.0)	(20.7)	(18.1)	(8.7)	(6.8)	(8.4)
RSFSR	1.6	20.8	35.9	25.6	8.9	4.6	2.6
	(12.4)	(26.3)	(19.7)	(19.6)	(9.0)	(5.7)	(7.3)
			Ferma Leader				
USSR	1.0	12.8	34.0	29.1	11.6	6.8	4.7
	(10.9)	(26.0)	(20.7)	(18.1)	(8.7)	(6.8)	(8.4)
RSFSR	1.3	14.3	32.8	29.5	11.5	6.3	4.1
	(12.4)	(26.3)	(19.6)	(19.0)	(9.0)	(5.7)	(7.3)

Sources: TsSU, *Itogi vsesoiuznoi perepisi naseleniia 1959 goda, SSSR* (Moskva: Gosstatizdat, 1962), p. 136; *RSFSR*, pp. 238-239.

Note: Age distribution of kolkhoz population (both sexes) given in brackets. All data in percentages.

agement is recruited from among brigade and ferma leaders, this pattern would be sensible, though such a method of recruitment remains to be demonstrated.[7]

If women play a minimal role in top management posts, what can be said in

[7] In fact, promotion to the position of chairman from within apparently declined in the 1950s. See Jerry F. Hough, "The Changing Nature of The Kolkhoz Chairman," in James R. Millar (ed.), *The Transformation of The Soviet Rural Community* (Urbana: University of Illinois Press, 1971), pp. 103-120.

regard to their participation in managerial duties at the brigade and ferma level? First, it is evident (see Table 8-6) that the findings reported by Norton Dodge can generally be supported. Thus as one moves from top to bottom in the managerial hierarchy, women play an increasingly important role. Indeed, women are dominant at the link level in many regions. Second, there is a considerable degree of variability among different types of brigades, the field brigade generally having the smallest proportion of female leaders.[8] Third, there is a degree of regional variation. The lower level of female participation in the Central Asian republics can be explained by persistent Moslem prejudices regarding the proper role of women. In the case of Estonia, as an example of the Baltic republics, the age and education distribution of male and female kolkhoz members is not significantly different. However, there is in the population of the kolkhozy a rather significant female-male imbalance. Thus in 1959, of the total number participating in the public sector of the kolkhozy, 57.9 percent were women.[9] However, in spite of a similar age distribution and an emphasis upon female kolkhoz mem-

Table 8-6
Proportion of Women as Middle Level Managers (Kolkhozy), 1959

	Field Brigadier	Animal Brigadier	Ferma Leader	Link Leader
USSR	8.3	12.7	15.0	87.3
RSFSR	12.7	18.2	20.1	88.3
Ukraine	4.3	7.1	9.3	96.4
Uzbekistan	2.8	1.9	2.8	14.0
Georgia	2.6	3.2	7.5	30.9
Kazakhstan	4.0	5.6	6.4	58.5
Azerbaidzhan	1.8	2.5	6.6	63.0
Lithuania	1.9	17.3	17.9	32.3
Moldavia	1.9	5.9	8.5	40.0
Latvia	6.4	71.4	54.0	10.2
Kirgizia	2.1	6.7	5.4	51.6
Tadzhikistan	4.0	...	3.7	10.6
Armenia	3.0	3.9	2.4	58.0
Turkmenistan	4.4	...	11.3	21.3
Estonia	15.7	73.4	67.4	...

Source: TsSU, *Itogi vsesoiuznoi perepisi naseleniia 1959 goda* (Moskva: Gosstatizdat, 1962), all volumes.

[8] If we consider the present-day brigade as roughly comparable to the typical kolkhoz of fifteen years ago, this conclusion is important. Further, the very small proportion of women as brigadiers of field brigades is numerically of great importance given the relatively large numbers of field brigades vis-a-vis other forms of production brigades.

[9] Tsentral'noe statisticheskoe upravlenie SSSR (TsSU), *Itogi vsesoiuznoe perepisi naseleniia 1959 goda, Estonskaia SSR* (Moskva: Gosstatizdat, 1962), p. 32.

bers, the proportion of female link leaders in the Baltic republics as compared with the Soviet Union as a whole is relatively very low.

Comparing Tables 8-7 and 8-6, it would appear that as a brigadier of ferma leader, younger women are more likely to prevail than younger men. Thus while the proportion of women in middle and upper management positions are broadly similar for the age bracket 50 years and over, there are relatively fewer women in the age bracket 30-50 years at the middle levels, offset in part by relatively more at this level in the below 29 year age category.[10] Finally, for both sexes, the age distribution for middle and upper level managerial personnel is broadly

Table 8-7
Age Distribution of Middle Level Managerial Personnel (Female) on Collective and State Farms, 1959

	-20	20-29	30-39	40-49	50-54	55-59	60 Plus
			Brigadier Field Brigade				
USSR	3.1	21.0	41.0	24.8	6.5	2.6	1.0
	(10.4)	(24.4)	(22.1)	(21.8)	(9.5)	(6.3)	(5.5)
RSFSR	2.3	19.0	42.1	25.8	7.1	2.6	.9
	(10.0)	(23.0)	(21.0)	(24.2)	(10.5)	(6.2)	(5.1)
			Brigadier Animal Brigade				
USSR	4.7	31.9	37.1	19.4	4.6	1.7	.6
	(10.4)	(24.4)	(22.1)	(21.8)	(9.5)	(6.3)	(5.5)
RSFSR	4.3	32.3	39.1	18.6	4.2	1.1	.3
	(10.0)	(23.0)	(21.0)	(24.2)	(10.5)	(6.2)	(5.1)
			Ferma Leader				
USSR	3.7	20.9	37.7	26.2	6.8	3.4	1.3
	(10.4)	(24.4)	(22.1)	(21.8)	(9.5)	(6.3)	(5.5)
RSFSR	3.9	20.7	37.4	26.3	7.1	3.4	1.1
	(10.0)	(23.0)	(21.0)	(24.2)	(10.5)	(6.2)	(5.1)

Sources: TsSU, *Itogi vsesoiuznoi perepisi naseleniia 1959 goda, SSSR* (Moskva: Gosstatizdat, 1962), p. 143; *RSFSR*, p. 253.
Note: Figures in brackets represent age distribution of all female kolkhoz members. Note that no data is given pertaining to female leaders of tractor brigades or of complex brigades. All data in percentages.

[10]To the extent that promotion to top management is from the brigade and ferma levels, the relatively greater (though absolutely small) importance of young women in these middle-level managerial posts may, in the future, result in some increase in the proportion of women in the top managerial positions. While the likelihood of this happening apparently declined during the 1950s, there is some evidence of increased internal managerial recruitment during the 1960s. See Jerry F. Hough, op. cit. At the same time, to the extent that women were present in lower-level posts in the past but are not now chairmen, there has been discrimination or an absence of internal recruitment.

similar, though, at the middle level, there is a slightly increased emphasis upon youth.

Party Status and the Route to Management

For a long period of time, economists and others have been interested in the nature of the managerial function and indeed, what characteristics and qualities are necessary prerequisites of a "good" manager. While managerial selection may be highly centralized *within* large western corporations, it remains true that for the market economies as a whole, the selection process is highly decentralized. We can, therefore, study the characteristics of those who have "made it" in an attempt to define "good" management and hence simplify and improve selection procedures for the future. In the case of the Soviet collective farm, it is apparent that the Communist Party actively selects managerial personnel. Thus to further illuminate the role of management in a different socio-economic setting, it is necessary to examine the method of selection and, especially, the criteria required for selection of these personnel.

Throughout the history of the collective farm in the Soviet Union, chairmen have been recruited both by centralized mass campaigns and by individual selection at local levels.

In the only major mass recruitment of the post Stalin era, a decree of March 25, 1955, issued by the Central Committee of the CPSU and the Soviet Ministers ordered not less than 30,000 new collective farm chairmen dispatched to the fields by July 1, 1955.[11] The rationale for this movement was twofold. First, weak leadership has long been seen as a major cause of weak collective farms, a theme constantly stressed in the 1950s. Second, while normal recruitment processes would remain operative, these it was thought, could not serve to raise the educational level of collective farm chairmen within a short period of time. Some action was taken in 1951-52 when 12,000 agricultural specialists were placed at the head of collective farms. However, given the existence of 121,353 collective farms in 1950, the action was relatively minor and was deemed inadequate to cope with the problem.[12]

Throughout the 1950s, Khrushchev stressed the need for well trained farm chairmen. Indeed, as of July 1, 1953, only 18 percent of all collective farm chairmen had a higher or secondary education, and of this number, only 2.6 percent had complete higher education.[13] The new importance attached to the position of chairman was demonstrated in 1954 when it was placed upon the

---

[11] "O merakh po dal'neishemu ukrepleniiu kolkhozov rukovodiashchimi kadrami," as cited in *Sbornik*, pp. 224-228, and especially p. 226. There were 85.6 thousand agricultural artels in 1955.

[12] A.N. Karamelev, "Dvizhenie tridtsatityshiachnikov i ukreplenie kolkhozov," *Voprosy Istorii KPSS*, No. 1 (1962), p. 115.

[13] *Sel'khoz-1960*, p. 474.

nomenklatura of the Obkom, Kraikom and Central Committee of the Communist Party of the union republics.[14]

The mass recruitment of kolkhoz chairmen (1955) was a Party campaign throughout, and in some respects, set new guidelines for the desirable characteristics of farm chairmen.[15] Not unexpectedly, most of the newly recruited chairmen were Party members, and the selection procedure was by no means limited to those who were agricultural specialists by educational background. The data assembled in Table 8-8 gives a summary picture which, with some exceptions that we shall indicate, can be taken as representative of the entire recruitment campaign. Of those recruited in Belorussia, for example, about 29 percent were leadership workers of Obkom, Gorkom and Raikom Party organs and secretaries of local Party organizations (notably higher than the 12.4 percent of "leading Party workers" in Smolensk oblast); about 10 percent were leading workers of the oblispolkom, gorispolkom and raiispolkom organs (significantly lower than the 54.4 percent recruited from the soviets in Smolensk oblast); 8 percent were leadership workers of agricultural organs and from among agricultural specialists; 9 percent were from higher and secondary educational institutions; 12 percent from komsomol workers, newspapers, political organs of the railways, legal courts, procurators, war service personnel; and finally, about 29 percent from

Table 8-8
Characteristics of New Collective Farm Chairmen Recruited in Smolensk Oblast, 1955

Total number recruited in 1955:	362	100.0%
Of which:		
With higher education		25.0%
With incomplete higher or secondary education		40.5%
Communist Party members		93.0%
Background of newly recruited chairmen:		
Leading Party workers		12.5%
Komsomol		0.8%
Soviets		54.4%
Workers of agricultural organs		3.9%
Industrial enterprises		24.0%
Other organs		4.4%

Source: A.N. Karamelev, "Dvizhenie tridtsatityshiachnikov i ukreplenie kolkhozov," *Voprosy Istorii KPSS*, No. 1 (1962), p. 119.

[14] "O dal'neishem uvelichenii proizvodstva zerna v strane i ob osvoenii tselinnykh i zalezhnykh zemel,' " as cited in *Sbornik*, pp. 114-146, and especially p. 145.

[15] Throughout this discussion we rely heavily upon one of the few available detailed articles on the "thirty thousanders," or that group of chairmen directed to their posts in 1955. See A.N. Karamelev, op. cit., pp. 115-126. For a Western discussion, see Jerry F. Hough, op. cit.; Robert C. Stuart, op. cit.

economic organs and industrial organizations.[16] Of this group in the aggregate, approximately 92 percent were members of the Communist Party, a proportion said to be representative of all new kolkhoz chairmen placed during the 1955 campaign.[17]

In that campaign, emphasis seems to have been upon those persons who were educated, though not necessarily in agriculture; able to demonstrate leadership capability by prior performance in a *wide variety* of leadership positions; and who were Party members. The data in Table 8-9 suggests that even among factory personnel sent to the countryside, education and leadership record were important.

From the limited statistical evidence on the 1955 recruitment campaign, it is apparent that much effort was devoted to assuring its success. First, the state guaranteed a supplementary payment of 1500 rubles to the chairman in his first year, 1200 rubles in his second year and 1000 for the third year.[18] This was undoubtedly a major incentive at that time. It will be recalled from Chapter 5, that our calculation of managerial money earnings (monthly) based upon farm money income indicated that for 1953, 58.4 percent earned between 25 and 125 old rubles, while for 1957, this had dropped to 18.9 percent, and 54.9 percent were earning between 125 and 175 old rubles. If in fact the guaranteed ruble supplements were in addition to, and quite apart from the size of, normal managerial earnings, the proposition was indeed attractive even though it would be safe to assume that many of these newly recruited managers probably were sent to relatively backward farms.

Second, courses developed by the Ministry of Agriculture were given to the

Table 8-9

Previous Positions of Workers of Industrial Enterprises Recruited as Kolkhoz Chairmen in Belorussia, 1955

Total number of new kolkhoz chairmen recruited from industrial enterprises:	149	100.0%
Of which:		
Workers (rabochii)	13	8.7%
Foremen	25	16.8%
Engineering and technical workers	48	32.2%
Superintendents of shops	32	21.5%
Heads of an enterprise	31	20.8%

Source: A.N. Karamelev, "Dvizhenie tridtsatityshiachnikov i ukreplenie kolkhozov," *Voprosy Istorii KPSS*, No. 1 (1962), p. 120.

[16] A.N. Karamelev, op. cit., pp. 119-120.

[17] Ibid., p. 120.

[18] Ibid., p. 117.

new recruits on a three week basis followed by a two month practical training period on a "good" farm.[19] However, the rapidity of placement of these new chairmen would indicate that in many, if not most cases, the practical training period was never utilized.

In terms of the initial goals of this campaign, it was a success. In 1955 alone, 23 percent of collective farm chairmen were changed. Ultimately, 32,078 new collective farm chairmen (there were over 85,000 collective farms in 1955) were considered to be members of the so-called "thirty thousanders."[20]

According to Soviet reports, the number of applicants typically exceeded requirements and the number of successful recruits. Thus in Moldavia, as one writer recounts, with a requirement of 136 new chairmen, 419 requests were received from which Party organs ultimately selected 105.[21] The placement of new recruits was relatively quick. By the 2nd of June, 1955, 23,323 new chairmen had been placed on collective farms (presumably as trainees). The majority were placed sometime in 1955, though a few remained for placement in early 1956. Most were placed at the head of collectives, but some found themselves as assistant chairmen.

Significant data on the Party status of collective farm chairmen is spotty. Nevertheless, it is apparent that the campaign of 1955 was a continuation of a policy of placing Party members at the head of collective farms. From Table 8-10 it can be seen that as of July 1, 1953, 79.6 percent of collective farm chairmen were Party members. This figure had risen to 90.5 percent by April 1, 1956, undoubtedly strengthened by the newly appointed farm chairmen. Comparable shifts can be seen in the Ukraine and Belorussia, and were such data available for all republics, the results undoubtedly would be similar.

If Table 8-8 can be taken as roughly representative of the recruitment campaign as a whole, it represented a significant and continuing step in the improvement of educational levels of farm chairmen. Among 18,000 new chairmen recruited in 1955 in the RSFSR, Ukraine, Belorussia and Kazakhstan, about 55 percent had higher or secondary specialized education.[22] This figure might be compared with the collective farm chairmen of the USSR as of April 1, 1955, 29.3 percent of whom had higher or specialized secondary education.[23] The Soviet experience in raising the educational level of farm chairmen, and especially the significant push in this direction throughout the 1950s, is summarized in Table 8-11.

Although the available data is not clear on this point, it would seem that most

---

[19]"O merakh po dal'neishemu ukrepleniiu kolkhozov rukovodiashchimi kadrami," as cited in *Sbornik*, p. 227.

[20]A.N. Karamelev, op. cit., p. 121. This classification may include double counting since we do not know how turnover for this group compared with other farm chairmen.

[21]Ibid., p. 119. It is difficult to know whether this sort of response can be generalized to the country as a whole.

[22]Ibid.

[23]*Narkhoz-1958*, p. 531.

Table 8-10

Proportion of Collective Farm Chairmen who are Members of the Communist Party

| | July 1 | | | April 1 | | | | |
	1950	1952	1953	1956	1957	1958	1959	1960
USSR	...	79.4	79.6	90.5	91.2	92.6	93.5	95.3
RSFSR	...	...	...	...	...	...	94.0	...
	(1946)	(1951)						
Ukraine	40.2	74.2	...	83.3	95.7	94.4	97.1	...
Belorussia	...	...	...	...	...	...	96.5	...
Uzbekistan	...	...	...	...	...	...	93.1	...
Kazakhstan	...	...	...	...	...	...	95.4	...
Georgia	...	...	...	...	...	...	93.8	...
Azerbaidzhan	...	...	...	...	...	...	92.6	...
Lithuania	9.2	...	48.5	72.1	73.0	70.6	72.6	...
Moldavia	...	...	...	...	...	...	96.0	...
Latvia	...	...	...	...	...	...	81.3	...
Kirgizia	...	...	...	...	...	...	98.1	...
Tadzhikistan	...	...	...	...	...	...	96.9	...
Armenia	...	...	...	...	...	...	99.7	...
Turkmenistan	...	...	...	...	...	...	92.7	...
Estonia	...	...	...	...	...	...	76.0	...

Sources: *Narkhoz-1959*, p. 452, *Sel'khoz-1960*, p. 475; M.P. Panchenko, *Vidtvorennia suspil'nogo produktu v kolgospakh (Kiev: Kiev University, 1963), p. 121; TsSu, 20 let Sovetskoi litvy* (Vil'nius: Gosstatizdat, 1960), p. 215.

of the new farm personnel recruited in 1955 found themselves heading farms rather than serving as assistant chairmen. This interpretation would be in line with the evidence presented in Table 8-12 which suggests, for the relevant period, a decline in the number of farm chairmen served by a full time assistant. The recent tendency to expand the proportion of chairmen served by a full time assistant (although with very significant regional differentials) may be a delayed response to excessive amalgamation, in a sense, recognition of the growing complexity of the top managerial position.[24]

While the recruitment campaign of 1955 had a significant impact upon the composition of upper level managerial personnel, this procedure, so far as we know, has not subsequently been repeated. Accordingly, it is necessary to examine what in recent years has come to be the more typical recruitment procedure.

---

[24]The presence of a full time assistant chairman in 1969 does seem to correlate roughly with the size of the kolkhozy in the given region (measured by aggregate sown area per kolkhoz). For example, the smallest kolkhozy (in increasing order of size) are in Georgia, Armenia, Azerbaidzhan, Lithuania and Estonia. As Table 8-12 indicates, all these republics for the most part have kolkhozy without full-time assistant chairmen.

Table 8-11
Proportion of Collective Farm Chairmen with Complete Higher and Specialized Secondary Education (Percentage)

	1946	1950	July 1 1951	1952	1953	1955	1956	April 1 1959	1963	1966	1969
USSR	...	...	...	15.1	18.0	29.3	37.1	50.4	63.3	69.6	78.1
RSFSR	...	...	...	...	16.0	...	...	45.0	56.8	63.7	73.4
Ukraine	8.6	...	14.9	...	...	...	35.7	62.3	73.1	78.5	85.6
Belorussia	...	...	...	...	13.6	...	...	51.4	63.6	70.1	79.2
Uzbekistan	...	...	...	...	...	...	...	52.3	73.3	77.6	80.9
Kazakhstan	...	...	...	...	...	...	...	63.1	77.9	77.6	84.7
Georgia	...	...	...	...	...	...	...	55.6	68.7	69.9	76.5
Azerbaidzhan	...	...	...	...	...	...	...	65.0	61.3	72.9	74.8
Lithuania	...	3.8	...	...	5.5	14.6	22.0	38.2	52.5	57.8	68.9
Moldavia	...	...	...	...	32.3	39.8	48.6	73.8	83.7	90.2	95.2
Latvia	...	...	...	...	...	...	...	52.6	64.1	70.9	78.8
Kirgizia	...	...	...	11.5	15.8	18.2	30.4	31.7	85.4	74.6	83.1
Tadzhikistan	...	...	...	...	...	...	...	39.8	61.4	60.2	68.3
Armenia	...	...	...	...	...	...	...	62.1	73.9	76.2	84.3
Turkmenistan	...	...	...	...	...	...	...	50.9	59.9	74.5	78.8
Estonia	...	...	...	...	...	...	...	40.2	54.7	59.6	67.5

Sources: *Narkhoz-1961*, p. 466; *Narkhoz-1962*, p. 373; *Narkhoz-1965*, p. 440; *Narkhoz-1968*, p. 451; *Narkhoz RSFSR-1962*, p. 355; *Narkhoz Kirgiz SSR-1957*, p. 109; *Narkhoz Moldavian SSR-1962*, p. 198; *Sel'khoz-1960*, pp. 474-475; *20 let Sovetskoi Litvy*, p. 215; *Dostizheniia Sovetskoi Belorussii za 40 let*, p. 87; M.P. Panchenko, *Vidtvorennia suspil'nogo produktu kolgospakh* (Kiev: Kiev University, 1963), p. 121.

Table 8-12

Proportion of Collective Farm Chairmen Served by a Full Time Assistant Chairman (Percentage)

	December 1	April 1			
	1956	1959	1963	1965	1969
USSR	40.8	50.1	41.7	35.4	47.6
RSFSR	...	55.0	45.0	36.9	42.0
Ukraine	...	49.7	48.7	43.3	68.2
Belorussia	...	44.4	36.5	23.2	39.7
Uzbekistan	...	93.5	91.6	96.0	104.6
Kazakhstan	...	83.7	70.6	68.9	67.8
Georgia	...	15.0	3.4	4.0	1.9
Azerbaidzhan	...	21.9	10.2	5.0	5.4
Lithuania	...	36.2	11.4	1.8	22.6
Moldavia	...	78.5	77.4	76.7	88.2
Latvia	...	5.6	4.5	2.4	17.4
Kirgizia	...	69.5	75.7	76.6	67.3
Tadzhikistan	...	85.3	26.3	33.5	52.0
Armenia	...	2.5	4.9	1.5	.8
Turkmenistan	...	53.2	84.4	72.7	69.0
Estonia	...	6.9	7.5	4.9	15.9

Sources: TsSU, *Dostizheniia Sovetskoi vlasti za 40 let v tsifrakh* (Moskva: Gosstatizdat, 1957), p. 192; *Narkhoz-1963*, p. 372; *Narkhoz-1964*, p. 424; *Narkhoz-1968*, p. 451.

In theory, the chairman and members of the management board of the kolkhoz are elected by the general meeting of the kolkhoz. While a new chairman can be and most likely is brought before a general meeting, rejection is most uncommon. The "success" of the 1955 campaign would surely be strong support for this view. On the matter of how a candidate is selected in reality, Soviet writings have little to say.

Although details have probably varied over time, apparently both state and Party organs play an important role. If, for example, a farm is performing poorly and not meeting delivery targets, the raion authorities will be aware of this fact, and in due course, steps will be taken to secure a new manager. Under present procedures, the raion administration (under which both the kolkhozy and the sovkhozy fall), maintains a "personnel file" *(nomenklatura)* or list of names of those persons who might be suitable for such a position. Although the precise nature of this list is not known, it is most likely composed of those persons, the successful performance of whose tasks has made them known to upper level officials.[25] Undoubtedly education and Party status are important, but of even

[25] Based upon interviews conducted by the writer in Slav'iansk raion, Krasnodarskii krai, during August of 1966.

greater importance is the previous work record and the performance of the individual in his previous posts. In particular, there seems to be a good deal of weight placed upon a successful period in an administrative post, where it is thought leadership abilities can be examined.[26] However, after initial selection of a candidate by the raion administration, the candidacy will be discussed by the Party committee (at the raion center), at which time a member of the raion administration will be present. After there is agreement upon the candidate, he will be "recommended" to the collective farm, and in most cases, will be ratified by the general meeting. Thus any notion that a collective farm selects its manager is simply a myth.

There is little discussion about the selection of managerial personnel other than the chairman, though certain guidelines are known to prevail. First, it is anticipated that the chief specialists will be members of the management board. Second, it is apparent that the chairman, once selected, has considerable power in suggesting the composition of the management board. In addition to the specialists, one might expect to find the secretary of the Party organization, and possibly some middle level managers (brigadiers, ferma leaders, etc.) on this board. After the chairman's views are made known and approval of state and Party organs is ascertained, the members of the management board will be "elected" by the general meeting of the kolkhoz.

Party influence upon the selection of managerial personnel is great. This influence, however, neither begins nor terminates with placement. In particular, while Soviet leaders have placed great emphasis upon formal education *(obrazovanie)*, they also place continuing emphasis upon the proper upbringing *(vospitanie)* of those persons who may hold leadership posts. The latter is not the same as the former, and while there is a tendency to judge managerial capability by performance in lower level positions, there is also considerable effort to "train" managerial personnel.

Education for Managers

In the sense distinguished by Leibenstein, the stock of entrepreneurial talent, however this might be defined in the Soviet case, is a growth agent capable of executing growth producing activities.[27] While there seems to be a strong recognition of Leibenstein's general characterization by the Soviets, there is an absence of any clear notion of the admittedly difficult concept of managerial capacity. In almost all of the author's interviews with officials both at and above the collective farm level, there was a strong tendency to disclaim the notion of a

---

[26]The increasing emphasis upon administrative experience for collective farm chairmen appointed in the 1950s is stressed by Hough, op. cit.

[27]Harvey Leibenstein, *Economic Backwardness and Economic Growth* (New York: John Wiley & Sons, Inc., 1957), pp. 120-125.

special managerial talent.[28] One the other hand, if one examines Soviet behavior vis-a-vis the development of managerial personnel in the collective farm sector, one might suggest that in many cases, they act "as if" such a special talent did in fact exist (in terms of recruitment, training, and promotion) and must be further developed. In addition, there has been a continuing tendency to blame the existence of weak collective farms upon bad management.[29] Since we are fundamentally interested in the Soviet conception of this managerial capacity, it must be understood less by what they say it is, and more by how they try to achieve it in practice. The sphere of education is certainly important in this respect.

The Soviet educational system, even as it applies to farm management, has been relatively complex. There has been a good deal of institutional change during the period under study, though the fundamental purpose and content of managerial education has not changed radically. Rather than trace in detail these institutional changes, the presentation here will develop a broad picture of specific educational organs pertaining to farm management training and, the quantitative and qualitative success of these programs.

Broadly speaking, Soviet educational institutions can be subdivided into three levels as follows:

1. Higher level—Universities, institutes. (Higher education)
2. Intermediate level—Technicums, oblast agronomical schools and schools for preparation of kolkhoz chairmen. (Specialized secondary education)
3. Lower level—Training for mechanics.

While managerial training has been carried out at each of these levels, the bulk of formal training for top level farm management seems to have been at the secondary level. For this purpose, there exist a net of secondary agricultural schools in all oblasts, krais and republics. At the third level, there is a net of schools with training programs varying in length from six months to two years. These programs provide basic training for higher and lower level managerial personnel, and in addition, provide re-training in the form of short term refresher courses, some of which combine theoretical training in the classroom with practical training on a "good" collective farm.

Until 1951, persons destined to be appointed as chairman of a collective farm would enroll in a two year program.[30] The core of this training apparently centered upon "technical" subjects, and only secondarily, if at all, upon economics. After 1951, many of the one and two year programs were shifted to a single

[28]It is difficult to form a significant conclusion from this result, given that the nature of the question itself would tend to generate a negative response from many Soviet respondents.

[29]This was a theme continually pushed by Nikita Khrushchev and can be found in his writing and also in those of Soviet economists who have written on the matter of backward collective farms. See, for example, V.P. Rozhin, *Nekotorype voprosy pod'ema ekonomiki slabykh kolkhozov*, (Moskva: Ekonomizdat, 1961), Ch. III.

[30]There is a concise discussion of the system as it worked during these early years in *Sel'skokhoziaistvennaia entsiklopediia*, Vol. 3 (Moskva: Sel'khozizdat, 1953), p. 431.

three year period (full time), and, thus, at the middle level their graduates would, in Soviet statistics, be classified as having "specialized secondary education." The writer's examination of the educational system in the Krasnodar region provides some interesting insights into the educational process and the question of managerial mobility, although generalizations to the entire country must be made with care.

First, it must be emphasized that the structure of, and participation in, the rural educational programs is in large measure centralized and thus does not lie within the hands of those who would participate. The potential participant does not weigh the pros and cons of further education and accordingly decide whether or not to participate.[31] This picture tends to prevail whether we speak of a short-term refresher course or a longer run training program which might shift the individual to a higher level position. The basic reason for this pattern is the rigidity introduced by the specification in the plan of participation in the educational process. For example, the farm chairman is expected to participate in a refresher course once every five years.

One would suspect that there are channels, for example the Party apparatus (and this would in itself encourage membership for the ambitious), through which one could make his desires known. On balance, however, there appears to be a degree of rigidity which must hinder the upward mobility of those who would aspire to managerial positions, especially insofar as formal education is heavily weighted as a "success indicator."[32]

In Krasnodarskii krai for example, there exists a six month course (October-March), previously a one year course, for the purpose of raising specialists to chief specialists, and chief specialists to farm managers. Course content is planned by the Ministry of Agriculture. For those selected, salary is maintained, room and board is provided and a stipend is paid. It is, therefore, an attractive proposition. For those elevated to a managerial position after completion of the course, re-location will most likely be necessary. For those starting from a lower level (specialists and brigade leaders) re-location is less likely and hence the prospect of participation may be more appealing.

Apparently selection is the responsibility of the Kraikom Party and Bureau, while placement is the responsibility of the krai administration. For potential participants, there is an upper age limit, though in fact most fall in the 35-42 age range. Course content is a combination of theory (approximately 3½ months) and practical training (approximately 1½ months). The latter portion of the training program will take place on a large wealthy farm and will be executed under the supervision of a faculty member from the institute where the theoreti-

---

[31] The exception to this pattern would be the young who have not participated in the labor force and who are embarking on a university career or training in an institute.

[32] Although it is a matter of judgment, this writer would suggest that performance in the completion of formal educational qualifications is not a major indicator for managerial success, if by success we mean movement into and upward within managerial ranks.

cal training has been completed. Placement into practical training is a joint decision of the institute faculty and the krai administration of agriculture.

In addition to those courses that result in a shift upwards for successful participants, there are short-term (three month) courses which serve only a refresher function. The kolkhoz chairman, as we have noted, is expected to participate in such a course once every five years. During his absence, the assistant chairman will take over the farm. Upon completion of the course, the chairman will return. There are similar courses for other personnel, for example a two month course for the specialists.

It is apparent that within the total educational structure, there is a significant emphasis upon practical training and experience of one type or another. Within individual kolkhozy and indeed for farms within a region, there is emphasis upon the frequent presentation of seminars, field trips and evening courses. These events vary from those of a basically political nature to those of a technical nature, and are normally carried out throughout the year. For the evening courses operative during the winter (frequently planned and executed by the kolkhoz Party organization), attendance is typically compulsory, though not always appreciated by the participants. Upon successful completion of the program, a certificate of some type is awarded.

It is very difficult to assess the performance of this system. Quantitatively, while we can examine the growth in educational level of farm chairmen, we do not know in many cases what *type* of education this is, nor do we know the *source* of this education (type of school, on-the-job training, etc.). These difficulties stem in part from lack of statistical data pertaining to the typical routes to management. Thus we cannot distinguish between two managers, both of whom have "specialized secondary education" but one of whom has been trained in engineering and plucked from industry into agriculture, while the other has training in agronomy gained through the routes described for Krasnodarskii Krai. Qualitatively, we have little or no idea as to the degree of correlation between "success" as a manger and educational level. Thus it is difficult to assess the extent to which educational achievement has been either the proper type or amount.

Throughout the 1950s and 1960s, the educational level of collective farm chairmen has risen significantly. In large part, specialized secondary education, or that type carried out in the course structure that we have described, has been responsible for this pattern. But, if the educational level of chairmen has improved, what can be said for other managerial personnel?

As one moves downward in the managerial hierarchy, the level of educational attainment declines. (See Tables 8-13 through 8-15). Although for the most part showing increases over time and regionally, educational levels are very low at the brigade and ferma levels.[33] It should also be noted, that the Soviet practice of

[33]This is an important conclusion given the significant structural expansion of the brigade during the 1950s and the potentially expanded decision-making role of the brigadier. Although educational achievement for brigadiers and ferma leaders has improved in recent years, it remains well below that of farm chairmen and specialists.

Table 8-13

Proportion of Full Time Assistant Chairmen Having Complete Higher and Specialized Secondary Education

	1959	1963	1965	1966	1969
USSR	22.3	33.8	40.6	44.4	58.9
RSFSR	15.4	19.7	24.7	24.3	38.6
Ukraine	34.7	46.2	52.8	57.5	70.7
Belorussia	12.3	22.2	27.2	28.5	59.6
Uzbekistan	48.7	68.5	69.2	72.1	80.4
Kazakhstan	34.2	48.8	60.0	50.8	64.2
Georgia	40.0	65.3	49.1	47.6	76.9
Azerbaidzhan	34.3	46.4	44.9	59.4	46.5
Lithuania	7.5	13.5	20.7	37.5	71.2
Moldavia	48.8	76.7	81.5	83.3	87.9
Latvia	17.4	57.5	57.9	58.6	73.2
Kirgizia	48.8	70.0	82.6	78.7	83.8
Tadzhikistan	27.5	41.1	45.2	45.5	55.8
Armenia	65.0	45.2	12.5	44.4	75.0
Turkmenistan	39.0	42.2	44.0	52.6	56.0
Estonia	9.6	27.9	26.0	38.5	39.3

Sources: *Narkhoz-1962*, p. 373; *Narkhoz-1964*, p. 424; *Narkhoz-1965*, p. 441; *Narkhoz-1968*, p. 451; *Sel'khoz-1960*, pp. 470-471.

combining, for statistical reporting, personnel with higher *or* secondary education tends to cloud the result, since the proportion of the total with secondary education tends to increase as one moves downward in the structure. Second, it is worth drawing attention to the universally high educational level of the agricultural specialist. The significantly higher formal qualifications of the specialists vis-a-vis the managers is evidence of the necessity for more theoretical training for staff specialists.

Soviet statistical series for the most part do not report the *types* of education received by managerial personnel. In the top management category, those with higher education (a relatively small proportion of all top managers) are most likely agricultural specialists. According to Nicholas De Witt, out of 91,070 "professionals" (higher education) engaged in Soviet agriculture as of December, 1959, 18,153 were engineers, 66,936 were agricultural specialists and the remainder, various unspecified specialists.[34]

For one republic (kirgiz) we do have data on the type of education of collective farm chairmen (Table 8-16). First, as is true for the country as a whole, specialized secondary education is the most important in this republic. Second,

[34]Nicholas De Witt, *Education and Professional Employment in the USSR* (Washington, D.C.: U.S. Government Printing Office, 1961), p. 519.

Table 8-14

Proportion of Brigade and Ferma Leaders with Complete Higher and Specialized Secondary Education (Percentage)

	1959[a]		1963		1966		1969	
	Brigadier	Ferma Ldr	Brigadier	Ferma Ldr	Brigadier	Ferma Ldr	Brigadier	Ferma Ldr
USSR	5.1	5.6	8.5	9.0	10.4	10.9	15.6	15.4
RSFSR	3.2	3.5	4.6	4.2	5.7	5.6	9.2	8.7
Ukraine	7.1	4.9	10.7	9.4	13.5	10.3	19.0	14.3
Belorussia	1.7	2.3	2.0	2.7	4.3	6.1	14.7	20.0
Uzbekistan	7.0	13.3	11.5	22.9	10.0	23.3	11.6	27.8
Kazakhstan	8.6	8.3	13.8	17.0	13.0	20.4	16.5	22.7
Georgia	15.4	24.9	22.4	34.2	22.3	33.7	29.8	38.7
Azerbaidzhan	9.9	12.3	20.1	25.2	15.3	19.7	20.9	25.2
Lithuania	8.4	1.7	4.4	9.5	25.2	32.7	42.6	43.4
Moldavia	10.6	7.4	17.6	16.8	19.2	17.7	24.9	21.4
Latvia	9.4	12.3	14.1	18.4	24.5	22.8	32.9	25.7
Kirgizia	6.2	12.4	13.9	27.4	15.3	32.6	22.7	41.3
Tadzhikistan	4.8	8.2	5.6	13.8	3.8	15.6	5.0	20.8
Armenia	15.6	18.7	21.1	24.4	21.7	25.0	31.7	35.7
Turkmenistan	7.0	12.5	7.9	18.9	9.1	27.6	10.6	29.0
Estonia	6.7	14.8	15.0	23.4	32.0	28.8	46.8	33.5

Sources: *Narkhoz-1962*, p. 373; *Narkhoz-1965*, p. 440; *Narkhoz-1969*, p. 451; *Sel'khoz-1960*, pp. 470-471.

[a]As of April 1, for each year.

Table 8-15
Proportion of Agronomists and Zoötechnicians with Complete Higher and Specialized Secondary Education (Percentage)

	1959 Agron.	1959 Zoötech.	1966 Agron.	1966 Zoötech.	1969 Agron.	1969 Zoötech.
USSR	96.4	91.8	94.6	91.0	95.7	93.1
RSFSR	96.3	91.7	94.4	88.4	95.7	91.4
Ukraine	97.6	92.4	97.0	94.4	97.2	96.1
Belorussia	97.8	93.2	97.1	89.0	96.8	93.5
Uzbekistan	90.5	88.9	86.5	92.5	90.3	93.3
Kazakhstan	91.6	89.0	93.2	91.3	92.8	87.7
Georgia	98.3	97.4	90.7	92.6	94.2	92.9
Lithuania	96.2	89.4	96.1	91.4	97.7	93.3
Azerbaidzhan	97.3	94.0	90.7	92.6	93.2	93.2
Moldavia	97.8	96.0	96.3	98.3	97.9	93.3
Latvia	97.4	84.5	97.8	86.0	99.0	87.6
Kirgizia	95.7	93.4	93.9	95.4	95.3	94.7
Tadzhikistan	80.0	84.7	77.6	90.6	80.2	94.5
Armenia	96.3	96.8	92.4	92.7	92.2	94.0
Turkmenistan	96.0	93.1	94.4	96.0	94.4	94.0
Estonia	94.8	85.6	96.5	84.3	95.8	87.1

Sources: *Narkhoz-1965*, p. 440; *Narkhoz-1968*, p. 451; *Sel'khoz-1960*, pp. 472-473.

Table 8-16
Amount and Type of Education of Collective Farm Chairmen of the Kirgiz Republic (Percentage)

	July 1 1953	April 1 1955	1956	1958	1959	1960	1961
Portion of all chairmen with higher and secondary spec. ed.	15.8	18.2	30.4	33.2	31.7	45.0	54.7
Of which:							
Higher ed.	1.7	1.6	3.1	3.9	7.0	12.1	15.5
of which:							
agronom. zoötech. & vet doctor	1.0	1.0	1.2	1.7	...	...	...
Secondary spec. education	14.1	16.6	27.3	29.3	24.7	32.9	39.2
of which:							
agron. zoötech. & vet doctor	8.7	12.4	12.7	11.2	...	...	...
other spec.	5.4	4.2	14.6	18.1	...	...	...

Source: *Narkhoz Kirgizskoi SSR v 1960 godu* (Frunze: Gosstatizdat, 1961), p. 140.

while for the early 1950s agricultural education was relatively more important than other specialties, this position has been weakened in recent years. One explanation for this pattern may be the thrust by Soviet leaders (amply demonstrated by the recruitment campaign of 1955) to place educated persons in managerial positions, and above all, persons of intelligence and demonstrated leadership capacity, quite apart from specific training.[35] Further, there has been a recent trend towards the generalization of training for lower level personnel. One might anticipate some impact of this thinking at higher levels. Thus in part as a response to seasonal labor problems, there has been increasing emphasis upon the training of specialists with a "wide profile." Soviet agricultural education, at least for the lower levels, has tended to be highly specialized. In the case of the Kirgiz republic, the upsurge of "other specialists" does occur in the period 1955-58, and thus to some extent may have been a result of the 1955 campaign. Unfortunately, we lack such data for the post-1958 period.

To the extent that decision making has become an increasingly important and complex task of collective farm management, one might expect an infusion of personnel trained at a minimum in the skills of accounting, and more likely, the general expansion of economic knowledge commensurate with the needs of the decision makers. Such does not seem to be the case.

As recently as 1960 (Table 8-17) almost one-half (47.4 percent) of all accounting workers on Soviet collective farms had no accounting training. At the same time, while only 2.1 percent of all chief accountants had no accounting training, the comparable figure for the brigade and ferma level was a whopping 77.4 percent. This is surprising in view of the sharply growing accounting needs of collective farms and the inability to sub-contract for such services in the Soviet Union, and most notably the expanding importance of decision making at the brigade level.

In recent years there has been a considerable amount of discussion centering upon the need for improved training in accounting and economics, although there is no evidence to suggest that any significant changes have taken place. In many cases, collective farm leaders know little about these subjects, and those who do, have only a formalized training. Much of the training of a bookkeeper apparently centers upon acquiring routine skills for such tasks as the completion of plan documents. In some collective farms, a planning department has been established headed either by a planner or an economist-planner, or alternatively, there may be an economist conducting such operations within the accounting department. Likely the latter system prevails, though the number of trained economists is minimal. This will also mean that even given proportional managerial recruitment among all types of specialists, very few managers will be economists or accountants, given the exceedingly small numbers of these specialists

[35]This conclusion is derived mainly from the increase in the proportion of "other specialities" under the secondary educational level. As such, it is not a very strong conclusion and therefore must not be seen as seriously conflicting with other conclusions in the present chapter.

Table 8-17

Educational Level of Accountants, Bookkeepers and Counters on Soviet Collective Farms, 1960 (Percentage)

	Accountants Head of Kol. Accounting	Accountants Bookkeepers in Office	Bookkeepers & Counters in Brig. & Ferm	All Accounting Workers in Kol.[a]
Working in kolkhozy	100.0	100.0	100.0	100.0
of which:				
Complete higher ed.	0.5	0.2	0.1	0.2
Complete secondary specialized ed.	10.5	7.5	1.9	5.5
graduates:				
Agr. schools for kol. accountants	35.4	23.4	4.2	16.8
All-Union extension accounting courses	29.4	13.4	3.3	11.5
Short-term courses for bookkeepers	22.1	23.0	13.1	18.6
Total:	97.7	67.5	22.6	52.5
Without bookkeeping training:	2.1	32.5	77.4	47.4

Source: V.P. Rozhin, *Nekotorye voprosy pod'ema ekonomiki slabykh kolkhozov* (Moskva: Ekonomizdat, 1961), p. 52.

Note: As of January 1.

[a]Not including bookkeeper-adjustors.

vis-a-vis the agronomists and zoötechnicians. The absence, until recently, of a decree *(polozhenie)* about economists and their role on collective farms, and lack of support on these matters from above suggest that improvement will be slow.[36]

According to V.P. Rozhin, as of December 1, 1959, there were 197.7 thousand economists and economic-statisticians with higher education in the Soviet economy and 337.5 thousand statisticians and planners with specialized secondary education.[37] How have the kolkhozy fared in obtaining the services of this group?

[36]There has been a good deal of criticism in the Soviet press pertaining to the lack of economists on collective farms. Frequently they simply don't exist and their tasks fall to others who are inadequately prepared. There have been frequent requests for a "polozhenie" or definitive statement as to their proper role in the collective farm, but such a statement has not materialized. See, for example, "Ob ekonomiste kolkhoza," *Uchet i finansy v kolkhozakh i sovkhozakh*, No. 1 (January 1962), pp. 28-32. A similar criticism was voiced in 1964. See A. Grigor'siants, "Kolkhoznyi ekonomist," *Kolkhoznoe-sovkhoznoe proizvodstvo Uzbekistana*, No. 11 (November 1964), pp. 41-43. Another recent article is critical of the Ministry of Agriculture of the RSFSR for lack of assistance in the improvement of economic training in the Ryazan agricultural institute. See M.F. Gainetdinov, "Ob ikonomickeskoi podgotovke spetsialistov sel'skogo khoziaistva," *Uchet i finansy v kolkhozakh i sovkhozakh*, No. 3 (March 1963), pp. 39-40.

[37]V.P. Rozhin, op. cit., p. 54.

While data for the country as a whole is not available, in Krasnordarskii Krai, one of the most advanced agricultural regions in the Soviet Union, the following ratios prevailed in 1959: 13.4 agronomists, zoötechnicians, veterinarians and engineers with higher or specialized secondary education per collective farm; and an economist-planner similarly trained for every third collective farm.[38] The situation has improved somewhat in the Krasnodar region. In 1965, there were 308 economist-planners with higher or specialized secondary education for approximately 338 collective farms.[39]

The absence of significant training in accounting, economics and related subjects for rural personnel would seem to be a decisive restriction in any realistic decentralization effort, especially introduction of khozraschet at the brigade level.

**The Kolkhoz Chairman —
A Profile**

From the various formal characteristics examined in this chapter, a profile of the collective farm manager emerges. Typically, the kolkhoz chairman is a male, 40 years of age with a specialized secondary education. He was selected for the position by the Party, and would be a Party member. He will have shown formal educational achievement (especially education in an agricultural specialty), political reliability and, above all, administrative experience in previous positions. While this experience was probably gained outside the kolkhoz during the 1950s, there is some evidence to suggest that for the 1960s, promotion from within became increasingly likely.[40]

In a very real sense, the recent past is evidence of a continuing effort to create a "professional" kolkhoz manager—a rural counterpart of the industrial plant manager. Those managers interviewed by the author were of this type and indeed they managed highly successful farms.[41] They were, in almost all instances, impressive personalities—in fact prototypes of the popular conception of the American executive—continually on the move, prone to ulcers and other disorders, constantly on the telephone and so on. These managers were knowledgeable about their farms. One had the feeling that they were in touch with operations in the most remote corners, and for decisions such as when to begin the harvest in a particular field of a given brigade, the managerial voice would be important. These managers were definitely models of a new "professional" manager.

Managerial personnel and the nature and importances of offices which they

[38] *Narkhoz Krasnodarskogo Kraia* (Krasnodar: Statistika, 1965), p. 291.
[39] Ibid.
[40] Jerry Hough, op. cit., p. 118.
[41] Based upon personal observations of the author on several good collective farms of the Krasnodar region during August of 1966.

hold cannot, however, be summarized simply in terms of age, sex and similar sorts of variables. The managerial achievement is, after all, part of a more general career pattern in which one assumes a measure of upward mobility. In this respect, there may be much to be done in upgrading collective farm management. Our interviewees were, after all, a select group from among the best and thus cannot be taken to represent the vast bulk of farm chairmen. Further, the position of chairman may enjoy a good deal of respect within the rural sector, though the evidence suggests that this respect is not found in the urban sector. The position of chairman has tended to be an end position with little likelihood of promotion to higher levels—indeed as Jerry Hough has pointed out, such promotion is a relatively more complicated procedure in agriculture than it would be for the industrial manager moving up within the ministerial system.[42]

Finally, the patterns of managerial selection have fluctuated quite significantly during the past twenty years. These waverings may in fact suggest the absence of any well defined state policy on "professionalization" of the managerial group in collective agriculture, for indeed much of the qualitative improvement that we have noted can be explained as a by-product of the amalgamation and conversion movements.

[42] Jerry Hough, op. cit., p. 119.

9 Conclusions

The Soviet collective farm is in no sense a cooperative organization insofar as the significant aspects of its structure and operation are concerned. This seemingly simple conclusion lays to rest many of the imagined though non-existent differences between the kolkhoz and the sovkhoz as forms of agricultural organization in the Soviet Union.

The practical operation of the kolkhoz seems to differ significantly from its theoretical underpinnings. The kolkhoz, rather than being a self governing, semi-autonomous unit maximizing a member dividend, is, in fact, an organization almost wholly subservient to the planning apparatus and operating within a net of institutional, legal and economic controls serving to constrain the kolkhoz within operational bounds differing little from those of regular state organizations.

In this respect, the effect of monetization on the kolkhoz has been quite limited and developed almost entirely within the traditional planning apparatus. This apparatus remains based, in large measure, upon physical input-output patterns, the expressions of which in ruble terms are of doubtful theoretical or practical relevance for purposes of economic decision making. In this latter respect, it is apparent that a fundamental similarity exists between industrial economic reform and the changes examined in the collective farm sector. This similarity is reflected in the need for fundamental improvement in the nature of the *price system*, and, for the agricultural sector, the need to come to grips with costing problems, most notably the inclusion of land rental charges and appropriate charges for capital.

At the same time, the period since the early 1950s has been one of important and positive change in Soviet collective agriculture. The educational level of farm chairmen has improved and they, along with the farm members, have come to enjoy significantly increased rewards. Also, there is evidence of important, if limited, expansion of managerial authority in combination with the introduction of new, even though crude, decision making tools. Can we consider the trends outlined in this study as representing a significant shift away from the methods of collective farm operation as applied to an era when extensive cultivation was appropriate and towards those methods necessary in the search for intensive methods? The answer to this question must necessarily be hesitant, for while individual changes in the collective farm sector have been viewed with some clarity, these changes, when viewed in broad perspective, appear in many instances to be sharply contradictory. Indeed, the contradictions become most apparent when the period is appraised in terms of degrees of decentralization of decision making. To gain insight into these changes, we first borrow an interpretative model as developed for the study of Soviet industrial management, and second, examine the contradictory aspects of collective farm development in the light of this model.

While discussing industrial management in the Soviet Union, David Granick has argued that, in effect, two managerial systems (the "fundamental" and the "khozraschet") exist simultaneously, and yet given the non-feasibility of incorporation of the two models, one typically dominates the other.[1] The simultaneous existence of both models, it is argued, represents an ambivalence on the part of Soviet leaders who, recognizing the difficulties associated with the fundamental model, turn to the khozraschet model for an improved managerial system.[2] In spite of the difficulty of determining at any point in time the degree to which these two models have in fact been incorporated, the general interpretation of Soviet management suggested by Granick and applied to the agricultural sector by Karcz can lend significant assistance to our understanding of recent trends in the management of collective farms.

The period since 1950, when viewed in the framework developed by Granick, can be represented as a shift away from the fundamental model and towards the khozraschet model for the management of the collective farm. This interpretation avoids a not atypical western habit of viewing economic reform, in particular, expansion of the khozraschet model, as a unidirectional shift away from the rigidities of a highly centralized command model and, therefore, it is not difficult to conclude, towards a decentralized profit-oriented system.[3]

Our initial hypothesis suggested that the developments of the 1950s and 1960s tended to move Soviet collective agriculture away from a rigidly centralized and physically targeted planning system towards a semi-decentralized "value-targeted" model. This shift, it was suggested, could be found in the nature of the managerial framework, the decision making tools utilized by management and indeed the quality of the managers as potential decision makers. Evidence has been presented to suggest that indeed such a shift has in fact oc-

---

[1]The fundamental model in simplistic form can be equated with the traditional command model—a high degree of centralization, planning largely in physical terms with multiple objectives, formal and informal managerial response to a rigid incentive structure and so on. The khozraschet model, on the other hand, is a prototype of a market model—a measure of decentralization of decision-making, greater reliance upon a cost-profit calculus etc. For a detailed development of these decision-making models and their applicability in Soviet industry, see David Granick, *Soviet Metal-Fabricating and Economic Development* (Madison: University of Wisconsin Press, 1967), Ch. 7.

[2]The difficulties with the fundamental model—inappropriate success indicators, managerial emphasis on the short run, stress upon capital intensity and so on, are so well known to the student of the Soviet economy that they need not be repeated here. For elaboration, see David Granick, op. cit. For an interesting application of these models to agriculture, see Jerzy F. Karcz, "An Organizational Model of Command Farming," op. cit.

[3]Thus both the fundamental and the khozraschet system operate simultaneously, the latter being introduced to alleviate problems arising from the dysfunctional features of the fundamental model. The sympathy of planners, however, remains largely with the fundamental model.

curred, and yet its magnitude has been limited precisely because the khozraschet model of Soviet management is itself widely misunderstood and frequently grossly overstated as being a decentralized variant of a cost-profit framework. The hesitancy of Soviet leaders on the question of economic reform in the collective sector of Soviet agriculture is most evident when one examines the sharp contradictions in the trends outlined in this study—in particular, trends of both centralization and decentralization of decision making. Thus a sense of balance is most difficult to achieve. In what sense can we argue that the introduction of khozraschet is a limited achievement for the collective farm and where indeed are the contradictions?

First, khozraschet, as we have suggested, is only in a very limited sense anything more than an accounting system and the value representation of an otherwise physically directed variable. While it is true that khozraschet has been pushed broadly in the collective farm sector (even at the brigade level), this development has not itself significantly altered the power of the farm manager to structure the input-output mix. More important, where managerial flexibility seems to have expanded, much of the earlier "physical" (fundamental) system remains in the form of guidance norms, or, systems of controls which have been elaborated to direct appropriately (primarily in accordance with central wishes) the khozraschet system. At best, therefore, introduction of the khozraschet system is an attempt to improve the execution of planning, and it is very distant from a system in which managers respond to the "messages" of a decentralized cost-profit calculus.

Second, where a significant degree of local decision making flexibility has been introduced, difficulties, normally associated with the industrial manager, have been introduced to the farm manager. In this regard, one need only cite the case of farm machinery and equipment. Granted it rests in the kolkhoz, probably even at the brigade level, and yet the absence of storage space and spare parts is reminiscent of a short-term planning horizon and similar defects of the industrial planning and supply system. In this respect, it may be that the second of the famous "two bosses" referred to by Khrushchev, once concentrated in the MTS, is now fragmented, parts of which are to be found in the Raion, the agricultural supply system and the tolkach who rides his motorcycle from farm to farm in search of spare parts.

Third, to the extent that the collective farm managerial system is moving towards the khozraschet model, the pattern is similar to that experienced in the industrial sector some years ago. Would it not be possible to learn from the industrial experience, especially since the khozraschet model in that sector has been the subject of so much reform discussion in recent years? In effect, the collective farm system is introducing an intermediate step, and thus it is not surprising to find, in the agricultural sector, some of the problems associated with planning in the industrial sector. If this interpretation is reasonable, it may be some years before significant improvement in agricultural management can be expected. In particular, it will be necessary to implement in agriculture some of the much discussed reforms of the industrial sector—notably reduction of tutelage over management, simplification of plan targets and norms, and significant improvement in the price system and associated costing procedures.

It might be objected that a direct comparison of agricultural and industrial khozraschet leads to unreasonable conclusions given the relatively primitive level of development of the former as opposed to the latter. Certainly to the extent that the khozraschet system and its components (cost accounting for example) are introduced into the collective farm sector in a meaningful way, undesirable aspects of the planning system may be perceived in sharper focus and corrective state and Party directives may be forthcoming. Indeed, the introduction of cost accounting in 1956 brought the severity of the pricing problem into sharp relief, to which Soviet leaders responded with price increases and significant if most limited changes in the methodology of price formulation and adjustment. To the extent that these sorts of changes can introduce even the beginnings of intensive cultivation, they will have been beneficial, and yet we must recall, the marriage of the khozraschet and fundamental models has never been especially successful.[4]

Thus we have suggested that the events of the past twenty years have not served to alter, in any fundamental sense, the parametric framework in which collective farm managers operate—there is no intention of instigating a full cost-profit calculus to direct economic activity. Rather, there is an effort to improve the efficiency of plan performance. To interpret more liberally the shift from a fundamental to a khozraschet model would, we suggest, seriously overstate the perceived gains of the latter model. This has been argued in terms of the very limited nature of the khozraschet model. Let us now turn to the significant contradictions, in effect, the attempts to curtail even the limited khozraschet model.

While many of the changes that we have examined can in a simple sense be described as decentralization of decision making, there has nevertheless been a significant thrust towards centralization.

First, in spite of important regional differentials in amalgamation and the continuing conversion of kolkhozy to sovkhozy, the general trend of amalgamation has been clear: the typical kolkhoz is, today, significantly larger than in the past, bringing it, in a sense, "closer" to the Raion and other external and superior organs. In this light, control from above might well be greater rather than less.

Second, the amalgamation process has re-structured the brigade such that in both size and pattern of operation, in many instances it closely resembles the kolkhoz of the past. Not only is the typical brigade larger, many are producing multiple products with a permanent operational base. If expansion of decision

---

[4]This question is really fundamental to reform in the planned economies. It involves, in essence, the extent to which plan and market mechanisms can be effectively combined in a single system, where political leaders are unwilling to place exclusive reliance upon a single system.

making power within the kolkhoz is to have anything more than a formal significance, surely the relevant comparison is the *brigade* of 1970 and the *kolkhoz* of 1950. Our analysis of the managerial system when viewed in this light would suggest that the sorts of improvements outlined may have in fact been much less significant than they at first appeared to be. The introduction of cost accounting has certainly been a major improvement, and yet at the brigade level, it remains of very limited significance. Not even at the kolkhoz level do we find improvement in the volume of talent concentrated in the accounting and economic areas. Also, our examination of improvement in managerial quality (Chapter 8) suggests that while quite significant, this improvement has been concentrated almost totally at the kolkhoz level with only very marginal improvement at the brigade level.

To characterize the changes since 1950 within a framework of centralization and decentralization, it is apparent that some changes have offset others, the net result being at best a limited measure of decentralization of decision making. That there has been a limited measure of decentralization seems evident, for while there is both contradictory and negative evidence involving in a sense a rather subjective weighting of the evidence, some of the changes pointing to decentralization must be considered as especially significant in the Soviet agricultural schema. The abolition of the MTS is a significant example of this sort of change. At the same time, it must be noted that in the Soviet Union, regional differences are usually very important, and while the conclusions of this study are based upon what appear to be generally prevailing patterns, especially the concept of simple amalgamation, this has not been the pattern at all times.

Finally, it must be stressed that the concept of decentralization is very difficult to characterize with any degree of precision. The present study has concentrated upon developments within the kolkhozy. But, decentralization is more than this and above all must include consideration of decision making external to but vitally connected with the operations of the kolkhoz.

Thus far the changes in decision making procedures on Soviet collective farms have been characterized within the framework of the fundamental and khozraschet decision making models. However, the sorts of conclusions drawn thus far require a broader interpretation which can be found in the long standing features of Soviet agricultural policies and their ideological underpinnings.

First, even to the degree that Soviet leaders do in fact correctly perceive the difficulties of generating efficient agricultural production, they do not see solutions to existing problems in the absence of rather active state intervention. Quite apart from a long standing Soviet predilection towards a general and active role for the state in economic affairs, Soviet leaders see in the agriculturally "successful" countries (notably the United States), a record of market failure and continuing state intervention on a significant scale. Apart from the merits of this view, it seems that the message, however crude, is not lost in the continuing debate as to appropriate forms of organization for agricultural production.

Second, agriculture seems to be viewed by at least some Soviet leaders as inherently inferior to industry. Partly this is reflected in the extent to which an active role for the state is pursued, but it is also reflected in the continuing ambivalence as to the relative merits of the kolkhoz vis-a-vis the sovkhoz. Although we return to this question shortly, suffice it to say at this point that the state farm networks around large cities were in part created to utilize the perceived superiorities of the sovkhoz in solving the problem of potato-vegetable shortages. Partly, however, it has been argued that large sums of investment were necessary, and these could only come from direct state intervention.

Third, while some Soviet economists and possibly a handful of Soviet leaders may appreciate the niceties of an economic system directed by prices operating in a general cost-profit calculus, this form of "rationality" is not destined to play an important role in collective agriculture for at least two broad reasons. First, the mathematical generation of scarcity prices is still a great distance from becoming operational reality. Second, quite apart from the traditional and lasting Soviet distrust of the market mechanism and its "anarchy," the *plan* is seen as a far superior instrument for the rapid and accurate direction of economic activity. These thoughts, while not in themselves especially profound, are reflected in the Soviet development experience.

There seems to be a general tendency for economists in the West to downplay the role of ideology in the formation and execution of Soviet economic policy—the quotations from Marx are not infrequently seen as the usual window dressing of orthodoxy required prior to any real discussion of the subject at hand. However, the changes in Soviet collective agriculture over the past twenty years, when viewed in an ideological framework, appear to conform rather well to basic ideological positions.

The collective farm, as we have seen, has been considered as ideologically inferior to the state farm. Reform, therefore, might well be viewed within a narrow context since, in Soviet eyes, the normal path of historical development will "strengthen" the kolkhoz as an organizational form to a point where it, along with the existing state farms, will merge to create a new organizational form capable of combining and utilizing the best features of both and appropriate for the future Soviet (Communist) society. Whether these sorts of changes are historically "necessary" is a question that need not be pursued here.

Viewed in historical perspective, however, the *raison d'etre* for the collective farm, namely, manipulation of rural living levels and appropriation by the state of an agricultural "surplus", however we may ultimately appraise the success of that venture, has disappeared with the Soviet economy at a higher level of economic development. What was historically perceived to be the most important feature of the kolkhoz may prove to be, at a later stage of economic development, a negative feature.[5] To the extent that the kolkhoz as an organization

---

[5] As noted in the Introduction, Jerzy Karcz has argued that in fact, the product contribution of Soviet agriculture to the development process has been held down in the long run due to the solidification of, and hence apparently permanent nature of the negative features of the kolkhoz as a production organization. See Jerzy F. Karcz, "From Stalin to Brezhnev: Soviet Agricultural Policy in Historical Perspective," op. cit.

cannot be converted to the needs of intensive agricultural production, it does not bode well for the utilization of this type of organizational form in the less developed countries—unless its contribution at an earlier stage, possibly within the peculiar context of collectivization and all that that implies, is seen as paramount.

It may well be wide of the mark to even suggest that there is any predisposition on the part of Soviet leaders to re-structure the managerial system in kolkhozy, especially along the lines of a cost-profit calculus. Where kolkhozy have performed well, there is a tendency to leave them alone, and yet where performance is inadequate, conversion has been a popular reform mechanism. One might suggest that the kolkhoz is not a viable organizational form for the present level of Soviet development since in many instances it does not serve the needs of efficiency and change, except in selected instances, in which cases Soviet researchers do not seem able to isolate the reasons for "success" and transfer the knowledge to less fortunate farms. The "good" kolkhoz may be less a function of the organizational form as such and more a function of other factors, for example natural conditions and state credits. In the Soviet planning framework, state assistance can be more effectively channeled through the sovkhoz. At the same time, the organizational changes in the collective farm sector may be a continuing part of the perpetual Soviet search for the solution of economic problems through organizational shuffling and an appropriate definition of optimal size of farm organizations.

Maybe we ought to be asking different questions, and in particular focusing directly upon the kolkhoz as it is, rather than its ability to adapt to change, and its relevance as an organizational mechanism in developing countries. Whether significant decentralization of decision making and a concomitant change in the kolkhoz managerial system would, under present circumstances prevailing in the Soviet Union, improve performance is a moot question; these sorts of changes have occurred only to a very limited degree. One might conclude that, since Soviet leaders are presumably in the best position to perfect the kolkhoz within their own environment, it may be that within the prevailing political and other constraints the kolkhoz is not capable of being significantly altered to perform new tasks.

Whether the kolkhoz could be made to work differently under differing political, institutional and economic conditions is an open question. In the present Soviet case, however, to the extent that reform of the kolkhoz rather than conversion to sovkhozy is utilized as a mechanism for change, the dysfunctional features of the khozraschet model in the industrial sector may become pervasive in the agricultural sector. If trends of the recent past continue, it may be necessary to analyze these developments within the sovkhoz sector, or at a minimum, within kolkhozy that bear very little resemblance to those of the past.

Appendixes

Appendix A

Standard Charter of an
Agricultural Artel[1]

Standard Charter of an Agricultural Artel Approved by the Second Convention of Shock Workers of the Collective Farms and Confirmed by the Council of People's Commissars of the U.S.S.R. and by the Central Committee of the All-Union Communist Party *(Bolsheviki)* on February 17, 1935.

I. Aims and Purposes

1. The toiling peasants of the village (settlement, hamlet, *khutor, kishlak, aul*) of . . . . in the district of . . . . voluntarily band together into an agricultural artel in order to establish, with common means of production and with organized common labor, a collective, i.e., a joint farm, to insure complete victory over the kulaki, over all the exploiters and enemies of the toilers, over want and ignorance, over the backwardness of small individual farming, to create high productivity of labor and, by this means, to insure the well-being of the members.

The path of collective farming, the path of socialism, is the only right path for the toiling peasants. The members of the artel take upon themselves the obligation to strengthen their artel, to work honestly, to distribute the collective farm income according to the amount of work done, to guard the common property, to take care of the collective farm property, to keep the tractors and machinery in good order, to tend the horses carefully, to execute the tasks imposed by the workers' and peasants' government in order to make theirs a bolshevist collective farm and all its members prosperous.

II. The Land

2. All bounds that have hitherto divided the land allotments of the members of the artel shall be abolished, and all individual allotments in the fields shall be converted into one great solid piece of land, which shall be in the collective use of the artel.

Land occupied by the artel (like any other land in the U.S.S.R.) is governmental property of all the people. Under the laws of the workers' and peasants' State the use of the land shall be secured to the artel for an indefinite period,

---

[1] Reproduced by permission of the University of Michigan, from Vladimir Gsovski, *Soviet Civil Law* (Ann Arbor: University of Michigan Law School, 1949), pp. 441-462.

that is to say, forever, and may be neither sold nor bought nor let by the artel.

The executive committees of the district soviets shall issue to each collective farm a government title deed securing the use of the land for an indefinite period and fixing the size and exact boundaries of the land used by the artel; this land may not be decreased, but may be increased, either out of the free government land reserve or the extra land occupied by independent peasants, always, however, preserving the land of the collective farm in one block.

A small tract of land shall be allocated from the collectivized landholdings for the personal use of each household in the collective farm in the form of a house-and-garden plot (vegetable garden, garden, orchard).

The size of plots assigned for individual use by households (exclusive of the site of the house) may vary from one-quarter hectare [0.62 acres] to one-half hectare [1.24 acres], and, in certain districts, to one hectare [2.47 acres], depending upon regional and district conditions, as determined by the people's commissariats for agriculture of the constituent republics on the basis of directions issued by the U.S.S.R. People's Commissariat for Agriculture.

3. The land enclosure of the artel may in no case be diminished. It is forbidden to parcel allotments out of the artel's land enclosure to such members as leave the artel. Departing members may receive allotments only out of the free lands of the government land fund.

The land of the artel shall be divided into separate fields to correspond with the established system of crop rotation. Each field brigade is to work on the same portion of land during an established period of crop rotation.

Collective farms which possess large stockbreeding farms may, in case of need, and if they have a sufficient amount of land, parcel out certain tracts of land to be attached to the stockbreeding farms and used for the cultivation of fodder for the animals.

III. Means of Production

4. The following objects shall be owned only collectively: all draught animals, agricultural implements (plows, sowing machines, harrows, threshing machines, mowing machines, et cetera) seed reserves, forage necessary for collectively owned livestock, buildings needed for collective farming, and all establishments processing agricultural products.

The following objects shall not be pooled in the collective capital and shall remain in the personal use of the household of a collective farmer: dwellings, personal cattle, and poultry, as well as buildings necessary for keeping such cattle.

When farming implements are pooled, minor implements needed for tilling the house-and-garden plots shall be left to the individual households.

The management of the artel may, if necessary, allot a few horses out of the total number of collectively owned draught animals to serve the personal needs of the members, but on the condition that these services are to be paid for. The artel shall organize a mixed stockbreeding farm or, if there are a large number of animals, several specialized stockbreeding farms.

5. In the regions of cultivation of grain, sugar beets, cotton, flax, hemp, potatoes and vegetables, tea and tobacco, each household in the collective farm may have in its individual possession one cow, not more than two calves, one sow with sucklings or, if the management of the collective farm should think it advisable, two sows with sucklings, not more than ten sheep and goats together, an unlimited number of fowl and rabbits, and not more than twenty beehives.

In agricultural regions with developed stockbreeding, each household in the collective farm may have in its individual possession two or three cows with their calves, two or three sows with sucklings, twenty or twenty-five sheep and goats altogether, an unlimited number of fowl and rabbits, and not more than twenty beehives. Such districts are, for instance, the agricultural districts of Kazakstan not bordering on nomadic districts, forest districts of White Russia, the Chernigov and Kiev provinces of the Ukraine, the districts of the Baraba Steppes and Altai districts of Western Siberia, the Ishim and Tobolsk groups of districts of the Omsk province, the hilly part of Bashkiria, the eastern part of Eastern Siberia, the agricultural districts of the Far Eastern area, and the Vologda and Holmogory groups of districts in the northern area.

In nonnomadic or seminomadic stockbreeding regions, where agriculture is of small significance and stockbreeding plays the leading part in agriculture, each household in the collective farm may have in its individual possession four or five cows with their calves, thirty or forty sheep and goats in all, two or three sows with sucklings, an unlimited number of fowl and rabbits, not more than twenty beehives, and also one horse or one milking mare or two camels or donkeys or two mules. Such, for instance, are the following districts: the stockbreeding districts of Kazakstan bordering on nomadic districts, the stockbreeding districts of Turkomanistan, Tadjikistan, Kara-Kalpakia, Kirghizia, Oirotia, Khakassia, the western part of Buryato-Mongolia, the Kalmyk autonomous region, the hilly districts of the Daghestan autonomous republic, the Chechen-Ingush, Kabarda-Balkarsk, Karachaevsk and Ossetin autonomous provinces of the Northern Caucasus, and also the hilly parts of the Azerbaijan, Armenian, and Georgian soviet socialist republics.

In the districts of nomadic stockbreeding, where agriculture has almost no significance and where stockbreeding is the all-embracing branch of farming, each household in the collective farm may have in its individual possession eight or ten cows with their calves, 100 to 150 sheep and goats in all, an unlimited number of fowl, up to ten horses, five or eight camels. Such districts, for instance, are the nomadic districts of Kazakstan, the Nogai district, and the nomadic districts of Buryato-Mongolia.

*IV. The Work of the Artel and
Its Management*

6. The artel binds itself to conduct its collective farming according to plan, observing exactly the plans of agricultural production drawn up by the agencies of the workers' and peasants' government and the duties of the artel towards the government.

The artel shall accept for precise execution the programs of sowing, fallow plowing, weeding, harvesting, threshing, and autumn plowing prescribed in consideration of the condition and peculiarities of collective farms, and also the government plan for the development of stockbreeding.

The management and all the members of the artel bind themselves:

(a) To increase the fertility of the fields of the collective farm by the introduction and observance of correct rotation of crops, deep plowing, extermination of weeds, increasing and improving the fallow and autumn plowing, timely and careful hoeing of cotton plantations, putting in manure taken from the stockbreeding farms and from households belonging to the collective farms, putting in mineral fertilizers, extermination of pests, timely and careful harvesting without losses, tending and cleaning the irrigation constructions, safeguarding the forests, planting trees to shelter the fields, and the strictest observance of all agricultural and technical regulations established by the local land authorities;

(b) To select the best seeds for sowing, to purify them from any admixture to keep them safe from damage and pilfering, to store them in clean, well-ventilated premises, to increase the sowing of purebred seeds;

(c) To increase the area sown by utilization of all land at the disposal of the artel, by improvement and cultivation of waste lands, by plowing up virgin land, and by introduction of effective land distribution within the collective farm;

(d) To make full use, on a collective basis, of all draught animals and traction engines, of all implements and agricultural machinery, of seeds, and of all other means of production which the artel possesses, and also of all tractors, motors, threshers, combines, and other machinery which the workers' and peasants' government supplies to the collective farms through the machine-tractor stations, to tend livestock and machinery correctly, and to make every endeavor to keep animals and machinery in the collective farm in good order and condition;

(e) To organize stockbreeding farms and, in those localities where conditions are favorable, horsebreeding farms, to increase the number of animals, to improve the breeds and the fecundity of animals, to help members who work honestly on the collective farm, in purchasing cows and small cattle, to mate cows, mares, et cetera, with improved and purebred bulls, stallions, et cetera, not only those collectively owned, but also those cows, mares, et cetera, which are individually owned by members, and to observe the established zoological, technical, and veterinary regulations with respect to stockbreeding;

(f) To increase the production of fodder, to improve meadows and pastures, to render assistance to members who conscientiously work in common production, and to ensure for them, so far as possible, the use of the pastures of the collective farm, and also to give them, so far as possible, fodder for the cattle owned by them individually, on account of labor days credited to them;

(g) To develop all other branches of agricultural production in correspondence with local natural conditions, and also to develop home industries in correspondence with the conditions prevailing in the district, to take care of ponds and keep them clean, to dig new ponds and stock them with fish;

(h) To organize the construction of communal farm buildings by common labor;

(i) To improve the labor qualifications of the members, to assist the members in training for such duties as brigadiers, tractor drivers, combine operators, drivers, veterinary surgeons and sanitary experts, stablemen, sow herders, cowmen, shepherds, field laboratory assistants;

(j) To raise the cultural standard of the members, to introduce newspapers, books, radios, to establish clubs, lending libraries, and reading rooms, to build public baths and hairdressing shops, to construct clean and airy field-camps, to keep the village streets in good order, to plant various trees, especially fruit-bearing trees, to assist the members in improving and decorating their houses;

(k) To draw the women into the work of the collective farm and the social life of the artel, to appoint capable and experienced women members to managerial posts, so far as possible to free women from domestic work by establishing crèches, playgrounds for children, and so forth.

V. Membership

7. Admission to membership shall be granted by the general meeting of the members, which confirms the lists of new members submitted by the management.

All toilers, women as well as men, who have attained the age of sixteen, may join the artel.

No kulaki nor persons deprived of the franchise shall be admitted to the artel.

Note: From this rule shall be exempt:

(a) Children of the disfranchised who, for a number of years, have been engaged in publicly useful work and who are working conscientiously;

(b) Former kulaki and members of their families who, having been deported for their anti-soviet and anti-collectivist activities, have proved at the place of their deportation for a period of three years, by their honest work and by their support of the measures passed by the soviet government, that they have reformed.

Independent peasants who have sold their horses in the two years preceding their entering the artel, or who have no seed, shall be admitted to the artel on

the condition that they bind themselves to refund the cost of a horse by install-
ments out of their income over a period of six years and to surrender the
required quantity of seed in kind.

8. Members may be expelled from the artel only by a resolution of the general meeting at which not less than two thirds of the total number of the members
are present. The number of members present at the general meeting and the
number of votes cast for expulsion should be explicitly stated in the minutes of
the meeting. If an expelled member appeals his expulsion to the District Executive Committee, the case shall be decided finally by the presidium of the District
Executive Committee of Soviets in the presence of the chairman of the artel and
the appellant.

VI. Funds of the Artel

9. A member admitted to the artel shall pay an entrance fee of from twenty
to forty rubles according to his economic capacity. The entrance fee shall go to
the indivisible fund of the artel.

10. From one quarter to one half of the value of the collectively owned
property of the members (draught animals, machinery, farm buildings, et cetera)
shall go into the indivisible fund of the artel; the more well-to-do the member,
the larger the proportion of his property which shall go into the indivisible fund.
The remaining portion of the property shall be considered the share of the
member.

When the relationship of a member with the collective farm is severed, the
management shall settle accounts with the departing member and shall return to
him his share in money; the departing member may obtain a land allotment only
outside the land enclosure belonging to the artel. As a rule, the settlement of
accounts is effected at the end of the agricultural season.

11. Out of the crops gathered and the animal products raised, the artel shall:

(a) Fulfill its obligations towards the State with respect to deliveries of products and the return of seed loans; pay the machine-tractor station in kind for the
work done by the station, in accordance with the contract, which has the force
of the law, and fulfill other contracts entered into;

(b) Store seed for the next year's sowing and fodder for animals for the whole
year, and create permanent, annually renewed seed and fodder funds of from 10
to 15 per cent of the annual needs, in order to insure itself against failure of
crops or a shortage of fodder;

(c) In accordance with the decision of the general meeting, create funds to
assist disabled, old, or sick people and poor families of Red Army soldiers, and
to support crèches and waifs; all these funds should not exceed 2 per cent of the
total annual production;

(d) Fix the proportion of the products which, in accordance with the decision of the general meeting, are to be sold to the government or on the free market;

(e) Distribute all the remaining portion of the crops and animal products produced by the artel among its members according to the number of labor days credited to each member.

12. From its cash proceeds, the artel shall:

(a) Pay to the government taxes established by law and insurance premiums, and repay money loans of preferential status;

(b) Defray expenses necessary to cover the current needs of production, such as current repairs of agricultural machinery and implements, medical treatment of animals, the combating of pests, et cetera.

(c) Defray administrative expenses of the artel to the extent of not more than 2 per cent of the total income in money;

(d) Assign money for cultural needs, such as training personnel of the collective farms, organizing crèches and children's playgrounds, purchasing radios, et cetera;

(e) Replenish the indivisible funds of the artel for the purchase of cattle, agricultural machinery, and building materials, and for paying wages to workers hired for building operations;

The total sum assigned for replenishing the indivisible fund in grain regions shall be not less than 12 per cent and not more than 15 per cent of the total cash income of the artel and in regions of industrial crops and animal husbandry shall be not less than 15 per cent and not more than 20 per cent of such income;

(f) The remaining cash proceeds of the artel shall be distributed among the members in accordance with the number of labor days credited to each member.

All sums received by the artel shall be entered in the books on the day when the money is received.

The management shall prepare an estimate of revenue and expenditures for the ensuing year, which estimate shall become effective only upon approval by the general meeting.

The management may make expenditures only in accordance with the appropriations provided for in the estimate; arbitrary shifting of appropriations from one item of the expenditure estimate to another shall not be permitted, and the management shall obtain the consent of the general meeting to transfer appropriations from one item to another.

Before the final outlook for the crops is ascertained, the management may spend for the production needs of the artel not more than 70 per cent of the appropriations provided for in the annual estimate of expenditures approved by the general meeting of members of the collective farm. The other 30 per cent shall remain in reserve and shall be spent only after the final ascertaining of the outlook for crops and the decision of the general meeting of members of the collective farm.

The artel shall keep its money in current account with a bank or a savings bank. Debits in the current account shall be made only by order of the management, which order is valid when signed by the chairman and by the accountant (as amended December 4, 1938, U.S.S.R. Laws, text 308).

VII. Organization and Remuneration of Labor and Labor Discipline

13. All operations in connection with the running of the business of the artel shall be performed by the personal labor of its members in accordance with the rules of internal organization approved by the general meeting. Nonmembers may be engaged for agricultural operations only when they possess special knowledge and training (agronomists, engineers, technicians, and so forth).

The hiring of outside casual labor shall be permitted only under exceptional circumstances, when urgent operations cannot be performed in time by the members working at full speed, and also for building and construction operations.

14. The management shall create production brigades from the members of the artel.

Members of field brigades shall be assigned for a full period of crop rotation.

A field brigade shall work the same plot for a full period of crop rotation. The management shall, under a special instrument, secure to each field brigade all necessary machinery, draught animals, and farm buildings.

Members of stockbreeding brigades shall be assigned for a period of not less than three years.

The management shall secure to each stockbreeding brigade productive cattle, as well as implements, draught animals, and buildings necessary for carrying on animal husbandry.

Work shall be distributed among the members of the brigade by the brigadier, who must make the best possible use of each member of his brigade, not permitting himself to be influenced by family or other personal considerations in distributing tasks, and taking into account the qualifications, experience, and physical fitness of each member, and, in cases of pregnant or nursing women, the necessity of alleviating their work; a woman shall be free from all work for a period of one month before and one month after giving birth, and during these two months shall receive remuneration equal to one half of the average number of labor days she normally earns.

15. Agricultural operations shall be performed on the basis of piecework remuneration.

The management shall work out and the general meeting shall confirm the required standard of output and the rates of remuneration in terms of labor days for each separate job for all agricultural operations.

Such standard of output shall be fixed for each operation according to what a conscientious collective farmer can produce with the draught animals, machinery, and soil at hand. Each operation, as, for instance, to plow one hectare, to sow one hectare, to hoe one hectare of a cotton plantation, to thresh one ton of grain, to dig out two hundredweight of sugar beets, to gather one hectare of flax, to moisten one hectare of flax, to milk one litre of milk, and so on, is to be valued in fractions of a labor day in accordance with the qualifications required of the laborer and the complexity, difficulty, and importance of the operation for the artel.

The brigadier shall, not less than once a week, compute all the work which has been done by a member and, in accordance with the established remuneration, enter the number of credited labor days in the labor book of the member.

The management shall display every month a list of the members showing the number of labor days credited to each member during the preceding month.

The annual amount of work and the income earned by each member shall be certified by the brigadier and the chairman of the artel in addition to the accountant. The list showing the number of labor days earned by each member shall be publicly displayed not later than a fortnight before the date of the general meeting which is to confirm the distribution of the income earned by the artel.

Should a field brigade, by its good work, harvest crops from its plot exceeding the average crops obtained by the artel, or should a stockbreeding brigade, by its good work, show an increased output of milk per cow, fatten cattle more successfully, or more fully ensure the preservation of young animals, the management shall increase the remuneration of the members of such brigades to the extent of 10 per cent of the total labor days credited to them; the best shock workers in the brigade are entitled to a 15 per cent increase, and brigadiers of stockbreeding farms to a 20 per cent increase.

Should an agricultural brigade, as a result of bad work, gather crops from its plot below the average yield obtained by the artel, or should a stockbreeding brigade, as a result of bad work, show a poorer output of milk per cow, poorer fattening of cattle, or greater mortality among young animals, the management shall reduce the credit in labor days of the members of such brigades to the extent of 10 per cent of the number credited to them.

The distribution of income among the members shall be made exclusively according to the number of labor days credited to each member.

16. Money may be advanced to a member during the year in an amount not to exceed 50 per cent of the sum credited to him for his work.

Advances in kind shall be made to the members of the artel by the management after the threshing is begun, and from 10 to 15 per cent of the threshed grain left for the needs of the artel may be used for this purpose.

An artel cultivating industrial crops shall not have to wait for the completion of delivery to the government of cotton, flax, sugar, tea, tobacco, et cetera, but may make money advances to its members not less than once a week in the course of delivery to the extent of 60 per cent of the money received for the delivered products.

17. All members of the artel shall assume the obligation to take good care of the property of the artel and the government-owned machinery used in the fields of the artel, to work honestly, to observe the provisions of the charter, to carry out the resolutions of the general meeting and the orders of the management, to follow the rules of internal organization of the artel, to execute conscientiously the tasks and social duties imposed upon them by the management and brigadiers, and to observe strictly labor discipline.

Members who fail to take good care of or who neglect the collective property, who fail to report for work without a justifiable reason, who work badly, or who violate labor discipline or the charter, shall be punished by the management in accordance with the rules of internal organization. For example, such member may be ordered to do the poor work over again without any credit in labor days, he may be warned, reprimanded, or reproved at the general meeting, or his name may be put on the blackboard, he may be fined up to five labor days, he may be demoted to a lower paid job or suspended from work.

In cases where all measures of an educational and penal nature applied by the artel have failed, the management shall bring before the general meeting a motion for expulsion of the incorrigible member.

Expulsion shall be carried out in accordance with the procedure provided for in Section 8 of the present Charter.

18. Any dissipation of collective and government property as well as reckless handling of the property and livestock of the collective farm and the machines of machine-tractor stations shall be deemed by the artel a betrayal of the common cause of the collective farm and aid to enemies of the people.

Persons guilty of such criminal undermining of the mainstays of collective farming shall be delivered to the court to be punished in accordance with all the severity of the laws of the workers' and peasants' State.

VIII. Management of the Artel

19. The business of the artel shall be managed by the general meeting of the members, and, in the intervals between the meetings, by the board of managers elected by the general meeting.

20. The general meeting shall be the highest authority in the management of the artel. The general meeting shall:

(a) Elect the chairman and the members of the board of managers of the artel and also the auditing committee of the artel; the auditing committee shall be confirmed by the District Executive Committee of Soviets;

(b) Admit new members to and expel members from the artel;

(c) Confirm the program of annual production, the estimate of revenue and expenditures, the building program, the standards of normal output, and the remuneration rates in terms of labor days;

(d) Confirm the contract with the machine-tractor station;

(e) Confirm the annual account of the mangement, which shall be accompanied by the opinion of the auditing committee, and also the reports of the management on the most important agricultural undertakings;

(f) Confirm the size of various funds to be put aside and the amount of produce and money to be distributed per labor day;

(g) Confirm the rules of internal organization governing the conduct of the business of the artel.

The decisions of the board of managers affecting the matters enumerated in the present section of the Charter shall be null and void if not confirmed by the general meeting.

A quorum for the general meeting shall be not less than one half of the membership of the artel; this quorum may decide all matters except the election of a chairman and members of the board of managers, the expulsion of members, and the size of various funds; for resolutions upon these matters, the presence at the general meeting of not less than two thirds of the membership shall be required.

Resolutions at the general meeting shall be made by a majority of votes, and the voting shall be effected by show of hands.

21. To run the business of the artel, the general meeting shall elect for a period of two years a board of from five to nine managers, depending upon the size of the artel.

The board of managers shall function as the executive committee of the artel and shall be responsible to the general meeting for the work of the artel and for the fulfillment of its obligations to the government.

22. For the discharge of the day-to-day direction of the work of the artel and its brigades, and for day-to-day checking on the execution of the decisions of the board of managers, the general meeting shall elect a chairman of the artel, who shall also be chairman of the board of managers.

The chairman shall convoke the boards of managers not less than twice a month to discuss the current business and to make the necessary decisions.

Upon the recommendation of the chairman, and to assist him, the board of managers shall elect a vice-chairman from among the members of the board.

The vice-chairman in all his work shall follow the directives of the chairman.

23. Brigadiers and managers of stockbreeding farms shall be appointed by the board of managers for a period of not less than two years.

24. To keep accounts and records of property, the board of managers shall appoint from among the members of the artel, or shall hire from outside an accountant. The accountant shall keep the accounts and records in accordance with the prescribed forms and shall be absolutely subordinate to the board of managers and to the chairman of the artel.

The accountant shall have no right to dispose of the funds of the artel independently, to make advance payments, or to expend the stocks of produce. Such right shall belong only to the board of managers and the chairman of the artel.

All orders for payment must be signed by the chairman or the vice-chairman of the artel in addition to the accountant.

25. The auditing committee shall verify all the economic and financial activities of the board of managers, i.e., shall ascertain whether all revenues in money and in kind are duly credited to the artel on the books, whether the procedure prescribed by the Charter of the artel for expenditures is followed, whether the property of the artel is kept adequately safe, whether there has been any misappropriation of property or embezzlement of funds of the artel, whether the artel meets its obligations to the government, whether the artel pays its debts and collects from its debtors.

In addition, the auditing committee shall carefully ascertain how the artel settles its accounts with its members and shall bring to light any case of fraudulent accounting, inaccurate credit of labor days, delay in distribution of income for labor days, or any other violation of the interests of the artel and its members.

The auditing committee shall audit the accounts four times a year. The auditing committee shall report to the general meeting its opinion on the annual accounts submitted by the board of managers, which opinion shall be heard by the general meeting immediately after the accounts of the board of managers.

The auditing committee shall be responsible for its activities to the general meeting of the members of the artel.

Appendix B *

The Model Collective Farm Charter
as Adopted, November 28, 1969[a]

I. Goals and Tasks

1. The___(name)___ Collective Farm in_____ District, _____
Region,_____Province (Territory),_____Republic, is a cooperative
organization of voluntarily associated peasants for the joint conduct of large-
scale socialist agricultural production on the basis of communal means of production and collective labor.

2. The collective farm sets as its chief tasks: to strengthen and develop the
communal sector in every way, steadily to increase labor productivity and the
effectiveness of communal production [and to instill in collective farmers the
spirit of a communist attitude toward labor] ; to increase the production and sale
to the state of agricultural output by means of the intensification and further
technical re-equipment of collective farm production, the introduction of integrated mechanization *and electrification* and the broad implementation of
chemicalization and land reclamation; *under the leadership of Party organizations, to conduct work on the communist upbringing of the collective farmers,
on drawing them into public life and on developing socialist competition; to satis-*
fy more fully the growing material and cultural requirements of the collective
farmers, to improve their living conditions and gradually to transform rural vil-
lages into well-appointed settlements.

*II. Membership in the Collective Farm and
the Rights and Obligations of Collective
Farm Members.*

3. Any citizen [of the U.S.S.R.] who has reached the age of 16 and expresses
a desire to participate through his labor in the communal sector of the collective
farm may be a member of the collective farm.

Admission to collective farm membership is carried out by the *general meet-*

*Translation copyright © 1970 by *The Current Digest of the Soviet Press*, published weekly
at the Ohio State University, Columbus. Reprinted by permission. From the *Current Digest*,
Vol. XXI, No. 50 (January 13, 1970), pp. 9-15.

[a]The draft Model Charter for the Collective Farm was published in The Current Digest of
the Soviet Press, Vol. XXI, No. 17, pp. 3-8. Changes in and additions to the draft version are
underlined. Substantive passages dropped from the draft are enclosed in brackets. Some
changes have been made in the translation, the most important being the substitution of
"communal sector" for "public economy."

ing of collective farmers [by the board of the collective farm] , *upon the recommendation of the board of the collective farm and in the presence of the person submitting the application* [upon application from a prospective member; the decision of the board is ratified by a general meeting of the members of the collective farm, in the presence of the individual who submitted the application] .

An application for admission to collective farm membership is considered by the collective farm board within one month's time.

A collective farmer's labor booklet—these are of a single form—is kept for each member of the collective farm.

4. A member of the collective farm has the right: to receive work in the communal sector of the collective farm with guaranteed pay in accordance with the quantity and quality of the labor he contributes; to participate in the administration of the collective farm's affairs, to elect and to be elected to its administrative bodies; to submit proposals for improving the collective farm's activity and for eliminating shortcomings in the work of the board and of officials; to receive assistance from the collective farm in increasing his production skills and in acquiring a speciality; to use a personal plot of land for conducting auxiliary farming, for the construction of living quarters and farm buildings, and also to use the collective farm's pastures, communally owned draft animals and transportation for personal needs, under the procedure that has been established on the collective farm; to social security, cultural and everyday services and assistance from the collective farm in the construction and repair of living quarters and in the provision of fuel.

5. A member of the collective farm is obligated: to observe the collective farm's charter and its regulations, to carry out the resolutions of general meetings and the decisions of the collective farm board; to labor conscientiously in the communal sector, observe labor discipline and master advanced methods and procedures of work; to participate actively in the administration of the collective farm's affairs, to care for, protect *and strengthen* state and collective farm property, not to tolerate mismanagement for a negligent attitude toward communal property, to utilize rationally and correctly land in communal and personal use.

6. Collective farm membership is retained by individuals who temporarily leave the collective farm, in the following cases: a tour of active military duty; election to an elective position in a Soviet, public or cooperative organization; enrollment in studies making it necessary to leave production; *assignment to work in an inter-collective farm organization*, departure for work in industry or another branch of the national economy for a period established by the collective farm board.

Collective farm membership is also retained by collective farmers who have stopped working because of old age or disability, if they continue to live on the collective farm.

7. A collective farmer's application to leave the collective farm must be con-

sidered by the collective farm board *and the general meeting of collective farm members* [with subsequent ratification of the board's decision at the next general meeting of collective farm members], no later than three months from the day the application was submitted.

The collective farm board settles all accounts with a former collective farmer as of the end of the economic year, no later than one month after the collective farm's annual report is approved.

III. The Land and Its Use

8. In accordance with the U.S.S.R. Constitution, the land held by the collective farm is allotted to it for free and permanent use, i.e., in perpetuity.

The land allotted to the collective farm is *state property* [the property of all the people and of the state], i.e., it is the common property of the nation, and it cannot be the object of purchase or sale, rental or other transactions.

The executive committee of the district (or city) Soviet issues to every collective farm a state deed on the right to use of the land, indicating the dimensions and precise boundaries of the land allotted to the collective farm.

The land allotted to the collective farm is subdivided into land for communal use and land for personal plots. The personal plots are separated by natural boundaries from the land given over to communal use.

9. The collective farm is obligated to make the fullest and most correct utilization of the land allotted to it, constantly to improve this land, to increase its fertility; *to bring unused land into agricultural production*; to carry out measures for land irrigation and drainage, for combating soil erosion and *for creating field shelter-belt plantings*; to care for collective farm land and strictly protect it from wasteful use; to observe established regulations for *the protection of nature and for* the use of forests, sources of water and useful minerals (sand, clay, stone, peat, etc.).

The board, executives and specialists of the collective farm are responsible for the highly productive use of the land.

10. A reduction in the area of the collective farm's land or changes in the boundaries of the collective farm's landholdings occasioned by state or public needs are carried out only when a general meeting of the collective farmers has given its consent and by decision of the appropriate state agencies. Moreover, the assignment for nonagricultural needs of irrigated or drained land, plowland or plots of land occupied by plantings of perennial fruits and vineyards is prohibited, as a rule.

The collective farm is entitled to compensation for losses connected with a reduction in the area of collective farm land or *the temporary occupation of this land* [changes in the boundaries of the collective farm's landholdings]. *Compensation for losses is carried out* in accordance with the procedure established by legislation now in effect.

IV. The Collective Farm's
Communal Property

11. The collective farm's communal property, along with state ownership of the land, constitutes the economic basis of the collective farm.

The collective farm's communal property consists of enterprises, buildings, installations, tractors, combines and other machinery, equipment, means of transportation, draft animals and productive livestock, perennial plantings, land-reclamation and irrigation installations, output, money and other collective farm property. *The collective farm's communal property also includes the property and resources of inter-collective farm and state-collective farm organizations and enterprises on the basis of shares.*

12. For the implementation of its activities and the further growth of the communal sector, the collective farm creates, utilizes in a planned and efficient way and replenishes fixed production assets and working capital. These assets are indivisible (they are not to be distributed among the members of the collective farm) and are used only for their designated purposes.

Fixed assets for nonproductive purposes are also indivisible.

13. The right to dispose of the property and monetary resources of the collective farm belongs only to the collective farm itself and to its administrative agencies. *The collective farm does not permit the diversion of resources for purposes not connected with its activity.*

The acquisition, sale, withdrawal from use and writing off of fixed assets and other material assets is carried out according to the procedure established by the general meeting of collective farm members and on the basis of legislation now in effect.

Collective farm members who cause the destruction, spoilage or loss of collective farm property [through their negligence or carelessness], as well as those guilty of the unauthorized use of tractors, motor vehicles, farm machinery or draft animals [or productive livestock] and those who cause material damage to the collective farm are obligated to compensate the collective farm for these actions.

The amount of actual damage is determined by the collective farm board. Penalties for damage done *are exacted in the amount of the actual damage, but no more than one-third of the basic monthly earnings of the collective farm member, if the damage was caused by carelessness in work. When the damage is inflicted deliberately, and also in cases provided for by legislation, the collective farm member is materially liable for the full amount or a higher amount. Penalties for damage done are exacted by the collective farm board, while disputed cases are settled by the people's courts* [may be set by the collective farm board, with consideration of the specific situation in which it was inflicted, in amounts up to one-third of the basic monthly earnings of the collective farm member, and larger amounts may be fixed by the people's court. A decision by a collective farm board setting a penalty for damage may be appealed to a people's court by the collective farmer involved.].

V. The Production-Economic and Financial Activity of the Collective Farm.

14. The collective farm conducts its economic activity according to a plan that is approved by the general meeting of collective farmers, employing the most progressive and scientifically substantiated forms and methods of the organization of production, which ensure the obtaining of maximum amounts of high-quality output with minimum expenditures of labor and resources.

In drawing up its plans, the collective farm proceeds from the necessity of the expanded reproduction of the communal sector, fulfillment of the plan for state purchases, contract agreements for the sale of agricultural products and the above-plan sale of grain and other output necessary to the state, and the satisfaction of the material and cultural requirements of the collective farmers.

15. The collective farm's production-financial activity is carried out on the basis of economic accountability and the wide application of moral and material incentives aimed at developing production and increasing the farm's profitability.

16. The board and all the members of the collective farm are obligated to ensure: the rational conduct of agricultural production, by means of its intensification and specialization and the preponderant development of those branches for which the best natural-economic conditions exist; an increase in the harvest yield of agricultural crops on the basis of an upswing in the standards of farming, *the observance of crop rotations, the improvement of seed growing, the systematic application of fertilizers, and the implementation of other measures*; the all-around development of animal husbandry, an increase in the productivity of livestock and poultry, the improvement of pedigreed stock breeding, the observance of zootechnical and veterinary regulations, and the creation of a firm and stable feed base for animal husbandry; the introduction in production of new machinery and progressive technology, integrated mechanization, electrification and the achievements of science and advanced experience; the conduct of land reclamation and chemicalization; the efficient use and maintenance of tractors, combines, motor vehicles and other machines, draft animals and productive livestock, buildings and installations; the construction of production buildings and cultural and service facilities, dwellings and children's institutions, roads, water-supply and other installations, in accordance with plans for the development of the farm and the buildup of communities.

17. For the purpose of the fuller and more even utilization of manpower and local sources of raw materials and of increasing the profitableness of the communal sector, the collective farm creates and develops, *without detriment to*

agricultural production, auxiliary enterprises and various sidelines *[promysly]* ; it can enter into contractual relations with industrial enterprises and trade organizations for the creation on the collective farm of branches (shops) for the production of various articles and commodities by the collective farmers in the periods that they have free from agricultural work.

18. The collective farm may take part on a voluntary basis in the activity of inter-collective farm and state-collective farm enterprises and organizations, and it may join associations and unions.

19. By decision of the general meeting of collective farmers, the collective farm may pool part of its resources with the resources of local Soviets, state farms and other state and cooperative enterprises and organizations for the construction [on the collective farm], on the basis of shares, of cultural and service facilities and public amenities and for other measures aimed at the development of collective farm production and the improvement of cultural and everyday services for the collective farmers.

20. The collective farm concludes contracts with state, cooperative and public organizations for the sale of agricultural output, the purchase of machinery, materials, livestock and other property, for the sale of semifinished products and articles made by auxiliary enterprises and sidelines, for the performance of various jobs and the provision of services, and also enters into other contractual relations in accordance with the goals of its activity.

21. The collective farm opens an account with an institution of the U.S.S.R. State Bank for the settling of accounts and the safekeeping of monetary resources and makes all deposits and settles all accounts in accordance with established regulations.

The transfer or payment of monetary funds from the account that the collective farm keeps in an institution of the U.S.S.R. State Bank is carried out on instructions from the collective farm board.

The collective farm may make use of state short-term and long-term credits.

The instructions of the collective farm board for the transfer or payment of funds from the collective farm's account and the collective farm's obligations with respect to credits are valid if they bear the signatures of the chairman and the chief bookkeeper of the collective farm.

22. The collective farm keeps bookkeeping, operational and statistical records, introduces advanced methods and forms of record-keeping, compiles reports according to approved forms and submits them to the appropriate agencies within the established deadlines.

23. The collective farm is not responsible for the obligations and debts of collective farm members. The members of the collective farm have no property liability where the obligations and debts of the collective farm are concerned.

VI. Labor Organization, Pay and Discipline.

24. All work in the communal sector of the collective farm is performed by the personal labor of the collective farmers.

The hiring of specialists and other personnel from outside is permitted only in instances in which the collective farm does not have the appropriate specialists or in which agricultural and other jobs cannot be performed by the collective farmers themselves within the requisite time period.

The collective farm introduces the scientific organization of labor and shows concern for the full and most rational utilization of manpower in communal production.

25. The length and detailed schedule of the working day on the collective farm, the procedure for granting days off and annual paid vacations, and also the minimum labor participation in the communal sector by able-bodied collective farmers, are governed by the collective farm's regulations.

26. The forms of the organization of production and labor—sectors, livestock sections, brigades, teams and other production units—are established and applied by the collective farm in accordance with the specific conditions of the farm and the level of the mechanization, specialization and technology of production.

Collective farmers are selected for membership in production units *on the basis of the interests of the development of the communal sector and* with consideration of their qualifications, work experience, skills, place of residence and personal desires.

Plots of land, tractors, machinery and equipment, draft animals and productive livestock, the necessary buildings and other means of production are assigned to the collective farm's production units [for a number of years].

The activity of the collective farm's production units is carried out on the basis of the intrafarm settling of accounts.

27. The chief source of the collective farmers' incomes is the communal sector of the collective farm. Payment for labor on the collective farm is carried out in accordance with the quantity and quality of the labor contributed by each collective farmer to the communal sector, according to the principle of higher pay for good labor, for the best results. *Increases in the pay of collective farm members are to be carried out on the basis of the preponderant growth of labor productivity*.

The collective farm employs piecework *and job-rate payment* for labor, for volume of work done or output produced, *time-rate pay*, a combination of time-rate and bonus pay, *or other systems of pay* [according to established pay scales and rates]. Work that is done poorly through the fault of the collective farmer is not paid for, or the amount of pay for it is reduced accordingly.

Output norms and pay scales for agricultural and other jobs are worked out and, when necessary, reviewed with the broad participation of the collective farmers and specialists, proceeding from the *standard output norms and with consideration of the* specific conditions of the farm, and are approved by the collective farm board.

28. The collective farm establishes guaranteed pay for collective farm members for work in communal production.

For the purpose of raising the material interest of the collective farmers in increasing agricultural output, improving its quality and lowering its unit cost, supplementary payments and other forms of material incentives are used, in addition to the basic pay.

Collective farm members who fail to fulfill the established minimum for labor participation in the communal sector without valid reasons, *and also those guilty of absenteeism*, may, by decision of the collective farm board, be partially or completely deprived of supplementary payments and other forms of material encouragement.

29. To satisfy the collective farmers' requirements for agricultural products, a payment-in-kind fund [for distribution according to labor] is created on the collective farm; a certain portion of the gross harvest of grain and other products, as well as of feed, is allocated to this fund. These products and this feed are issued *as pay* or sold to the collective farmers in quantities and under the procedure established by the general meeting of collective farm members.

30. The collective farm board ensures the prompt payment of the earnings due the collective farmers. In the process, money is paid at least once a month, and produce in kind is issued as it is received.

The final settling of accounts with the collective farmers is carried out no later than one month after the collective farm's annual report has been approved.

31. The collective farm board, guided by this Charter, draws up *regulations and* statutes on pay and on the intrafarm settling of accounts, which are ratified by the general meeting of collective farmers.

32. All jobs on the collective farm are performed with observance of the established safety rules and the requirements of production sanitation.

The collective farm allocates the necessary resources for the conduct of safety measures and production sanitation and for the acquisition of special clothing, special footwear and protective devices for issuance or sale to the collective farmers according to established norms.

33. Women collective farm members are entitled to pregnancy and childbirth leave; pregnant women are given lighter work; women with breast-fed babies are provided with the necessary conditions for nursing their infants at the proper time, and they may be granted additional leave.

The collective farm establishes a shorter working day and other privileges for adolescents.

34. For the achievement of high results in production, the elaboration and introduction of rationalizers' proposals, effecting savings in communal resources, irreproachable work for many years in collective farm production and other services to the collective farm, the general meeting of collective farm members or the board employs the following measures of encouragement for collective farmers: a declaration of gratitude; the issuance of a bonus or the award of a valuable gift; the award of a Certificate of Honor; inscription on the Roll of Honor or in the Book of Honor; conferral of the titles Honored Collective Farmer and Distinguished Collective Farmer.

Other measures of encouragement may also be established, at the discretion of the general meeting of collective farm members.

The titles of Honored Collective Farmer and Distinguished Collective Farmer are conferred by decision of the general meeting of collective farm members, in accordance with the regulations approved by the collective farm.

35. For violations of labor discipline, the charter of the collective farm *or its regulations*, the general meeting of collective farmers or the collective farm board may impose the following penalties on the guilty parties: censure; a reprimand; strict reprimand; transfer to a lower-paying job [for a period of up to three months] ; dismissal from the position held; warning of expulsion from collective farm membership.

Expulsion from collective farm membership may be employed as an extreme measure against individuals who regularly violate labor discipline or the collective farm's charter, after other sanctions have been used against these individuals. A resolution of the general meeting of collective farmers on expulsion from collective farm membership may be appealed to the executive committee of the district (or city) Soviet.

Individuals expelled from collective farm membership are deprived of the rights of a collective farm member as established by this Charter.

Penalties may be imposed on the chairman of the collective farm, the chairman of the inspection commission, members of the board and members of the inspection commission by the general meeting of collective farmers; penalties may be imposed on chief (senior) specialists, the chief bookkeeper and the leaders of production units by the general meeting or by the collective farm board.

The procedure for imposing and removing penalties is determined by the collective farm's regulations.

*VII. Distribution of the Collective
Farm's Gross Output and Income.*

36. In the distribution of income, the following must be ensured: the correct combination of accumulation and consumption, the continuous growth of production assets, insurance funds and communal funds for cultural and everyday purposes, and a rising living standard for the collective farmers.

The material expenditures on the production of the collective farm's output (depreciation of fixed assets, outlays of seeds, feed, fertilizer, petroleum products, expenditures on current repairs, etc.) are reimbursed out of the collective farm's gross output.

The collective farm forms a fund for labor payments out of gross income received.

The collective farm uses its net income: to pay taxes and to make monetary payments to the state; to increase fixed assets and working capital; to create a fund for cultural and everyday purposes and a fund for social security and material assistance to collective farmers; for material incentives to collective farmers and specialists; to form and replenish a reserve fund, and for other purposes.

Allocations for increasing fixed assets and working capital are mandatory; the amounts of the allocations are established annually, taking into account the requirements for resources to ensure the continued steady growth of communal production.

37. From the in-kind output of crop cultivation and animal husbandry; the collective farm: creates a seed fund to cover the farm's total requirements; fulfills the plan for the sale of agricultural products to the state, repays loans in kind, creates an in-kind stock of grain and other products for issuance *as pay* or sale to the collective farmers and, when possible, sells over and above the plan grain and other output needed by the state; allocates feed for communally-owned livestock and poultry to cover annual requirements, and also for issuance or sale to the collective farmers; forms insurance and carryover funds of seeds, fodder and foodstuffs; allocates products for public catering and for the upkeep of children's institutions and orphans; assigns a portion of products and animal feed for assistance to pensioners, invalids and needy collective farm members.

The collective farm sells its remaining output to the consumers' cooperatives or on the collective farm markets, or uses it for other needs at its discretion.

38. The collective farm uses the money obtained from the sale of output and other sources primarily for settling accounts with the collective farmers for their labor, to cover other production expenditures, to make payments to the state, to repay monetary loans, and to form and replenish the collective farm's public funds.

VIII. Social Security for
Collective Farmers

39. Collective farm members, in accordance with legislation now in effect, receive old-age and disability pensions and pensions for the loss of a breadwinner *through the resources of the centralized Union social security fund for collective farmers;* in addition, women receive pregnancy and childbirth allowances [from the centralized Union social security fund for collective farmers].

40. *In accordance with established procedure, collective farm members receive allowances for temporary disability and passes to sanatoriums and rest homes, and also are granted other forms of social insurance, through the centralized social insurance fund for collective farmers.*

By decision of the general meeting, the collective farm can make supplementary payments to all forms of pensions established for collective farmers and can establish personal pensions for veterans of collective farm construction and individuals performing special services in the development of the collective farm's communal sector.

[By decision of the general meeting, the collective farm can, out of its own funds, pay collective farm members allowances for temporary disability, purchase passes for collective farmers to sanatoriums and rest homes and provide other forms of social insurance, and also make supplementary payments to all forms of pensions established for collective farmers.]

The collective farm gives material assistance out of its own resources to disabled collective farm members who do not receive pensions or allowances. By decision of the general meeting of collective farmers, the collective farm can allocate resources for the construction of collective farm and inter-collective farm sanatoriums, rest homes, Young Pioneer camps and homes for the aged and invalids.

According to established procedure, the collective farm allocates resources to the centralized Union social security fund for collective farmers and to the centralized Union social insurance fund for collective farmers.

IX. *Culture, Everyday Life and Public Services and Amenities*

41. The collective farm takes steps to improve the cultural and everyday conditions of the collective farmers' lives *and displays day-to-day concern for strengthening the health of collective farm members and their families and for their physical training.*

To this end, the collective farm: builds and equips collective farm clubs, libraries and other cultural-enlightenment institutions *and sports installations*, assists in the development of physical culture and sports, and sets up kindergartens and nurseries; assists parents and the schools in the correct upbringing of children, maintains close ties with the schools, gives assistance to public education agencies in the production training of children, provides the schools with plots of land, machinery, seeds, fertilizer and means of transportation, and ensures the job placement of school graduates on the collective farm; when necessary, organizes public catering for collective farmers; gives assistance to the public health agencies in conducting curative and preventive measures on the collective farm and provides collective farm members with free and emergency transportation to take sick persons to medical institutions; provides public services and amenities, electricity and radio service for the collective farm communities and the collective farmers' homes *and assists in the organization of everyday services for collective farm members;* under the procedure established by the collective farm, gives assistance to the collective farmers in the construction and repair of dwellings, and provides housing space for specialists working on the collective farm who are in need of it.

The collective farm concerns itself with raising the production skills and cultural and technical level of the collective farm members; sends collective farmers, under established procedure, for study in higher and specialized secondary educational institutions and vocational-technical schools and in advanced training courses; *grants privileges provided by existing legislation to collective farmers who are successfully studying in correspondence and evening general-education and specialized educational institutions and who are conscientiously working on the collective farm* [creates conditions for collective farmers to take correspondence courses].

Collective farmers who graduate from educational institutions to which their collective farm has sent them are obligated to return to work in their specialty on that collective farm.

X. The Auxiliary Farming of the Collective Farmer's Family (Collective Farm Household)

42. The collective farmer's family (collective farm household) may own a dwelling, farm buildings, productive livestock, poultry, bees, and small agricultural implements for work on a personal plot.

The collective farmer's family (collective farm household) is granted the use of a personal plot of land, as a vegetable garden, an orchard or for other needs, up to 0.50 hectares in size, including land occupied by buildings, and up to 0.20 hectares on irrigated land.

The size of the personal plot, within the established norms, is defined by the collective farm's charter. At the same time, the sizes of existing personal plots established in accordance with the Charter of the Agricultural Artel previously in effect may be retained.

The personal plot of the collective farmer's family (collective farm household) is granted by decision of the general meeting of collective farm members, and its size is established with consideration for the number of members of the collective farmer's family (collective farm household) and their labor participation in the collective farm's communal sector. *

In carrying out the compact buildup of rural communities, the collective farm allots personal plots of a smaller size to collective farmers near their dwellings (or apartments), granting them the remaining portion of the land plot outside the residential zone of the community. In so doing, the total land area allotted for use by the collective farmer's family (collective farm household) must not exceed the size of the personal plot as stipulated by the collective farm's charter.

The use of personal plots in the sizes established by the collective farm is retained by collective farmers' families (collective farm households) in instances in which all members of the family (collective farm household) are unable to work because of old age or disability, in which the only able-bodied member of the family (collective farm household) is called up for a tour of active military

---

*[See the bracketed paragraph at the end of Art. 43.]

duty, is elected to an elective position, takes up studies or temporarily transfers to other work, with the consent of the collective farm, or in which only minors remain in the family (collective farm household). In all other instances, the question of the retention of the personal plot is decided by the general meeting of collective farm members.

A personal plot may not be transferred for use by other individuals or be cultivated with the use of hired labor.

The collective farm board gives assistance to collective farmers, under the procedure established by the collective farm, in the cultivation of personal plots; this assistance is rendered primarily to families in which there are no able-bodied individuals.

The collective farm board is obligated to exercise systematic control over the observance of the established sizes of personal plots. In the event of an unauthorized increase in the size of a personal plot, the excess land over the established norm is confiscated by the board and the harvest grown on this land is turned over to the collective farm, without compensation for expenses incurred during the illegal use.

43. The collective farmer's family (collective farm household) may have one cow with a calf up to one year of age, one heifer or bull up to two years of age, one sow with pigs up to three months of age or two hogs that are being fattened, up to 10 sheep and goats (combined), beehives, poultry and rabbits.

An increase in the norms for the keeping of personally-owned livestock by a collective farmer's family (collective farm household), or the replacement of some types of livestock by others in certain regions, taking national characteristics and local conditions into account, is permitted by decision of the Union-republic Council of Ministers.

The number and types of livestock that a collective farmer's family (collective farm household) may have within the established norms are defined by the collective farm's charter.

The collective farm board gives the collective farmers assistance in the acquisition of livestock, furnishes veterinary service, and also provides feed and pastures for livestock.

The keeping of livestock over and above the norms established by the charter is prohibited.

[The size of the personal plot and the number of livestock that a collective farmer's family (collective farm household) may keep are established by the general meeting of collective farm members, taking into account the number of members in the family and their labor participation in the collective farm's communal sector.]

44. By decision of the general meeting of collective farmers, the collective farm grants personal plots of land to teachers, physicians and other specialists who work in the rural locality and reside on the collective farm's territory. Workers, office employees, pensioners and invalids residing on the collective

farm's territory may, when vacant land for personal plots is available, be granted personal plots by decision of the general meeting of collective farmers.

The collective farm may also permit the aforementioned individuals to use pastures for their livestock, under the established procedure.

XI. The Collective Farm's Administrative Bodies and Inspection Commission

45. The administration of the collective farm's affairs is carried out on the basis of broad democracy and the active participation of the collective farmers in the resolution of all questions of collective farm life.

The collective farm's affairs are administered by the general meeting of collective farm members; during the period between meetings, they are administered by the collective farm board.

46. The general meeting of collective farm members is the highest administrative body of the collective farm.

The general meeting: adopts the charter of the collective farm and makes changes in and additions to it; elects the board and the chairman of the collective farm and the inspection commission of the collective farm; *decides questions* [approves decisions of the board] on the admission of collective farm members and [decides questions of] *on* the expulsion of collective farmers from collective farm membership; adopts regulations for the collective farm and statutes on pay and on the intrafarm settling of accounts; ratifies the collective farm's organizational-management plan and its long-range and annual production-financial plans; hears reports by the collective farm board and inspection commission on their activities; approves the annual report of the collective farm and the sizes of the collective farm's in-kind and monetary funds; approves decisions of the collective farm board on the appointment and release of chief (senior) specialists and the collective farm's chief bookkeeper; decides questions of the collective farm's participation in inter-collective farm and state-collective farm enterprises and organizations, of its affiliation with associations and unions, and of the enlargement of the collective farm or its division into smaller units; *reviews questions of changing the size of the collective farm's land or the boundaries of the land it uses.*

Decisions of the collective farm board on the questions listed above are not valid unless approved by the general meeting of collective farmers.

The general meeting of collective farmers also considers other questions of the collective farm's activity.

47. The general meeting of collective farm members is convened by the collective farm board at least four times a year. The collective farm board is also obligated to convene the general meeting of collective farmers if this is requested by at least one-third of the collective farm's members *or by the inspection commission.*

The general meeting is empowered to decide questions if the meeting is attended by at least two-thirds of the collective farm members.

Decisions are adopted at the general meeting of collective farmers by a simple majority of votes.

The collective farm board notifies the collective farmers of the convocation of a general meeting at least seven days in advance.

48. On large collective farms, where the convocation of general meetings of collective farm members is difficult, meetings of representatives may be convened to decide questions falling within the purview of the general meeting.

Representatives are elected at meetings of collective farmers in the brigades and other units of the collective farm. The norms of representation and the procedure for the election of representatives are *determined by the collective farm board* [established by the general meeting of collective farm members]. *Questions falling within the jurisdiction of meetings of representatives are given preliminary discussion at meetings of collective farmers in the brigades (units). The representatives report to brigade (unit) meetings on decisions adopted by the meetings of representatives.*

A meeting of representatives is empowered to decide questions if it is attended by at least three-fourths of all the representatives.

49. The collective farm board is an executive and administrative body that is responsible to the general meeting of collective farm members, and it exercises direction over all the organizational, production, financial, cultural, service and educational activities of the collective farm.

The collective farm board organizes fulfillment of the plans for the production and sale to the state of agricultural output, *ensures the rational utilization of land*, expends material and monetary resources in a careful and thrifty way, and takes steps to strengthen production and labor discipline.

In its activity, the collective farm board constantly relies on the broad collective farm *aktiv;* it develops and supports creative initiative on the part of collective farm members in perfecting the organization of communal production and raising labor productivity, shows constant concern for improving the working and living conditions of the collective farmers, and takes a sensitive and attentive attitude toward the consideration of their requests and proposals.

The collective farm board is elected for a term of three years. The collective farm board makes an annual report on its activity to the general meeting of collective farmers.

Meetings of the collective farm board are convened when necessary, but at least once a month; the board is empowered to decide questions if the meeting is attended by at least three-fourths of the board members.

The board adopts decisions by a simple majority of votes.

50. The general meeting of collective farmers elects the chairman of the collective farm, who is simultaneously the chairman of the collective farm board, for a term of three years.

The chairman of the collective farm exercises day-to-day direction over the collective farm's activity, ensures the fulfillment of the decisions of the general meeting and the board, and represents the collective farm in its relations with state agencies and other institutions and organizations.

The collective farm board elects from its membership one or two vice-chairmen of the collective farm.

[The chairman of the collective farm or board members who fail to justify the trust placed in them may be removed before the end of their terms by decision of the general meeting of collective farm members.] *

51. The collective farm board appoints a chief bookkeeper from among the collective farm members or hires a person for this post under a labor contract.

The chief bookkeeper organizes the keeping of records and the compilation of reports on the collective farm and exercises day-to-day control over the safekeeping and proper expenditure of monetary resources and material assets. The chief bookkeeper, together with the collective farm chairman, signs the annual report of the collective farm and documents certifying the receipt and expenditure of monetary resources and material assets.

52. To guide individual branches of the collective farm's activity, the board appoints specialists from among the collective farm members or hires persons for these posts under labor contracts.

Chief (senior) specialists bear responsibility for the condition of the branch that they guide and organize fulfillment of the production-financial plan. The instructions of chief (senior) specialists on questions falling within their purview are mandatory for collective farm members and also for the officials of the collective farm.

53. For the broader participation of collective farm members in the administration of communal production, meetings of collective farmers are convened in the brigades and other production units of the collective farm.

The meeting of the collective farmers of a brigade (or unit): elects a brigade leader (unit leader), whose election must subsequently be approved by the collective farm board; reviews the plan assignment, reports by the brigade leader (unit leader) on work done, and other questions of production activity; discusses measures for strengthening labor discipline and submits proposals to the collective farm board on measures of encouragement or penalties.

Meetings are convened by the leader of the production unit, by the board or by the collective farm chairman.

The meeting elects a brigade council (unit council). The leader of the respective unit is the chairman of the council. The rights and obligations of the council are defined by the collective farm board.

The instructions of the brigade leader (unit leader) relating to production activity are mandatory for all the collective farmers working in the given unit. In his work, the brigade leader (unit leader) is subordinate to the board and the chairman of the collective farm, and in specialized questions to the chief (senior) specialists as well.

*[See the last paragraph of Art. 56.]

54. The inspection commission, which exercises control over the economic and financial activity of the board and the officials of the collective farm, is elected for a term of three years. The inspection commission elects a chairman from among its members.

The inspection commission is guided by the collective farm's charter and by legislation now in effect, is accountable to the general meeting of collective farm members, and exercises control over observance of the collective farm's charter, the preservation of collective farm property, the legality of contracts and economic transactions, the expenditure of monetary resources and material assets and the correct keeping of records, compilation of reports and settling of accounts with collective farmers, and also over the prompt consideration by the collective farm board and officials of complaints and petitions from collective farmers.

The inspection commission conducts at least two inspections each year of the collective farm's economic and financial activity, carries out periodic checkups on the economic activity of the brigades and other production units, and offers its conclusions on the collective farm's annual report. Inspection documents are subject to ratification by the general meeting of collective farmers.

55. The inspection commission has the right: *to check on the proper utilization and preservation of agricultural output, seeds and fodder, material-technical and monetary resources, draft animals and productive livestock, buildings, installations and other property;* to demand that officials and members of the collective farm present the necessary documents for examination [to inspect warehouses and other building and enterprises of the collective farm] ; to submit proposals, *based on the results of checkups and inspections*, for consideration by the general meeting and board of the collective farm.

The proposals of the inspection commission are considered at the next general meeting; proposals submitted to the collective farm board are considered within 10 days.

56. The election of the board, the chairman of the collective farm and the inspection commission is done by open or secret ballot, at the discretion of the general meeting of collective farmers.

The number of members of the board and of the inspection commission is determined by the general meeting of collective farm members.

The collective farm chairman, the board members and the chairman and members of the inspection commission, if they do not justify the trust placed in them by the collective farmers, can be removed from office before the completion of their terms by decision of the general meeting of collective farm members.

57. The collective farm creates the necessary conditions for the successful activity of public organizations [that, under the guidance of the Party organizations, perform work having to do with the communist upbringing of the collective farmers, their enlistment in public life and the development of socialist competition] .

58. An economic council or a bureau of economic analysis, a cultural and everyday-service commission *or other commissions* operating on a volunteer basis, as well as a mutual aid fund [and other organizations], may be set up on the collective farm.

XII. The Adoption and Registration of the Collective Farm's Charter

59. The collective farm's charter, adopted by the general meeting of collective farm members on the basis of the Model Charter, is presented for registration to the executive committee of the district (or city) Soviet. Subsequent changes in and additions to the collective farm's charter are made by the same procedure.

60. The registered charter of the collective farm is filed with the collective farm board, the district agricultural agency and the executive committee of the district (or city) Soviet.

61. The collective farm is guided in its activity by the collective farm's charter and by legislation in effect.

The collective farm, as a socialist *agricultural* enterprise, enjoys the rights of a juristic person and has its own seal and banner.

Glossary of Terms

Glossary of Terms

Artel A group of persons working together, for example as a production unit, and sharing the returns.

Kolkhoz Collective farm of the artel type in which a group of peasants till the soil, held in perpetuity by the farm, and subject to the directives of the Soviet legal system and the planning organs. Property held by the kolkhoz is termed "kolkhoz-cooperative" and is utilized according to the dictates of the Ustav or kolkhoz Charter.

Ustav The charter or basic laws pertaining to a kolkhoz elaborating questions of structure and operation.

Kollegial'nost' Decision making by a board or group.

Edinonachalie The making of decisions and the bearing of responsibility for those decisions by a single individual.

Upolnomochennyi A plenipotentiary or authorized agent empowered to act on someone else's behalf.

Raiispolkom The executive committee of a raion soviet.

Pravlenie Governing body or management board.

Revizionnaia Komissiia Review, inspection or audit commission of the collective farm empowered to expedite basic auditing of accounting and other financial operations of the collective farm.

Sovet Council or advisory body attached to an administrative organ of the kolkhoz, for example, the council of the brigade.

Aktiv That group of people, who, as opposed to the masses participate actively in a given organization and who are expected to lead the masses.

Schetovod Bookkeeper or ledger clerk.

Pervichnyi	Local or primary; for example, a local Party organization.
Pravo Kontroliia	The right of control; the term control is normally used here in the sense of checking or verification.
Upravliat'	To administer, govern, rule or direct.
Rukovodit'	To guide; to act as a leader.
Zakon	A law.
Postanovleniia	A written resolution or decision arising from the collective action of a body empowered to make specific decisions.
Ukaz	A decree or edict which has legal force.
Resporiazhenie	A regulation or ruling.
Prikaz	An order, instruction or direction; for example, for a superior individual or organization to a lower level individual or organization.
Vedomost'	A list or register; for example of accounting or data records.
Upravlenie	Management, control or direction.
Reshenie	A decision.
Polozhenie	A decree, position paper or state of affairs; for example, a polozhenie outlining the duties of the kolkhoz economist.
Normativnoe Akt	An enforceable act setting forth standards, quotas, etc.
Dogovor	A contract, agreement or treaty.
Tipovoe Dogovor	A model contract, agreement or treaty.
Napravlenie	The direction or orientation of policy.
Velenie	Command or order.
Nedelimye Fondy	The indivisible funds or capital funds of the collective farm.

Denezhnyi Dokhod Money income of the collective farm.

Valovaia Produktsiia Gross output of animal breeding (value of livestock products not including slaughter or births and weight changes) plus the gross value of all crops plus changes in stocks and incompleted output.

Sebestoimost' Cost of production including purchases at actual purchase prices, internally produced materials at actual cost of production, amortization at state farm rates and labor at the value of actual distributions *or* state farm norms.

Zootechnician Veterinarian—concerned with the management of livestock.

Agronom Agronomist—Specialist in the management of field crops.

Bibliography

Bibliography

Books

English

Abramov, Fyodor. *The New Life*. New York: Grove Press Inc., 1963.

Ames, Edward. *Soviet Economic Processes*. Illinois: Richard D. Irwin, Inc., 1965.

Azrael, Jeremy A. *Managerial Power and Soviet Politics*. Cambridge: Harvard University Press, 1966.

Belov, Fedor. *The History of a Soviet Collective Farm*. New York: Frederick A. Praeger, 1955.

Bergson, Abram. *The Economics of Soviet Planning*. New Haven and London: Yale University Press, 1964.

Bergson, Abram and Kuznets, Simon (eds.). *Economic Trends in the Soviet Union*. Cambridge: Harvard University Press, 1963.

Berliner, Joseph S. *Factory and Manager in the USSR*. Cambridge: Harvard University Press, 1957.

Bienstock, Gregory, et al. *Management in Russian Industry and Agriculture*. Ithaca: Cornell University Press, 1948.

Cartter, Allan M. *Theory of Wages and Employment*. Homewood: Richard D. Irwin, Inc., 1959.

Dodge, Norton T. *Women in the Soviet Economy*. Baltimore: The Johns Hopkins Press, 1966.

Fainsod, Merle. *Smolensk Under Soviet Rule*. New York: Random House, 1963.

Granick, David. *Management of the Industrial Firm in the USSR*. New York: Columbia University Press, 1954.

_____. *The Red Executive*. New York: Doubleday & Company, Inc., 1961.

_____. *Soviet Metal-Fabricating and Economic Development*. Madison: University of Wisconsin Press, 1967.

Gregory, Paul. *Socialist and Nonsocialist Industrialization Patterns*. New York: Praeger Publishers, 1970.

Hubbard, Leonard E. *The Economics of Soviet Agriculture*. London: Macmillan, 1939.

Jasny, Naum. *The Socialized Agriculture of the USSR*. Stanford: Stanford University Press, 1949.

Kanovsky, Eliyahu. *The Economy of the Israeli Kibbutz*. Cambridge: Harvard University Press, 1966.

Karcz, Jerzy F. (ed.). *Soviet and East European Agriculture*. Berkeley and Los Angeles: University of California Press, 1967.

Kingsbury, Robert C., and Taaffe, Robert N. *An Atlas of Soviet Affairs*. New York: Frederick A. Praeger, 1965.

Kornai, Janos. *Overcentralization in Economic Administration*. Oxford: Oxford University Press, 1959.

Laird, Roy D., and Crowley, Edward L. (eds.). *Soviet Agriculture: The Permanent Crisis*. New York: Frederick A. Praeger, 1965.

Laird, Roy D. (ed.). *Soviet Agricultural and Peasant Affairs*. Lawrence: University of Kansas Press, 1963.

Lewin, M. *Russian Peasants and Soviet Power*. London: George Allen and Unwin, 1968.

Litterer, Joseph A. *The Analysis of Organizations*. New York: John Wiley & Sons, Inc., 1965.

Mellor, J.W. *Economics of Agricultural Production*. Ithaca: Cornell University Press, 1966.

Millar, James R. *Price and Income Formation in the Soviet Collective-Farm Sector Since 1954*. Unpublished doctoral dissertation, Cornell University, September 1965.

_____ (ed.). *The Soviet Rural Community*. Urbana: University of Illinois Press, 1971.

Miller, Robert F. *One Hundred Thousand Tractors*. Cambridge: Harvard University Press, 1970.

Mitrany, David. *Marx Against the Peasant*. New York: Collier Books, 1961.

Nimitz, Nancy. *Farm Employment in the Soviet Union, 1928-1963*. Santa Monica: The Rand Corporation, November, 1965.

Nove, Alec. *Economic Rationality and Soviet Politics*. New York: Frederick A. Praeger, 1964.

_____. *The Soviet Economy*. 2nd ed. rev. New York: Frederick A. Praeger, 1965.

Ploss, Sidney I. *Conflict and Decision-Making in Soviet Russia—A Case Study in Agricultural Policy, 1953-1963*. Princeton: Princeton University Press, 1965.

Schultz, Theodore W. *Transforming Traditional Agriculture*. New Haven and London: Yale University Press, 1964.

Simon, Herbert A. *Administrative Behavior*. 2nd ed. New York: The Free Press, 1965.

Strauss, Erich. *Soviet Agriculture in Perspective*. London: George Allen and Unwin Ltd., 1969.

United States Government, Joint Economic Committee. *Comparisons of United States and Soviet Economies*. Washington, D.C.: U.S. Government Printing Office, 1959.

_____. *Dimensions of Soviet Economic Power*. Washington, D.C.: U.S. Government Printing Office, 1962.

_____. *New Directions in the Soviet Economy*. Washington, D.C.: U.S. Government Printing Office, 1966.

Volin, Lazar. *A Century of Russian Agriculture: From Alexander II to Khrushchev*. Cambridge: Harvard University Press, 1970.

Ward, Benjamin N. *The Socialist Economy–A Study of Organizational Alternatives*. New York: Random House, Inc., 1967.

Washenko, Steve. *The Kolkhoz as a System of Agricultural Resource Organization*. Unpublished masters thesis, University of Maryland, 1966.

Wilber, Charles K. *The Soviet Model and Underdeveloped Countries*. Chapel Hill: University of North Carolina Press, 1969.

German

Wädekin, Karl-Eugen. *Privatproduzenten in der Sowjetischen Landwirtschaft*. Cologne: Wissenshaft und Politik, 1967.

Russian

Abramov, V.A. (ed.). *Ekonomika sel'skokhoziaistvennykh predpriiatii*. Moskva: Gospolitizdat, 1962.

Akademiia Nauk SSSR, Institut Ekonomiki. *Puti povysheniia proizvoditel'nosti truda v sel'skom khoziaistve SSSR*. Moskva: Nauka, 1964.

Akademiia Nauk SSSR, Institut Ekonomiki. *Material'noe stimulirovanie razvitiia kolkhoznogo proizvodstva*. Moskva: Izdatel'stvo Akademii Nauk SSSR, 1963.

Alekseeva, P.V. and Voronin, A.P. *Nakoplenie i razvitie kolkhoznoi sobstvennosti*. Moskva: Ekonomizdat, 1963.

Arutiunian, Iu. V. *Mekhanizatory sel'skogo khoziaistva SSSR v 1929-1957 gg.* Moskva: Nauka, 1960.

Ashcheulov, A.T., Bocharov, A.T. *Oplata truda rukovodiashchikh rabotnikov spetsialistov i mekhanizatorov kolkhozov*. Gosiurizdat, Moskva: 1962.

Bashmakov, G.S. *Pravovoe regulirovanie vnutrennego rasporiadka v kolkhozakh*. Moskva: Gosiurizdat, 1960.

Basiuk, T.L. *Organizatsiia sotsialisticheskogo sel'skokhoziaistvennogo proizvodstva*. Moskva: Ekonomika, 1965.

Bavarskii, A. *Kolkhoznaia partiinaia organizatsiia*. Moskva: Moskovskii rabochii, 1954.

Beliaeva, Z.S. and Pankratov, I.F. *Gosurdarstvennoe rukovodstva kolkhozami v period razvernutogo stroitel'stva kommunizma v SSSR*. Moskva: Gosiurizdat, 1961.

Boev, V.R. *Zakupochnye tseny i chistyi clokhod kolkhozov*. Moskva: Kolos, 1969.

Bondarev, A.I. *Upravlenie delami sel'skokhoaiaistvennoi arteli*. Sukhumi: Abkhazskoe gosudarstvennoe izdatel'stvo, Vypusk 14, 1956.

Borisov, Iu. S. *25-tysiachniki*. Moskva: Gospolitizdat, 1959.

Dmitrashko, I.I. *Vnutrikolkhoznye ekonomicheskie otnosheniia*. Moskva: Ekonomika, 1966.

Dmitrashko, I.I. *Oplata truda v sel'skom khoziaistve SSSR*. Moskva: Sotsekgiz, 1962.

Estrina, A.M. *Torgovye sviazi kolkhozov s promyshlennost'iu*. Moskva: Ekonomika, 1965.

Gataulin, A.M. *Sebestoimost' i sovokupnye zatraty truda v proizvodstve sel' skokhoziaistvennoi produktsii*. Moskva: Ekonomika, 1965.

Gladkova, I.A. (ed.). *Razvitie sotsialisticheskoi ekonomiki SSSR v poslevoennyi period*. Moskva: Nauka, 1965.

Grigor'ev, V.K. *Zakonodatel'stvo ob organizatsionno-khoziaistvennom ukreplenii kolkhozov*. Moskva: Gosiurizdat, 1961.

Grigor'ev, S.T. *Prava i obiazannosti revizionnykh kommissii kolkhozov*. Moskva: Gosiurizdat, 1955.

Ivin, I.A. *Oplata truda rukovoditelei i spetsialistov v kolkhozakh*. Moskva: Ekonomizdat, 1963.

Kolesnev, S.G. *Spetsializatsiia i razmery sel'skokhoziaistvennykh predpriiatii*. Moskva: Sel'khozizdat, 1963.

Kommunisticheskaia partiia kazakhstana v dokumentakh i tsifrakh. Alma-Ata: Kazakhskoe gosudarstvennoe izdatel'stvo, 1960.

Kommunisticheskaia partiia tadzhikistana v dokumentakh i tsifrakh. Dushanbe: "Irfon," 1965.

Kommunisticheskaia Partiia Kazakhstana v borb'e za osvoenie tselinnykh i zalezhnykh zemel', sbornik doumentov i materialov. Alma-Ata: Kazakhskoe gosudarstvennoe izdatel'stvo, 1958.

Korolev, A.I. *Prava i obiazannosti pravleniia kolkhoza*. Leningrad: Vsesiuznoe obshchestvo po rasprostraneniiu politicheskikh i nauchnykh znanii, Leningradskoe otdelenie, 1955.

Kosiachenko, G.P. (ed.). *Denezhnye doxody kolkhozov i differentsial'naia renta*. Moskva: Gosfinizdat, 1963.

Kotovoi, S.P., and Petrov, G.I. *Proizvodstvennye kolkhozno-sovkhoznye upravleniia*. Leningrad: Izd. Leningradskogo universiteta, 1963.

Kozachkovskyi, V.A. (ed.). *Kommunisticheskaia partiia Tadzhikistana v dokumentakh i tsifrakh*. Dushanbe: "Irfon," 1965.

Kozyr', M.I. *Imushchestvennye pravootnosheniia kolkhozov v SSSR*. Moskva: Nauka, 1966.

Kozyrev, D.F. and Nemtsov, V.F. (eds.). *Organizatsiia i planirovanie proizvodstva v kolkhozakh i sovkhozakh*. Moskva: Kolos, 1965.

Kuvshinov, I.S., Gumerov, M.N., and Lovkov, Ia. A. *Ekonomika sotsialisticheskogo sel'skogo khoziaistva*. 3rd ed. Moskva: Sel'khozizdat, 1963.

Kuznetsov, G. Ia. *Material'noe stimulirovanie truda v kolkhozakh*. Moskva: Mysl', 1966.

Kuznetsov, V.V., Rygalin, A.G., and Tverdov, A.A. *Spravochnik po zakonodatel'stvu dlia predsedatelia kolkhoza*. Moskva: Gosiurizdat, 1962.

Lapkes, Ia. B. *Tekhnicheskii progress i proizvoditel'nost' truda v sel'skom khoziaistve*. Moskva: Ekonomika, 1969.

Larionov, A.P. *Normirovanie i tarifikatsiia truda v kolkhozakh i sovkhozakh.* Moskva: Gosplanizdat, 1961.

Larionov, G.I. *Normirovanie truda v kolkhozakh i sovkhozakh.* Moskva: Sel'khozizdat, 1963.

Logvinov, A.D. *Differentsial'naia renta i ekonomika kolkhozov.* Moskva: Ekonomizdat, 1963.

Lopatin, I. Ia. *Rabota pravleniia kolkhoza s kadrami.* Penza: Penzenskoe knizhnoe izdatel'stvo, 1955.

Malafeev, A.N. *Istoriia tsenoobrazovaniia v SSSR (1917-1963 gg.).* Moskva: Mysl', 1964.

Mashenkov, V.F. *Ispol'zovanie trudovykh resursov sel'skoi mestnosti.* Moskva: Ekonomika, 1965.

Mikhailov, M.V. *Planirovanie i rezhim ekonomiki v kolkhozakh.* Moskva: Ekonomika, 1965.

Ministerstvo sel'skogo khoziaistva RSFSR, Glavnoe planovo-ekonomicheskoe upravlenie, *Ukazaniia po zapolneniiu tablits proizvodstvennofinansovogo plana kolkhoza na 1966 god.* Krasnodar, Statistika, 1965.

Mishchenko, A. *Novyi poriadok planirovaniia kolkhoznogo proizvodstva.* Moskva: moskovskii rabochii, 1957.

Mitiushkin, T.S. *Rentabel'nost' sel'skokhoziaistvennogo proizvodstva i khozraschet v kolkhozakh.* Moskva: Statistika, 1966.

Mitiushkin, T.S., Subbotin, V.P., Dvoirin, E. Iu., *Bukhgalterskii uchet v kolkhozakh.* Moskva: Statistika, 1964.

Moiseenko, N.A. *Proizvoditel'nost' truda, nakoplenie i potreblenie v kolkhozakh.* Leningrad: Lengosuniversiteta, 1964.

Morozov, V.A. *Trudoden', den'gi i torgovlia na sele.* Moskva: Ekonomika, 1965.

Nauchno-issledovatel'skii finansovyi institut, *Denezhnye dokhody kolkhozov i differentsial'naia renta.* Moskva: Gosfinizdat, 1963.

Nizhnii, N.I., Onishchenko, A.M., Romanenko, I.N., Storozhuk, A.A. *Denezhnaia oplata truda v kolkhozakh.* Sel'khozizdat, 1961.

Ostrovskii, V.B. *Kolkhoznoe krest'ianstvo SSSR.* Saratov: Izdatel'stvo Saratovskogo universiteta, 1967.

Okhapkin, K.A. *Ekonomicheskaia effektivnost' Denezhnoi oplaty truda v kolkhozakh.* Moskva: Gosplanizdat, 1960.

Olefir, K.I. (ed.) *Ekonomika i organizatsiia proizvodstva v sotsialisticheskikh sel'skokhoziaistvennykh predpriiatiiakh.* Moskva: Kolos, 1966.

Opyt izucheniia sebestoimosti kolkhoznoi produktsii. Moskva: Sel'khozgiz, 1956.

Pankratov, I.F. *Osnovnye prava i obiazannosti rukovodiashchikh kadrov kolkhoza.* Moskva: Gosiurizdat, 1957.

Pavlov, I.V. *Kompetentsiia raiispolkomov po gosudarstvennomu rukovodstvu kolkhozami.* Moskva: Izdatel'stvo Moskovskogo universiteta, 1961.

Pavlov, I.V. *Pravovye formy vnutrennogo khozrascheta v kolkhozakh.* Moskva: Gosiurizdat, 1961.

242

Pavlov, I.V. (ed.). *Pravovoe polozhenie kolkhozov v SSSR*. Moskva: Gosiurizdat, 1961.

———— (ed.). *Pravovye voprosy sblizheniia kolkhoznoi i obshchenarodnoi sobstevnnosti*. Moskva: Gosiurizdat, 1963.

————. *Razvitie kolkhoznoi demokratii v period razvernutogo stroitel'stva kommunizma*. Moskva: Gosiurizdat, 1962.

Pesin, A. *Garantirovaniia oplata i raspredelenie po trudu v kolkhozakh*. Minsk: Urozhai, 1969.

Piskunov, V. (ed.). *Voprosy organizatsionno-khoziaistvennogo ukrepleniia kolkhozov*. Moskva: Gospolitizdat, 1957.

Pokrovskii, I.F. *MTS–Opornyi punkt gosudarstvennogo rukovodstva kolkhozami*. Moskva: Gosiurizdat, 1957.

Pravdin, D.I. *Obshchestvennyi fondy potrebleniia v kolkhozakh*. Moskva: Kolos, 1964.

Rafikov, M.M. *Ekonomika, organizatsiia i planirovanie sel'skokhoziaistvennogo proizvodstva*. Moskva: Ekonomika, 1965.

Rogachev, S.V. *Proizvodstvennyi kollektiv i khoziaistvennaia reforma*. Moskva: Mysl', 1969.

Rozhin, V.P. *Nekotorye voprosy pod'ema ekonomiki slabykh kolkhozov*. Moskva: Ekonomizdat, 1961.

Rusakov, G.K., Miliavskii, I.O., Khabarov, N.F. *Planirovanie i khoziaistvennyi raschet v brigadakh i na fermakh kolkhoza*. Moskva: Gosplanizdat, 1960.

Ruskol, A.A., Denisov, A.A. *Proizvodstvennye kolkhozno-sovkhoznye upravleniia i ikh pravovoe polozhenie*. Moskva: Gosiurizdat, 1964.

Ruzskaia, E.A. *Perspektivy razvitiia i razmeshcheniia zhivotnovodstva v SSSR*. Moskva: Izdatel'stvo Akademii Nauk SSSR, 1959.

Selunskaia, V.M. *Rabochie-dvadtsatispiati-tysiachniki*. Moskva: Izd. Moskovskogo universiteta, 1964.

Seroshtan, I. *Rabota raikoma s rukovodiashchimi kolkhoznymi*. Moskva: Gospolitizdat, 1954.

Shaibekov, K.A. *Pravovye formy oplaty truda v kolkhozakh*. Moskva: Gosiurizdat, 1963.

Shevchenko, A.A. *Progressivnaia oplata truda kolkhoznikov*. Moskva: Ekonomizdat, 1963.

Shmelev, G.I. *Raspredelenie i ispol'zovanie truda v kolkhoaakh*. Moskva: Mysl', 1964.

Shukletsov, V.T. *Organizatsionno-khoziaistvennoe ukreplenie kolkhozov i pod'em material'nogo blagosostoianiia kolkhoznogo krest'ianstva v 1953-1957 godakh*. Moskva: Izd. VPSH i AON pri TSK KPSS, 1960.

Shumeiko, T.I. (ed.). *Ocherki po ekonomike Sel'skogo khoziaistva Turkmenskoi SSR*. Ashkhabad: Turkmengosizdat, 1962.

Sigov, I.I. *Razdelenie truda v sel'skom khoziaistve pri perekhode k kommunizmu*. Moskva, Ekonomizdat, 1963.

Sobolev, N.P. *Khozraschet v kolkhozakh.* Moskva: Sel'khozhiz, 1961.

_____. *Pod'em ekonomiki otstaiushchikh kolkhozov.* Moskva: Kolos, 1966. 1966.

Sokolov, M.M. *Tseny i tsenoobrazovanie na sel'skokhoziaistvennye produkty.* Moskva: Izd. Moskovskogo universiteta, 1964.

_____. *Organizatsionno-khoziaistvennoe ukreplenie kolkhozov.* Moskva: Gospolitizdat, 1948.

Spravochnik predsedatelia kolkhoza, kniga pervaia. Moskva: Sel'khozgiz, 1956.

Studentkova, N.M. *Metodika ischisleniia sebestoimosti produktsii v kolkhozakh i sovkhozakh.* Moskva: Ekonomika, 1965.

Sudarikov, V.F. (ed.). *Sbornik normativnykh aktov po kolkhoznomu pravu.* Moskva: Vsesoiuznyi iuridicheskii zaochnyi institut, 1965.

Suslov, I.F. *Ekonomicheskie problemy razvitiia kolkhozov.* Moskva: Ekonomika, 1967.

Tereshchenko, N.I. (ed.). *Dopolnitel'naia oplata truda v kolkhozakh.* Moskva: Sel'khozizdat, 1963.

Terent'ev, M.L. *Sebestoimost' kolkhoznoi produktsii.* Moskva: Sel'khozgiz, 1957.

Tiutin, V.A. *Ocherki ekonomiki kolkhozov nechernozemnoi polosy.* Moskva: Sel'khozgiz, 1957.

V Pomoshch' predsedateliu kolkhoza. Vypusk II. Moskva: Sel'khozgiz, 1955.

Venzher, V.G. *Ispol'zovanie zakona stoimosti v kolkhoznom proizvodstve.* Moskva: Nauka, 1965.

_____. *Kolkhoznyi stroi na sovremennom etape.* Moskva: Ekonomika, 1966.

Volkov, A.E. *Osnovy kolkhoznogo prava.* Moskva: Gosiurizdat, 1963.

Voropaev, V.I. and Belichenko, P.P. *Dopolnitel'naia oplata truda v kolkhozakh.* Moskva: Ekonomizdat, 1962.

Vovk, Iu. A. *Dogovornye otnosheniia kolkhozov s organizatsiiami i predpriiatiiami.* Moskva: Gosiurizdat, 1962.

Vsesoiuznyi Nauchno-issledovatel'skii Institut Ekonomiki Sel'skogo Khoziaistva. *Bukhgalterskii uchet v kolkhozakh pri vnedrenii khozrascheta.* Moskva: 1960.

Zakharov, A.I. and Perekrestov, V.N. *Organizatsiia i oplata truda v mekhanizirovannykh brigadakh i zven'iakh sovkhozov i kolkhozov.* Moskva: Rossel'khozizdat, 1969.

Zapisnaia knizhka brigadira kolkhoza. Moskva: Moskovskii rabochii, 1954.

Zapisnaia knizhka brigadira kolkhoza. Moskva: Moskovskii rabochii, 1955.

Zapisnaia knizhka predsedatelia kolkhoza. Moskva: Moskovskii rabochii, 1954.

Zapisnaia knizhka predsedatelia kolkhoza. Moskva: Moskovskii rabochii, 1955.

Zal'tsman, L.M. and Makarov, N.P. *Organizatsiia sotsialisticheskikh sel'skokhoziaistvennykh predpriiatii.* Moskva: Sel'khozizdat, 1963.

Zaslavskaia, T.I. *Raspredelenie po trudu v kolkhozakh.* Moskva: Ekonomika, 1966.

Articles

English

"Assure Each State and Collective Farm Its Own Seed." *Sovetskaia Rossia* (September 22, 1957), p. 1, translated and reprinted in *CDSP*, Vol. IX, No. 43 (December 4, 1957), p. 29.

Ballard, Allen B., Jr. "An End to Collective Farms?" *Problems of Communism*, Vol. X, No. 4 (July-August 1961), pp. 9-16.

Breus, F. "Party-Life: Be Honest with Both the Party and the People—From Plenary Session of the Pavlodar Province Party Committee." *Pravda* (March 28, 1961), p. 2, translated and reprinted in *CDSP*, Vol. XIII, No. 13 (April 26, 1961), p. 24.

Darmodekhin, V. "How Are Collective Farm Billions to be Realized?" Izvestia (February 19, 1960), p. 3, translated and reprinted in *CDSP*, Vol. XII, No. 7 (March 16, 1960), p. 30.

Diamond, Douglas B. "Trends in Outputs, Inputs, and Factor Productivity in Soviet Agriculture." *New Directions in the Soviet Economy* (Washington: U.S. Government Printing Office, 1969), pp. 339-381.

Domar, Evsey D. "The Soviet Collective Farm as a Producer Cooperative." *American Economic Review*, Vol. LVI, No. 4, Part I (September 1966), pp. 734-757.

"Double Labor Productivity on Collective Farms." *Izvestia* (March 29, 1959), p. 1, translated and reprinted in *CDSP*, Vol. XI, No. 13 (April 29, 1959), p. 30.

Durgin, Frank A. Jr. "Monetization and Policy in Soviet Agriculture Since 1952." *Soviet Studies*, Vol. XV, No. 4 (April 1964), pp. 375-407.

Durgin, F. "The Virgin Lands Programme, 1954-1960." *Soviet Studies*, Vol. XII (1961-62), pp. 255-280.

Granick, David. "Some Organizational Problems in Decentralized Planning." *Co-Existence*, No. 5 (1966), pp. 169-172.

Hough, Jerry F. "The Soviet Concept of the Relationship Between the Lower Party Organs and the State Administration." *Slavic Review*, Vol. XXIV, No. 2 (June 1965), 215-240.

Jackson, W.A.D. "The Virgin and Idle Lands Program Reappraised." *Annals of the American Association of Geographers*, Vol. LII (1962), pp. 69-79.

Johnston, Bruce F. and Mellor, John W. "The Role of Agriculture in Economic Development." *American Economic Review*, Vol. LI, No. 4 (September, 1961), pp. 566-593.

Kamensky, V. "Better Organization in Resettlement From Farmsteads." *Sovetskaia Belorrussia* (June 25, 1957), p. 3, translated and reprinted in *CDSP* Vol. IX, No. 27 (August 14, 1957), pp. 24-25.

Karcz, Jerzy F. and Timoshenko, V.P. "Soviet Agricultural Policy, 1953-1962." *Food Research Institute Studies*, Vol. 4, No. 2 (1964), pp. 123-163.

Khrushchev, N.S. "Successfully Implement Decision of February Plenary Session of C.P.S.U. Central Committee on the Intensification of Agricultural Production." *Pravda* (March 7, 1964), pp. 1-6, translated and reprinted in *CDSP*, Vol. XVI, No. 10 (April 1, 1964), pp. 17-18.

Klevakin, G. "Are There Virgin Lands in Georgia?" *Izvestia* (June 16, 1959), p. 2, translated and reprinted in *CDSP*, Vol. XI, No. 24 (July 15, 1959), p. 26.

Kozlitin, V. "In the Old Way." *Pravda* (March 3, 1959), p. 3, translated and reprinted in *CDSP*, Vol. XI, No. 9 (April 1, 1959), p. 68.

Kucherov, Alexander. "The Peasant." *Problems of Communism*, Vol. 14, No. 2 (March-April 1965), pp. 98-104.

Larionov, A. "On Establishing Norms for Collective Farm Labor." *Izvestia* (December 11, 1957), p. 2, translated and reprinted in *CDSP*, Vol. X, No. 47 (December 31, 1958), p. 14.

Loginav, V. "Without Taking the MTS' Needs Into Account." *Pravda* (May 25, 1957), p. 2, translated and reprinted in *CDSP*, Vol. IX, No. 21 (July 3, 1957), p. 37.

Makarov, S. "The Cost of Water." *Izvestia* (September 14, 1957), p. 2, translated and reprinted in *CDSP*, Vol. IX, No. 36 (October 16, 1957), pp. 22-23.

Matskevich, V. "Are RTS Needed Everywhere?" *Pravda* (November 11, 1959), p. 3, translated and reprinted in *CDSP*, Vol. XI, No. 45 (December 9, 1959), pp. 28-29.

"More Attention to The Production of Mineral Fertilizers." *Izvestia* (January 16, 1958), p. 1, translated and reprinted in *CDSP*, Vol. X, No. 3 (February 26, 1958), p. 29.

Nove, A. "The Kolkhoz System: Some Comments on Dr. Schlesinger's Article." *Soviet Studies*, Vol. III, No. 2 (October 1952), pp. 163-172.

_____. "Some Notes on the 1953 Budget and the Peasants." *Soviet Studies*, Vol. V, No. 3 (January 1954), pp. 227-233.

_____. "Problems of Economic De-Stalinization." *Problems of Communism*, Vol. VI, No. 2 (March-April 1957), pp. 15-21.

_____. "Soviet Agriculture Marks Time." *Foreign Affairs*, Vol. 40, No. 4 (July 1962), pp. 576-594.

_____. "Was Collectivization Inevitable?" *Problems of Communism*, Vol. 8, No. 4 (July-August 1959), pp. 56-59.

Nove, A. and Laird, Roy D. "Kolkhoz Agriculture in the Moscow Oblast." *The American Slavic and East European Review*, Vol. XIII, No. 4 (December 1954), pp. 549-565.

Oi, Walter Y. and Clayton, Elizabeth M. "A Peasant's View of a Soviet Collective Farm." *American Economic Review*, Vol. LVIII, No. 1 (March 1968), pp. 37-59.

"On Raising the Material Incentive of Collective Farmers in the Development of Communal Production." *Pravda* (May 18, 1966), p. 2, translated and reprinted in *CDSP*, Vol. XVIII, No. 20 (June 1966), p. 3.

Rudzinskas, A. "Drizzle From Big Storm Clouds." *Pravda* (February 28, 1961), p. 2, translated and reprinted in *CDSP*, Vol. XIII, No. 9 (March 29, 1961), pp. 26-27.

Schlesinger, R. "The Decisions on Agriculture." *Soviet Studies*, Vol. 5, No. 4 (January 1954), pp. 234-245.

———. "The Kolkhoz System: A Reply." *Soviet Studies*, Vol. III, No. 3 (January 1952), pp. 288-315.

———. "Some Problems of Present Kolkhoz Organization." *Soviet Studies*, Vol. II, No. 4 (April 1951), pp. 325-355.

Smith, R.E.F. "The Amalgamation of Collective Farms: Some Technical Aspects." *Soviet Studies*, Vol. VI, No. 1 (July 1954), pp. 16-32.

"Toward New Successes in the Development of Agriculture." *Pravda* (February 13, 1958), p. 1, translated and reprinted in *CDSP*, Vol. X, No. 7 (March 28, 1958), pp. 31-32.

Podgorny, N.V. "Toward a New Advance of Ukraine Agriculture." *Pravda* (February 27, 1958), pp. 3-4, translated and reprinted in *CDSP*, Vol. X, No. 9 (April 9, 1958), p. 28.

Podkhomutnikov, A. "Actions, Not Resolutions Needed." *Izvestia* (December 11, 1957), p. 2, translated and reprinted in *CDSP*, Vol. IX, No. 50 (January 22, 1958), pp. 30-31.

Pogodin, K. "Sowing Time is Approaching and There are Few Spare Parts." *Pravda* (March 12, 1959), p. 2, translated and reprinted in *CDSP*, Vol. XI, No. 10 (April 8, 1959), p. 34.

Polynsky, P. "Why are Frauds Shielded in Chernovtsy." *Sel'skoe Khoziaistvo* (September 12, 1957), p. 3, translated and reprinted in *CDSP*, Vol. IX, No. 42 (November 27, 1957), pp. 20-21.

Popel, D. "Save the Grain." *Izvestia* (October 23, 1958), p. 2, translated and reprinted in *CDSP*, Vol. X, No. 43 (December 3, 1958), pp. 23-24.

———. "What Happened to the Trucks?" *Izvestia* (August 11, 1956), p. 1, translated and reprinted in *CDSP*, Vol. VIII, No. 32 (September 1956), p. 25.

Ternovsky, P. "What Kind of Seed Do You Have?—Little Concern About Planting Select Hard Wheat in Chkalov Province." *Izvestia* (October 23, 1957), p. 2, translated and reprinted in *CDSP*, Vol. IX, No. 43 (December 4, 1957), pp. 29-30.

Yefimov, Y. "When Farming Standards are Ignored." *Izvestia* (January 29, 1957), p. 2, translated and reprinted in *CDSP*, Vol. IX, No. 4 (March 6, 1957), pp. 34-35.

Yeremin, A. "Do Not Violate Collective Farm Democracy." *Pravda* (February 21, 1961), p. 2, translated and reprinted in *CDSP*, Vol. XIII, No. 8 (March 22, 1961), pp. 36-37.

Zauberman, Alfred. "Liberman's Rules of the Game for Soviet Industry." *Slavic Review*, Vol. XXII, No. 4 (December 1963), pp. 734-744.

247

Russian

Abramov, G. "Revizionnye komissii–organy kontroliia." (Auditing Commission–Organ of Control). *Kolkhozno-Sovkhoznoe Proizvodstvo Moldavii*, No. 12 (December 1964), pp. 11-13.

Akhazov, T. "O podbore i vospitanii predsedatelei kolkhozov." (About the Selection and Training of Kolkhoz Chairmen). *Kommunist*, No. 2 (January 1954), pp. 55-64.

Barashev, V.F. "Ispol'zovanie pokazatelia sebestoimosti v rukovodstve khoziaistvom." (Utilization of cost indicators in the guidance of the economy). *Uchet i Finansy v Kolkhozakh i Sovkhozakh*, No. 6 (June 1958), pp. 24-27.

Berman, S. "Ocheredenye zadachi revisionnykh komissii kolkhozov" (The Order of Tasks for the Auditing Commission of Kolkhozy). *Kolkhoznik Sovetskoi Latvii*, No. 12 (December 1950), p. 28.

Bobrovnitskii, A. "Ispol'zovanie trudovykh resursov v sel'skom khoziaistve" (The Utilization of Labor Resources in Agriculture). *Voprosy Ekonomiki*, No. 3 (March 1961), pp. 146-147.

Chaikin, P. "Guaranteed Payment and Production." *Ekonomicheskaia Gazeta*, No. 9 (March 1968), pp. 28-29.

Doroshchenkov, G.D. "Raionnaia inspektsiia i uchet v kolkhozakh" (The Raion Inspection and Accounting in Kolkhozy). *Uchet i Finansy v Kolkhozakh i Sovkhozakh*, No. 12 (December 1958), pp. 46-48.

Dzhaidakbaeva, L. "Rezivionaia komissiia kolkhoza" (Auditing Commission of the Kolkhoz). *Sel'skoe Khoziaistvo Uzbekistana*, No. 5 (May 1965), pp. 59-61.

Evseev, A. "Ulichshit' Rabotu revizionnykh komissii v kolkhozakh" (Improve the Work of the Auditing Commission in Kolkhozy). *Kolkhozno–Sovkhoznoe Proizvodstva Kirgizii*, No. 1 (January 1963), p. 11.

Gainetdinov, M.F. "Ob ekonomicheskoi podgotovke spetsialistov sel'skogo khoziaistva" (about the Economic Preparation of Specialists of Agriculture). *Uchet i Finansy v Kolkhozakh i Sovkhozakh*, No. 3 (March 1963), pp. 39-40.

Galanov, A.M. "Ustranit' nedostatki v podgotovke kadrov" (Eliminate Inadequacies in the Preparation of Cadres). *Uchet i Finansy v Kolkhozakh i Sovkhozakh*, No. 5 (May 1961), p. 57.

Grigor'iants, A. "Kolkhoznyi ekonomist" (Kolkhoz Economist). *Kolkhoznoe-Sovkhoznoe Proizvodstvo Uzbekistana*, No. 11 (November 1964), pp. 41-43.

Karamelev, A.N. "Dvizhenie tridtsatityshiachnikov i ukreplenie kolkhozov" (The Thirty-Thousander Movement and the Strengthening of Kolkhozy). *Voprosy Istorii KPSS*, No. 1 (1962), pp. 115-126.

Karavayev, A. "Organizatsionno-khoziaistvennoe ukreplenie kolkhozov" (Organizational and Economic Strengthening of Kolkhozy). *Voprosy Ekonomiki*, No. 11 (November 1953), pp. 43-59.

Karimova, S. "Sovershenstvovat' upravlenie delami kolkhozov" (To Improve the

Administration of Affairs in Kolkhozy). *Sel'skoe Khoziaistvo Kazakhstana*, No. 8 (August 1959), pp. 17-21.

Kassirov, L. "Sebestoimost', tsena i khoziaistvennykh raschet v kolkhozakh" (Cost, Price and Economic Accounting in Kolkhozy). *Voprosy Ekonomiki*, No. 3 (March 1960), pp. 74-81.

Khavronin, K. "Iz opyta raboty pravleniia peredovoi sel'khozarteli" (From the Experience of the Work of a Management Board of an Advanced Agricultural Artel). *Zemledelie i Zhivotnovodstvo Moldavii*, No. 7 (July 1958), pp. 66-69.

Khlebnikov, V. "O dal'neishem ukreplenii ekonomiki kolkhozov" (About the Further Strengthening of the Economy of Kolkhozy). *Voprosy Ekonomiki*, No. 7 (July 1962), pp.

"Kolkhoznyi ekonomist" (Kolkhoz Economist). *Kolkhoznoe-Sovkhoznoe Proizvodstvo Moldavii*, No. 12 (December 1964), pp. 1-3.

Malakhov, I.P. and Kholodova, G.A. "Nekotorye voprosy deiatel'nosti kolkhoznogo ekonomista" (A Few Questions About the Activities of the Kolkhoz Economist). *Sel'skoe Khoziaistvo Severnogo Kavkaza*, No. 3 (March 1960), pp. 14-16.

Mel'nikov, V. "Voprosy podgotovki rukovodiashchikh kadrov kolkhozov" (Questions about the Preparation of Leadership Cadres for Kolkhozy). *Sotsialisticheskoe sel'skoe Khoziaistvo*, No. 8 (1951), pp. 16-24.

"O godovoi otchete kolkhoza" (About the Annual Accounts of the Kolkhoz). *Uchet i Finansy v Kolkhozakh i Sovkhozakh*, No. 6 (June 1961), pp. 10-13.

"Ob ekonomiste kolkhoza" (About the Economist of a Kolkhoz). *Uchet i Finansy v Kolkhozakh i Sovkhozakh*, No. 1 (January 1962), pp. 29-32.

Panin, N.A. "Revizionnym komissiiam nuzhna pomoshch' " (The Auditing Commission Must Help). *Uchet i Finansy v Kolkhozakh i Sovkhozakh*, No. 2 (February 1963), p. 37.

Podobedov, S.E. Raiispolkom i rabota revizionnykh komissii kolkhozov" (The Raiispolkom and the Work of the Kolkhoz Auditing Commission). *Uchet i Finansy v Kolkhozakh i Sovkhozakh*, No. 11 (November 1960), pp. 47-49.

"Presedatel' sel'skokhoziaistvennoi aretli—tsentralnaia figura kolkhoznogo proizvodstva" (The Chairman of Agricultural Artels—The Central Figure of Kolkhoz Production). *Sel'skoe Khoziaistvo Kazakhstana*, No. 6 (June 1955), pp. 1-5.

Totov, V. "P podbore i uluchshenii kachestvennogo sostava kadrov" (About the Selection and Improved Quality of Cadres). *Kommunist*, No. 5 (March 1955), pp. 49-60.

Usubaliev, T. "Proizvodstvennye upravleniia i kolkhoznaia demokratiia" (The Production Administration and Kolkhoz Democracy). *Kolkhozno-Sovkhoznoe Proizvodstvo Kirgizii*, No. 7 (July 1963), pp. 3-4.

Venzher, V. "O razvitii kolkhoznoi sobstvennosti na sovremennom etape" (About the Development of Kolkhoz Property in the Present Era). *Voprosy Ekonomiki*, No. 12 (December 1960), pp. 18-25.

Volkov, I. "Nekotorye voprosy denezhnoi oplaty truda v kolkhozakh" (A Few Questions About the Monetary Payment of Labor in Kolkhozy). *Sel'skoe Khoziaistvo Kazakhstana*, No. 10 (October 1959), pp. 46-50.

List of Periodicals

Russian

Ekonomicheskaia gazeta
Ekonomika sel'skogo khoziaistva
Finansy SSSR
Izvestia
Kolkhoznoe-sovkhoznoe proizvodstvo
Kolkhoznoe-sovkhoznoe proizvodstvo kirgizii
Kolkhoznoe-sovkhoznoe proizvodstvo moldavii
Kolkhoznoe-sovkhoznoe proizvodstvo RSFSR
Kommunist
Kommunist Tadzhikistana
Komsomolskaia pravda
Partiinaia zhin'
Planovoe khoziaistvo
Pravda
Sel'skaia zhizn' (Formerly Sel'skoe Khoziaistvo)
Sel'skoe khoziaistvo Kazakhstana
Sel'skoe khoziaistvo severnogo Kavkaza
Sel'skoe khoziaistvo Sibiri
Sel'skoe khoziaistvo Uzbekistana
Sovetskaia Litva
Sovetskaia Rossia
Sovetskoe gosudarstvo i pravo
Uchet i finansy v kolkhozakh i sovkhozakh
Voprosy ekonomiki

English

American Economic Review
The ASTE Bulletin
Bulletin of the Institute for Study of the USSR
Current Digest of The Soviet Press (CDSP)
Journal of Farm Economics
Problems of Communism

Problems of Economics
Slavic Review
Soviet Studies

Selected Reference Works
(With Abbreviations)

Direktivy KPSS i sovetskogo pravitel'stva po khoziaistvennym voprosam. Moskva: Gospolitizdat, 1958, Vols. 3-4. Cited as *Direktivy KPSS.*
Ekonomicheskaia zhizn' SSSR. Moskva: Gosudarstvennoe nauchnoe izdatel'stvo "sovetskaia entsiklopediia," 1961.
Entsiklipedicheskii sel'skokhoziaistvennyi slovar'-spravochnik. Moskva: Sel'khozgiz, 1959.
Itogi vsesoiuznoi perepisi naseleniia 1959 goda. Selected volumes. Moskva: Gosstatizdat, 1962.
Kommunisticheskaia Partiia sovetskogo soiuza v rezoliutsiiakh i resheniiakh. Moskva: Gospolitizdat, 1960. Cited as *KPSS v rezoliutsiiakh.*
Khrushchev, N.S. *Stroitel'stvo kommunizma v SSSR i razvitie sel'skogo khoziaistva.* Moskva: Gospolitizdat, 1962. 8 volumes.
Narodnoe khoziaistvo. Selected volumes for the USSR and Union republics. Cited as *Narkhoz.*
Sbornik reshenii po sel'skomu khoziaistvu. Moskva: sel'khozizdat, 1963. Cited as *Sbornik.*
Sel'skokhoziaistvennaia entsiklopediia. Vol. 3. Moskva: sel'khozizdat, 1953.
Sel'skoe khoziaistvo SSSR. Moskva: Sel'khozgiz, 1960. Cited as *Sel'khoz-1960.*

Index

251

About the Author

Robert C. Stuart was born in Chemainus, British Columbia in 1938. He graduated from the University of British Columbia in 1961 with a Bachelor of Commerce degree, having specialized in economics. Graduate study followed at the University of Washington and the University of Wisconsin. From the University of Wisconsin, he earned a Certificate of Russian Area Studies in 1965, a Master of Science degree in economics in 1966 and the Ph.D. in economics in 1969. He was awarded a Foreign Area Fellowship in 1964, a Ford Foundation Doctoral Dissertation Fellowship in 1966 and visited the Soviet Union in 1966 and 1969.

Under the auspices of the University of Toronto–Soviet Union Cultural Exchange Program, he spent January–October 1966 at the Timiriazev Agricultural Academy in Moscow, and during August of that year, lived on several collective farms in the Krasnodar region of the U.S.S.R. Upon returning to the United States, he continued research on Soviet agriculture at the Russian Research Center of Harvard University. He is currently assistant professor of economics at Douglass College of Rutgers University. He is married to the former Beverly McCaig, and they live with one son, Craig, in Belle Mead, New Jersey.